The New Poetries

The New Poetries

Poetic Form since Coleridge and Wordsworth

Donald Wesling

Lewisburg
Bucknell University Press
London and Toronto: Associated University Presses

Associated University Presses
440 Forsgate Drive
Cranbury, NJ 08512

Associated University Presses
25 Sicilian Avenue
London WC1A 2QH, England

Associated University Presses
2133 Royal Windsor Drive
Unit 1
Mississauga, Ontario
Canada L5J 1K5

Library of Congress Cataloging in Publication Data

Wesling, Donald.
  The new poetries.

  Bibliography: p.
  Includes index.
  1. English poetry—History and criticism. 2. English
language—Versification. 3. American poetry—History
and criticism. 4. French poetry—History and criticism.
5. French language—Versification. 6. Poetics.
I. Title.
PR508.V45W47 1985   821′.009   82-74493
ISBN 0-8387-5031-1

Printed in the United States of America

To the Departments of Literature in Colchester
(University of Essex, England) and La Jolla
(University of California, San Diego)

Contents

8　　　　　　　　　　　　*Contents*

Acknowledgments
and Note on Terminology

This book, *The New Poetries,* is the second of three related books on prosody. The first has already appeared as *The Chances of Rhyme: Device and Modernity* (1980); the set will be complete with *The Scissors of Meter: Grammetrics and Interpretation.*

Some pages from the Introduction appeared in *Poetry Nation Review* (Manchester, England, 1982). A section of Chapter 1 appeared in *Texas Studies in Literature and Language* (Austin, 1981) and is now somewhat revised. Chapter 5 is much revised from its first appearance in *Harvard Studies in English* 2 (Cambridge, 1971). I wish to thank the above for having given me permission to reprint.

Thanks are due to those who have inspected all or part of the manuscript and given advice. Edwin Fussell, magnificent reader, helped in sprightly and painstaking detail; he took pages to Rome and responded from there; he gave time to the whole when he could least afford it; and he disagreed sharply everywhere so that I can never hope adequately to convince (or thank) him. At various stages of revision I had useful comments on the whole from Willis C. Jackman, Fredric Jameson, Robert Kern, Roy Harvey Pearce, Andrew Wright, and anonymous readers from Bucknell University Press. Michael Davidson, Rhonda Levine, and William J. Lockwood asked productive questions about a very early draft of materials that made their way into the Introduction. I have corrected the sprung-rhythm chapter with remarks from T. V. F. Brogan, Charles Cooper, and Fred V. Randel; and I have corrected the prose-poem chapter with comments from Marjorie Perloff and Ron Silliman. At the last stage of revision in late 1981 and early 1982, I was reassured on the main lines of the book's argument by the visit to La Jolla of Hungarian scholar Enikö Bollobás, who turned out to be thinking similar thoughts on the relation of grammar to prosody.

Obviously these people are not responsible for my mistakes, yet they did help me to be more accurate. The objections of scholarly friends, who form a writer's first audience, must permanently modify a writer's thinking. These disagreements live forever in the book's pages, and wherever encountered they dignify the profession of literary criticism.

The Select Bibliography at the end of this book is notably briefer than it might have been because of the existence of lists on verse-form and general stylistics, respectively, in T. V. F. Brogan, *English Versification, 1570–1980: A Reference Guide with a Global Appendix* (Baltimore, Md.: The Johns Hopkins University Press, 1981) and Josephine Miles, *Style and Proportion: The Language of Prose and Poetry* (Boston: Little, Brown and Company, 1967).

I wish to thank the following publishers or holders of rights for having given me permission to quote from published works:

Atheneum Publishers, for permission to quote from W. S. Merwin, *The Carrier of Ladders,* 1970, and W. S. Merwin, *The Miner's Pale Children,* 1970.

Black Sparrow Press and the author, Michael Palmer, for permission to quote from Michael Palmer, *Blake's Newton,* 1972. Copyright © 1972, 1983 by Michael Palmer.

Georges Borchardt, Inc., Literary Agency, for permission to quote from Michael Benedikt's translation of Charles Baudelaire's "Get Drunk," in Michael Benedikt, editor, *The Prose Poem,* Dell Publishers, 1976.

University of California Press, for permission to quote from Robert Creeley, *Collected Poems of Robert Creeley, 1945–1975,* 1982.

University of California Press, for permission to quote from Josephine Miles, *Eras and Modes in English Poetry,* 1964.

Jonathan Cape, Ltd., London, and the author, Christopher Logue, for permission to quote from Christopher Logue, *War Music,* 1981.

Andre Deutsch, London, for permission to quote from Geoffrey Hill, *Mercian Hymns,* 1971.

Faber & Faber, Ltd., London, for permission to quote from John Berryman, *The Dream Songs,* 1969.

Farrar, Straus & Giroux, Inc., for permission to quote from "Dream Song #345" and "Dream Song #377" from John Berryman, *The Dream Songs,* 1969. Copyright © 1965, 1966, 1967, 1968, 1969 by John Berryman.

Librairie Ernest Flammarion, Paris, for permission to quote from Aloysius Bertrand, *Gaspard de la nuit,* edited by Jean Richer, Nouvelle Bibliotheque, 1972.

Four Seasons Foundation, for permission to quote from Edward Dorn, *The Collected Poems,* Copyright © 1975.

Éditions Gallimard, Paris, for permission to quote from Charles Baudelaire, *Oeuvres complètes,* 1954.

Éditions Gallimard, Paris, for permission to quote from Max Jacob, *Le Cornet à dés,* 1945.

Éditions Gallimard, Paris, for permission to quote from Stéphane Mallarmé, *Oeuvres complètes,* 1945.

Merrill Gilfillan, translator of Aloysius Bertrand's prose poem, "Le Maçon," Copyright © Merrill Gilfillan, 1981. Reprinted from *This 11,* edited by Barrett Watten.

Grossman Publishing in association with Cape Goliard Press, care of Jonathan Cape, Ltd., London, for permission to quote from Paul Blackburn, *In. On. Or About the Premises,* 1968.

Grove Press, Inc., for permission to quote from Robert Duncan, *The Opening of the Field,* 1960.

Harper & Row, Inc., for permission to quote from Ted Hughes, *Crow,* 1971.

Harvard University Press, for permission to use materials from Donald Wesling, "The Prosodies of Free Verse," from *Harvard Studies in English* 2 (1971).

Johns Hopkins University Press, for permission to quote from Karl Shapiro, "English Prosody and Modern Poetry," from *English Literary History* 14 (1947).

Kulchur Foundation, for permission to quote from David Antin, *Talking,* 1972.

London Magazine Editions, Ltd., London, for permission to quote from Tony Harrison, *The Loiners,* 1970.

Éditions Maisonneuve, Montréal, for permission to quote from Daniel Sloate's translation of "Villes," from Arthur Rimbaud, *Illuminations,* 1971.

New Directions Publishing Corporation, for permission to quote from Ezra Pound, *The Cantos,* 1934; from Ezra Pound, *Personae: The Collected Poems,* 1950; William Carlos Williams, *Pictures from Brueghel,* 1962; William Carlos Williams, *Illuminations,* 1970.

New York University Press, for permission to quote from Walt Whitman, *Leaves of Grass, Reader's Comprehensive Edition,* edited by Harold W. Blodgett and Sculley Bradley. Copyright © 1965 by New York University Press.

W. W. Norton, Inc., for permission to quote from Alfred, Lord Tennyson, *In Memoriam,* edited by Robert H. Ross, A Norton Critical Edition, Copyright © by W. W. Norton & Company, Inc. By permission of the publisher.

Harold Ober Associates, New York, for British rights permission to quote from W. S. Merwin, *The Carrier of Ladders,* and from W. S. Merwin, *The Miner's Pale Children,* 1970.

Ohio University Press, for permission to quote from Yvor Winters, *Collected Poems,* Swallow Press, 1960, reprinted with the permission of Ohio University Press, Athens, Ohio.

Peter Owen, Ltd., London, and Penguin Books, for permission to quote from Gertrude Stein, *Writings and Lectures 1909–1945*, edited by Patricia Meyerowitz, 1971.

Oxford University Press, for permission to quote from Robert Bridges, *Collected Essays, Papers, Etc.*, Vol II, 1930; Robert Bridges, *Milton's Prosody*, 1901; Robert Bridges, *New Verse*, 1925; Robert Bridges, *The Shorter Poems of Robert Bridges*, 1931; Samuel Taylor Coleridge, *The Poetical Works of Samuel Taylor Coleridge*, 1912; David Gascoyne, *Collected Poems*, 1965; Gerard Manley Hopkins, *The Letters of Gerard Manley Hopkins to Robert Bridges*, 1935; Gerard Manley Hopkins, *The Notebooks and Papers*, 1937; Gerard Manley Hopkins, *Poems*, fourth edition, 1967; John Keats, *The Poetical Works*, second edition, 1958; Charles Tomlinson, *The Way of a World*, 1969; William Wordsworth, *Poetical Works*, second edition, 1954.

Penguin Books, Ltd., Harmondsworth, Middlesex, for permission to quote from John Ashbery, *Three Poems*, 1977.

Penguin Books, Ltd., Harmondsworth, Middlesex and the translator, Keith Bosley, for permission to quote from *Mallarmé: The Poems*, translation © by Keith Bosley, 1977.

Princeton University Press, for permission to quote from Claudio Guillén, *Literature as System*, 1971.

Random House, Inc., for permission to quote from Gertrude Stein, *Four Saints in Three Acts: An Opera to be Sung*, Copyright © Random House, Inc., 1934.

Routledge, Ltd., London, for permission to quote from Donald Davie, *Collected Poems 1950–1970*, 1972.

Shoe String Press, for permission to quote from Paul Fussell, *The Theory of Prosody in Eighteenth Century England*, Archon reprint, 1966.

Sun and Moon Press, editor Douglas Messerli, for permission to quote from Michael Davidson, "Advancing Measures: Conceptual Quantities and Open Forms," in Norma Procopiow, *The New American Prosody*, 1983.

Viking Penguin, Inc. for permission to quote from Charles Rosen, *The Classical Style*, Copyright © 1971 by Charles Rosen.

I hyphenate *avant-garde* as noun and adjective, but have chosen to use the forms *avantgardism* and *avantgardist* because they look less obtrusive. Like many, I cringe at the term *avant-garde*. Just now, the term seems exclusively the property of a narrow range of writers whose dominant characteristic is lack of care for their medium. *Modernism* is perhaps a better noun to cover the tendencies discussed here, but its reference is exclusively to our own century, and my purpose is to trace lines back to probable origins in Romanticism. I have decided to keep the term *avant-garde* which deserves to be burnished, and to justify it as specifically as I can by reference to the post-1795 history of society and poetry; and to use *Modernism* and its subset *post-Modernism* where necessary, for phases of nineteenth- and twentieth-century poetics.

Perhaps I might also say why I use the phrase *form as proceeding* throughout, rather than the more usual and recent phrase, *poetry as process*. The Coleridgean phrase seems more exact and less liable to the misinterpretation that the poems it describes are poems where anything goes. Also, the intent is to show how Coleridge's idea of a poetics that outstrips versification retains its power for criticism even today.

The New Poetries

Introduction

Plurality of Styles in an Avant-Garde Era

Here are the openings of two Modern poems on the subject of fountains, the first, by Donald Davie, unrhymed but metered, traditional in its handling and yet a poem of our moment in the way the title leads into the syntax of the first line:

> The Fountain
>
> Feathers up fast, and steeples; then in clods
> Thuds into its first basin; thence as surf
> Smokes up and hangs; irregularly slops
> Into its second, tattered like a shawl;
> There, chill as rain, stipples a danker green,
> Where urgent tritons lob their heavy jets.[1]

The second, "The Memorial Fountain" by Roy Fisher, steps down the page differently in free-verse tiers, abandoning meter, rhyme, and equalized stanzas; also indenting and dividing unpredictably:

> The fountain plays
>   through summer dusk in gaunt shadows,
> black constructions
>   against a late clear sky,
> water in the basin
>   where the column falls
>   shaking,
> rapid and wild,
>   in cross-waves, in back-waves,
>   the light glinting and blue,
> as in a wind
>   though there is none.
>   Harsh
> skyline!
>   Far-off scaffolding
> bitten against the air.[2]

Here are already two instances of stylistic pluralism, the coexistence of diverse norms of structure. It remains to be seen whether they can be described by the same language, though surely it is plain from the outset that the conventional prosody of the handbooks will not suffice for the Fisher.

And here now is yet a third and equally valid poem, the twenty-seventh section of Geoffrey Hill's "Mercian Hymns":

> "Now when King Offa was alive and dead," they were all there, the funereal gleemen: papal legate and rural dean; Merovingian car-dealers, Welsh mercenaries; a shuffle of house-carls.
>
> He was defunct. They were perfunctory. The ceremony stood acclaimed. The mob received memorial vouchers and signs.
>
> After that shadowy, thrashing midsummer hail-storm, Earth lay for a while, the ghost-bride of livid Thor, butcher of strawberries, and the shire-tree dripped red in the arena of its uprooting.[3]

Traditional metered poetry, free verse, and the prose poem: the authors all happen to be British, but the same range in form may be found in American writers. And very likely the same range of possibility may be found in the work to date of any one of these three writers. The writers are, of course, exhibits from an era that lacks, or appears to lack, a period style.

In such an era—our era, stretching from 1795 to the present and with no end in view—poets and commentators alike find themselves enmeshed in a contradictory structure of thought, with no single, unquestioned definition of style, device, or literature. The era of diversity grew out of the era of uniformity. From the midst of the European Enlightenment came skeptical habits of mind, rebellion political and religious, a new industrial economy—among many other major changes that bear on poetry indirectly. After the 1790s the social practice of literature was put under tremendous new pressures by analytical-rational thinking, and by a social order more often than not antagonistic to mind and to humanitarian value. Literature's response was to devise for itself an ethos that continually thrust to the forefront certain intuitive notions of value, of reality. Rather than killing poetry by sinking it in technique, this habit of mind prefers the risk of sinking it in history, reference, and ordinary language. And a risk it is; this argument of poetry generates counterarguments, counterpoetics, which stress the literariness of literature, the corporeality of language. Fortunately for those who hope to find a pattern in the whole era, the arguments and counterarguments may be seen a forming a relation, a rapport-of-difference belonging to (and evolving within) the historical moment.[4]

The Scandal of Form

The idea of a poetic device is crucial to this hope, because successful use of the device—and of grammar treated as a device, as part of prosody—unites the twin virtues of the corporeality and the transparency of language.

Traditional rhyme and meter and metaphor and personification proclaim their literariness, but the mission of the poet (especially after Wordsworth and Coleridge) must be to make room for individual work by forgetting or suppressing the devices that represent the institution of literature. The very great interest of prosodic avantgardism is that it must fail in its project of abolishing style. It must fail because its means are themselves stylistic: abandoning form in and by form. Such is the invisible part of the subject. An art that sees beyond art to "reality" is never finished and often, one way or another, will comment on the inadequacy of its means to the great end it has proposed to itself—and if it fails to comment, its historians will.

Devices correspond to "shape as superinduced," which Coleridge opposed to his preferred notion of poetic method as continuous progression, "form as proceeding." As such there is something untouchable about these devices, though of course from Coleridge to the present day we have also known and continuously reaffirmed the truth that devices are necessary, inevitable, and the material condition of all verbal art.

Language, in the successful poem, is not only grammatical, it is also literary; it rhymes, it meters, it metaphors. In art sentences, a paradigm is extended into a system by a form of creative transgression. There is always a differential between literary and ordinary language, although it is exceedingly difficult to define, especially with the poets themselves working to exaggerate the difficulty. One of the special concerns of this study will be to show how in the Modern period methods, such as reliance on feints of grammar or logic, may be used to compensate for the lack of structures associated with discrete devices like meter or rhyme. In that way they attempt to elude the scandal.

I use the term *scandal* in its senses of a grossly discreditable circumstance, and "a cause of stumbling," a snare (an obsolete meaning). To speak in this way is to join in with a convention of mock horror, a hyperbole. Modern commentators often speak in this way when they deal with the contradictory relations between literary and ordinary language.[5] Nobody, I suppose, would argue that poetic form is literally a scandal, for in fact the apprehension of poetic form is a pleasure inseparable from the pleasure of poetry itself. For those who have bothered to take up this book, prosody is an aspect of the humanistic study of literature, worthy of anyone's prolonged attention. Nor do any of the poets and critics discussed in this study deny that poetic form is what constitutes the very literariness of literature. Nonetheless the radical deemphasis of those formal attributes which preexist the poem's making is the major method of post-Romantic writing. This suspicion of devices leads to perplexities that define conditions of possibility for a whole era of writing. The idea of the scandal of form comprises, then, both the necessity and the likely irrelevance of poetic technique. Thus the phrase may stand for the contradiction in culture and poetics that this book describes.

Whether we are sympathetic to the Modern mode of writing or not, we remain scandalized by the device, because that is our post-Romantic obligation. And yet, what looks like a scandal is a fact of art. Devices are best understood by reviewing the history of our ambivalences about their necessary role, and then by repositioning them within the movement, the cognitive curve of the text as a whole. The assignment is to see what devices and what elements in those devices can be emphasized, transformed, transcended at a given moment. Poets do this all the time. Their writings constitute a massive work of implicit theory, and every generation of poets renews the theory of devices. The story of how this happens is one that criticism must learn to tell.

Especially since the generation of Walt Whitman and Gerard Manley Hopkins, the renewal of devices has taken a particular turn toward the preprosodic structures of thought itself, and of the English sentence. Thinking exists independently of poetry; so does grammar. In the innovative prosodies this fact is emphasized as grammar tends to supplant traditional versification. The aesthetic element is somewhat swamped by the cognitive one, at least by contrast with traditionally made poems. Thus non-art evens its score *with* art—but *in* art. The scandal of form is that form should be necessary at all in an era of stylistic pluralism. There is in such periods of destructive discourse no final abolition of rule-governed behavior, though that is how some persons talk (praising or condemning the avantgardist spirit). Apparently, so long as there are set up in the text various equivalence systems of sound or of sense, it does not matter what equivalences are present. There is no abolition of rules, then; rather a perception that many different kinds of rules will serve to give language a corporeal body of the sort it needs to discriminate itself from ordinary discourse.

Grammar as Prosody

The very double-barreled terms that we use in naming sprung rhythm, free verse, and the prose poem contain seemingly irreconcilable impulses to marked and to unmarked language. Such categories, rather like the rhetoric of the apostrophe, where a text seems to gesture outside itself,[6] relate literature to communicative context and to language behavior outside literature, but at the same time they do not vaporize literature into something it is not. Such categories notably frustrate the attempt to maintain the distinctiveness of literature, its study in and by itself.

The New Poetries accounts for avant-garde practice by describing its assimilation of metrical and rhetorical devices into cognitive, syntactical, and grammatical procedures. This book describes the hermeneutics of the antihermeneutical, the poetics of the antipoetic. To phrase the design even thus briefly is to suggest how the innovative prosodies are, like all literary phenomena, "condemned (or privileged) to be forever the most rigorous and, consequently, the most unreliable language in terms of which man names and modifies himself."[7] While registering as completely as may be the unreliability Paul de Man describes in the passage just quoted, I should like to edge beyond his position—so suspicious of the world of reference, so insistent on the fictional status of literature—to defend the role avant-garde poems have in exemplifying a reconciliation among poetic form, history, and language.

In his "Semiology and Rhetoric" (1973), de Man reasserts an ancient distinction between rhetoric and grammar, and thereby disallows the reduction of figure to grammar he sees in recent anti-Formalist works. He draws a heavy line between natural language and literary language, resisting any attempts to image language as imprisonment, or to emphasize the hybrid nature of texts as partly literary and partly referential, or to take an interest in "writing and reading as potentially effective speech acts."[8] The attraction of reconciliation between form and meaning is doubtless, as de Man says, "the elective breeding-ground of false models and metaphors," and involves, often enough, "an inside/outside metaphor that is never being seriously questioned." And yet the present study does not deny that the epistemology of rhetoric is distinguishable from the epistemology of grammar, but rather sets out to describe why and how Modern meaning is, in de Man's words, "so anxious to blot out the obstacle of form." The difference between this account and de Man's is that I am taking the form-as-scandal ethos as deliberate overstatement, the heuristic gesture of a literature and criticism that understands ordinary language and historical experience as final values. By redefining literature and literary form, the tendency of theoretically central post-Romantic writing is to exaggerate the unreliability of literary language—literature's habit, in this period, of miming the conventions of unmarked discourse and speech. No cautions against the reduction of figure to grammar will suffice to stop this hunger for personal voice and the world of reference.[9]

The value of Paul de Man's insistence on the nonexclusive couple grammar-rhetoric is that, as he says, it "disrupts and confuses the neat antithesis of the inside/outside pattern," and forces us back to the perplexities of the tropological nature of the text. For de Man and others who are impelled by the same motives, language is the undoing of its own illusion of bridging a gap between word and world. The subject of this book, instead, is my own sense of the way the illusion is built up through determinate but nontraditional uses of language. The book supplements rather than contradicts deconstructive logics.

The attempt to blot out the obstacle of form is a historically specific feature of avantgardist thinking since 1795. When recent scholars have discovered similar attempts in Montaigne or Francis Bacon, they have been seeing themselves anticipated in the past, and their inquiries have been enabled by a post-Romantic mode of reading. Poems and poetic manifestos covering the whole period from Coleridge to Whitman to the 1980s, tend to value the text as an act, a voice, over the text as an object. For the literary documents of the period, in the depths everything becomes law, the intuitive has an inherent formal structure. In general, grammar is valued over poetic devices, and the motion of thought is valued over grammar. Working with these assumptions, Modern writing is at best an exercise of all the powers of language. The literary critic, however, is the analyst and historian of these assumptions, and for the critic there must remain a difference between thought and grammar, thought and poetic form. The critic who is not a linguist or philosopher or sociologist can never fully analyze the relation of language to thought, or the relation of linguistic to social context, which obtain within the chosen texts. Perhaps it is sufficient always to differentiate between the cognitive and the rhetorical, between the subject thought and spoken about, and the audience spoken to. In practice, this means keeping a lively sympathy for the attitudes that enable poets to write their poems, but means also a final refusal to affiliate with those attitudes.

Reading the poem written after 1795, we try to understand the way in which the tradition of English and American poetry has been adopted or rejected—searching absences, lines of most resistance; and understanding poetic influence, with Harold Bloom's example, as the late-coming poet's repression and misreading of the great predecessors' example. We see whether the Modernism is faint or extreme. We attempt, in form and theme, to see what is being negated. When we get down to cases in point of technique, we employ (always provisionally) concepts not only from traditional prosodic codes but also from an idea of natural language. At least at first, notions of grammar and syntax, of coincidence (or not) of sentence and line, of stress emphasis, of reader psychology through frustrated and affirmed expectation, will seem most valuable. One hears the poem as a kind of natural language genre, following its tone of voice and movement; at the same time or later, but without fail, the more highly formalized concepts of traditional prosody will be tried for their fit in each particular case. Working this way, we respect the poem's historical nature and its innovative ratio.

An adequate method for recovering and explaining poetry's structure in history has not been imagined by criticism, except in part. No single book can complete the task.

Beyond the Avant-Garde

My larger historical point is that, by and large, Modern poetic techniques tend rather to accelerate than to contradict Romanticism. In ethos and method, in their premise of a poetics that outstrips versification, Wordsworth and Coleridge are closer to T. S. Eliot than they are to Samuel

Johnson. Paradoxically, post-Romantic poetry refreshes language and literature by making us more aware of their conventionality, their limits. A whole
field not only of formal but of moral investigation is uncovered when form as
proceeding becomes a method and subject of art. Poetry as a system sees
beyond itself to the world on which it relies; it always did, of course, especially in Johnson, but never before with such urgency. Especially since 1945,
the "open" work in projective verse, the "happening," conceptual art, and
aleatory music have put into question the semiautonomous status of works
of art. This is the extreme extension of tendencies latent since Wordsworth.

A full theory of the way post-Romantic and Modern poetries are traditional would show, for the most recent and avant-garde directions, their
origins in the earlier period. Such a theory would show how the innovative
poetries are the response to human alienation in the sphere of poetic technique; it would show how this is related to the response in other areas of
social existence, where there is an equal insistence on the need for integration of the self. The avant-garde period is the same as the bourgeois period.
In its values, this time is individualist in the worst as well as the best sense,
plural with only an imagined reconciliation, a myth of community that would
enable an integration of self. The historical situation manifests itself, in the
realm of ideas, in these imaginings. A historical moment of increasing
anomie, whose conditions of possibility are largely fixed by the mode of
economic production and mediated by a complex of disunifying institutions,
has set against it a continuing imagination of a state of "more than usual
organic sensibility" (Wordsworth).

Some writers nurse the memory that a period style existed in a previous
time in English literary history (Samuel Johnson's time)—and the hope that
a period style might exist again. They base this hope upon their stubborn
sense that if we change literature, if we burnish the word, we will reform
consciousness itself and remake history and ourselves. This is the motive for
much in Eliot and Pound. Traditional Moderns, modern Augustans, modern
Metaphysicals, and New Critics all imagine a cultural change that might be
initiated among the arts themselves. If only the arts could redeem their
stylelessness and sloppiness! Then they might also redeem the time. Or at
least, beginning in this way with language and the medium, which are within
the writer's control, it might be possible to erase the symptoms of dec-
adence.

Thence derive a number of maneuvers within an avant-garde era, which
will permit writers to imagine that they have transcended the requirements
of their historical moment. The retrospective thinkers typically believe in
the forging of a Modern style, a Classicism to halt the slide toward disinte-
gration. The anticipatory thinkers, by contrast, argue that the avant-garde
has more or less lived out its role and we are now phasing into another era—
a new time, when the avant-garde is being adopted as a normative style and
thus being turned inside out, negating the negation, bringing us back to a

central style. Meanwhile, the avant-garde writers themselves are by their own definition obliged to throw themselves into the future, self-exiled there. Meanwhile, too, the retrenching antagonists of the avant-garde must batten off a previous moment and so absent themselves, in imagination, from the lineaments of the present scandal. Is anybody left in the present? In fact, all are here, in varying degrees of self-conscious Modernity.

The avant-garde tries to make contact with the others, the enemy, the unknown. Those within the avant-garde are separated from the mass, banded together in their isolation, militant if not military, needing to justify their loneliness and identity, requiring rich community within their group and contestation against the Others. It cannot be a healthy situation, whether the writer is consciously in advance or rather closer to the mass; there are degrees of more or less—within each career and from career to career in any writing generation—and yet all writers must be conscious of their lateness in literary history, their isolation, their shrillness of tone or the flat tone that comes of careful exclusion of many kinds of pitch, a kind of whispering but really saying the same things. Thus we push our artists into the future and so isolate them, even the consciously conservative ones who have no political or utopian gestures. All are infected by Modernity, all become imaginary time travelers within an avant-garde era. Only the rate of travel varies.

Perhaps it is not possible to think ourselves beyond the avant-garde. The very idea sounds like a contradiction in terms. Does it violate some Law of Progress even to mention the possibility? Must a philosophical literary criticism be deprived of the mode of the counterfactual, even as its subject, literature itself, takes its very nature from that mode?

Any movement forward out of this quagmire, where thought struggles, must be tentative. The requirements and the opportunities of another poetics might be projected from my own study of innovative poetries. I would like to suggest that within poetry and and criticism as we know them there may exist hints of a future poetry and thus of a future poetics. Such a future poetics, which could show (as we now cannot) the relation of poetry to history, of structure to function, could do worse than study, as I do in this book, a writing that uses preestablished logics and forms in order to subvert them. On the way to that more adequate poetics (adequate to our full humanity, adequate to a future poetry), commentators might try to understand the social and political basis for the contradictoriness, the scandal of literary form, at the same time as they undertake researches into form.

The task will be to show how through author and poem history itself is transmuted into precise literary form as one of its final articulations. Is criticism equal to the task? If my own study is any example at all, the demonstration will necessarily linger on certain moments—1795, 1855, 1910, perhaps 1960—when historical constraints and possibilities seem to be preternaturally clear. To understand an avant-garde era, poetic theory will tend to seek out relationships between poetic and broader contexts. Theory requires a monistic critical language to explain and (even to some degree) to match the works to be described. As it narrows the distance between description and interpretation, poetics should be able to fend off the temptation to relax into verification and taxonomy, those dualist forms of thought. The disproportion between what critical theory contains and what the poetry itself maintains will be the gap filled by the hyperbolic genre of the manifesto, so characteristic of the avant-garde period and so often misread as literal statement by enemies of avant-garde practice.

There are a number of versions of the resolved opposition between poetic and broader context. These are all dilemmas in logic, to be phrased not as binary oppositions but as resolved dualisms. A few of these may be listed: form as subversion of form; the 1795 transition as an epistemological break; literary history as progression through revolution; and prose as poetry (the prose poem). Here we have neither binary opposition nor a form of graduality mapping, but rather a relation of hyperbole, where the right-hand term is related to the left-hand term by overstating it. In such a relation, the elements require each other for self-definition, and create a special system by virtue of their locked-in-orbit repulsions. The poet's intent is to show how nothing is prior to the poetic utterance, no device independent of the process of his work. The right-hand elements in the list are hyperbolical forms of ordinary recognitions, and therefore they are avant-garde disguises, subsisting upon an expressionistic surplus of thought beyond the case.

In this way post-Romantic poetics frames and understands its working hypotheses as contested concepts, not to be settled by arguments. Utopian perhaps, expressing itself in the rhetorical mode of the manifesto, this poetics marshals a massive overdetermination beyond the fact of the art experience. Thus does it enact its distrust of Modernity, of the lack of interiority in a technological and business culture. Even in the most impersonal of poems, ego is the issue. Inscribed in every poem, in every smallest deflection of syllable and punctuation, is the process of the poem's own birth, and the process of authorial self becoming its own begetter. If the attempt by New Criticism and Deconstruction to halt and deny these processes has not succeeded, it is because of the tremendous continuing prestige of this Romantic aesthetic, whose power derives from the way it displaces value from the text to the world of ordinary events and language.

Literature in such a scheme would be understood as the condition of a process; with the poem as a notation, to be actualized in the humanizing practice of the reader's encounter with it. In that encounter, the categories of sound structure, grammar, syntax, and rhythmic cognition will be of as much importance as traditional categories of meter and rhyme. The language of poetry, especially since the Romantics, is a "regressive semiological system"

(Roland Barthes), always highlighting the word by devices of equivalence while also pointing back from word to thing. At once transparent and opaque, absent and present, the text must appear different in proportion as we emphasize its nature as literature or its nature as language. Yet obviously neither emphasis should exclude the other. Not all language is literary language; the sets overlap but do not coincide. Yet all literary language is language and uses language to provide most of its notations. To grasp the scandal of form as a reader, one method seems especially productive: read the work as language, as imaginary communication, as sentencing—while at the same time exhaustively valuing and integrating what is left over.

So the idea of post-Romantic writing is to build art with a system of conventions that point outside of art to ordinary perceptions of objects, events, and speechtones. For criticism to pursue the idea, it must trace the identity of the two scandals of poetic form and of Modernity, for each of these ends as "a falling away from literature and a rejection of history" (de Man). The programmatic violence of this form as proceeding in its historical moment may, it seems likely, lead us to a new knowledge of literature (like language and history, and representing them in this) as a human practice that calls its own mode of existence into question.

From the imaginary perspective of this future poetry and its poetics, there must be no question of our accepting or not accepting the scandal of form; for that ideal of organic form defines, for now, our horizon of thought. But fully to acknowledge that perhaps brings us closer to the future—if we want to get closer. Since 1795, every literary generation except the first has imagined itself the generation of, in Yeats's words, "the last Romantics," and yet none has been correct. Insofar as I have projected this I, too, am probably deluded. The history, indeed the very structure of post-Romantic poetry provides one of the most striking instances we have that the promise of art cannot be fulfilled by art.

Part One: *History and Theory*

1

The Transformation of Premises

The Literary Transition at 1795

Although the idea of genre is necessary to literary study, it tends to obscure or obliterate our sense of historical change. In their construction of genres, literary historians have often skipped over the major break at Romanticism. They have noticed that such forms as ode and elegy, rhyme and pentameter, are present on either side of 1795, but they have neglected the inventive distortion that is the stylistic differential on this side of the line.

The characteristic tendency, in fact, has been to read Romanticism backward. In an important essay of 1968, W. K. Wimsatt has expressed agreement with Robert Mayo's hope (1954) to submerge *Lyrical Ballads,* in form and content, into "what had grown to be a 'persistent' minority segment of the magazine verse of the 1790s. . . . Wordsworth's freedom and originality . . . will be found ultimately to consist in the fact that he is a better poet than most of his contemporaries at most moments."[1] A less subtle version of the same period concept is Geoffrey Tillotson's Byron Foundation Lecture of 1967, where the need for continuities leads to the statement that "Pope had written some of Wordsworth's poetry in advance," and that "if Pope had been born a century later he would have written Wordsworth's poems. He had the power to."[2] According to Tillotson, Wordsworth dropped the heroic couplet after his early poems, but since Dryden and Pope had helped to establish the diction and syntax of Modern English there was no wish to rethink other conventions. A third and final example comes from John Bayley's earlier book, *The Romantic Survival* (1957), which argues that "in verse the Romantics developed no new form. . . . Although in the sphere of the mind the movement was a revolution, in the sphere of form it was decidedly a revival. No new device was ready to the poet's hand like the decasyllabic line which had lent itself to the creative surge of the Renaissance and developed with it."[3] Looking for bold formal discoveries, Bayley misses the revolution in Romantic attitudes toward convention, language, and the reader; for his argument, there is no need, after this, to consider the finer subsequent question of how the premises shift to the metrics of avant-

gardism in sprung rhythm, free verse, and the prose poem in the next generation. Thus Bayley skirts all further explanation of the reason that, in his
words, Wordsworth and Coleridge "always refused to make any qualitative
distinction between poetry and prose," and he is left with the curiously
deficient notion that Wordsworth's blank verse lacked style: "The lucidity of
the great passages does not come to us in terms of style; we hardly think of
them as involved in a poetic medium."[4] Precisely; but that is not the admission of a lack, rather the signal triumph of a determinate style. Bayley has
registered the spontaneity, not the calculation, and so despite his suspicion is
just the reader Wordsworth anticipated. Like most of us most of the time, he
has been taken in by the executive fictions of a prosody that pretends to be
speech.

Romanticism's central thesis of the transparency of literary language is
still emergent—still, and rightly so, the subject of intense debate. In tracing
the origins of this thesis, one is led back continually to its beginnings in a
systematic conflict with Enlightenment poetry and poetics, with the only
truly unified period style in English literary history, here called Augustan
form. In the present chapter, I take up the question of epochs and their
exhaustion and generation, trying to explain the break at 1795; in the rest of
the book I turn to historical questions more narrowly, distinguising different
phases in the proceeding life of Romantic form.

Before I move on to show the transformation of Augustan into Romantic
premises, let me summarize my story and say how I propose to tell it.

No period in literary history was more vigorously ornamentalist in its
poetics than the eighteenth century. For Pope, even for Johnson as poet and
critic, the fitting together of form, style, and subject was not innocent (it
never is, but those periods when innocence is claimed are the fascinating
ones). Form during the period from 1660 to 1795 was decorous, programmatic, subservient to the hierarchy of genres. Ideas of Augustan form
created a state of affairs Wordsworth and Coleridge were always to deplore,
as they attempted to repossess the precritical innocence of a writing whose
prosody and meaning have a seamless fit. Ballads afforded a model of prosodic innocence, but so too did the work of Shakespeare and Milton,
megaliths beyond the far edge of the plain of Augustan achievement. However, as M. H. Abrams and others have remarked, a Wordsworthian poetic
theory that describes a spontaneous overflow of powerful feeling will always
imply a container from which the lyric emotion brims, and will therefore
entail more or less of a self-conscious separation between feeling and its
forms. Thus the wish from 1795 forward to resist what Coleridge called
"shape as superinduced," his synonym for Augustan form. More convincingly in the writing of poetry than in Romantic poetic theory, the ornamental-

ism of Enlightenment poetics helped to create its own undoing in the striving for form as proceeding. A major reorientation of theory and practice in Western literature—the attempt to disregard the rhetorical, generic, and prosodic theory of classical Greece—begins as a philosophical-stylistic aversion. In this process, it is difficult to separate out aversion from genuine innovation, the more so because the subsequent histories of the stylistic revolution are themselves part of the problem. However, in this case the innovation was so complete that from 1795 form as proceeding is the manner of writing all poets will have to contend with; in the work of Walt Whitman one sees the transition from the premises to the measures of this new poetry.

Many writers on prosody, critics as well as authors of manuals, speak of uniform prosodic premises of norm and variation. For them the history of prosody is not problematic. These evolutionary theories, which assume uniform prosodic premises from epoch to epoch, are open to challenge. However valuable it may be to work out descriptions of patches of continuity and genuine development, the method leaves no adequate way of dealing with prosodic innovation. Prosodic-epistemological breaks of greater or lesser magnitude do not happen in an entirely random way, of course; but neither do they add up to present-day perfection or a single way of writing. Any complete account of stylistic dynamism must supply, in addition, a theory of epochal discontinuity.

The present status of literary commentary, where no approach to texts is clearly dominant, reproduces in the realm of criticism the stylistic pluralism that we find in the texts of the Modern period. The uncertainties arise from the perception that perhaps, after all, literature can only be a denunciation of literature—so extravagantly does it call its own mode of existence into question that any statement about it is at risk, tangled in displacements of irony. There is a kind of philosophical commentary that pursues these very real complexities in the way language affects the representation, tracking metaphors to hidden lairs; and at the other extreme there is a critical technology that identifies and catalogs the literariness of the surface. But neither of these commentaries sets out to be historical in any credible way. They share the premise that it is now strictly impossible to do the narratives and analyses of works and oeuvres that were thinkable up to the very recent past; but neither moves far beyond this aversion to attempt another, more powerful historical construction. And so, at the very frontiers of theory, despite a growing bafflement about the proper contents of a history of literature, historical poetics remains one of the least-studied areas; avoided, even relegated.

In Anglo-American criticism the lifework of Josephine Miles is one of the few very distinguished examples of a strong, accurate theory of the relationship of eras and modes. Within the area of historical poetics, and notably in Miles's work, most studies very tightly calibrate their periodizations for analysis of the wave-and trough structure of literary phases. That work is admirable and largely reliable, and yet, looking at the same data with another reading of the historical series (eras), it is possible to defend another kind of periodization, at once cruder and less verifiable statistically, yet fruitful in speculation about post-Romantic writing and the current state of theory. This notion (which I will call the epistemological-prosodic break, and which derives from Thomas S. Kuhn's account of *The Structure of Scientific Revolutions* [1962; 1970]) differs from the usual by postulating certain rare crises in the history of poetry that carry all before them and institute for poets a new way of working with language. I am not proposing another template to lay over the top of existing theory. The concept of a break conveys the incommensurability of one part of the historical grid to another, and so more forcibly than existing theory includes the idea of continuity through revolutions.

To the skeptically inclined, such a term as *prosodic avantgardism,* like *free verse* and *organic form,* may sound self-contradictory, an unconventional prosody being no prosody at all, and a poem lacking meter and rhyme no poem. It goes better if we think of *prosody* as referring broadly to measure, form, and pattern in poetic writing, and *avantgardism* as the attempt by writers to appear unprecedented. The term derives from the literary historian's need for a theory of innovation, a graph of how change takes place within a genre and from genre to genre as these are destroyed and created, that is to say, changed. Just as question and answer in certain kinds of philosophy are strictly correlative, propositions being uttered as answers to specific questions, so a literary style may be said to be answerable to a previous style or styles. Literary innovation is as much a matter of aversion and reverse reflection as of original invention.

A period style is a probability system. To know what is probable one must also be saturated enough in the history of poetry to know what is possible in a given epoch and then, within that, in its schools and phases. The period style of 1795 and after fends off a great many of the premises and procedures of earlier writing, especially those of Augustan form. Literariness, marked language, was and remains the central issue. The early Romantics, the generation of writers who first tried to imagine the abolition of convention, first came to understand the need for their renewal by estrangement. The initiatory work, which dates from 1795, is Coleridge's "Eolian Harp"; the *experimentum crucis* for an insurgent meter is his "Christabel," begun in 1797; the vehicles of the new style are blank verse and the ballad stanza and the line of Blake's prophetic poems; the landmark collection in the new mode is *Lyrical Ballads* of 1798, with its fully developed manifesto in the 1800 preface. Further phases begin with the coming of a second, convinced generation of Romantics, the attacks in the quarterlies, Wordsworth's formal acceptance into the canon as laureate, and the wholesale adoption and deepening of Romantic premises by the Victorian poets and critics. Partly by repudiation of the public mode of Augustan form, we see here within the confines of the meanings and techniques of a traditional discipline the attempt to marshal all the reserve forces of interiority, producing not anarchy but arbitrariness, fragmentation, pluralism, and accelerating the processes of style change and canon formation. For the first time in modern literary history, an imagination of the transparence of the medium of language brings with it an exploratory understanding of the communal and plastic nature of the medium.

How does one distinguish a new paradigm or episteme from a variant articulation of an old one? In the present instance, the historical like the formal question has to be addressed as a dilemma in logic. For this reason, I shall describe the literary transition of 1795 by means of the hyperbole of the epistemological-prosodic break. Despite the bewildering variety of writing since 1795, there emerges a single premise—the cult of apparent styleless-ness—which dominates all writing between Wordsworth and yesterday. How, in more detail, this transition that is a break came to be is an argument whose details I now lay out by means of a table. The table plots history horizontally and theory vertically. The year 1795 is the dividing line of prosodic innovation. On each of seven topics, crucial to poetics, Romantic form as proceeding is a reversal-transformation of Augustan form. This table may serve to suggest how a single universe of discourse emerges coherently after the break, and how the break, in fuller description, is a conversion wherein concepts remain, but with meanings deepened or developed in unprecedented ways.

At this most volatile moment in English literary history, the rate of stylistic dynamism lurched into a rate of change so fast that to the observer the concept of transition disappears and becomes contrast. To affirm as much is to deny that Romanticism is producing the same kind of literature as usual, only with the reins relaxed. Romanticism is producing another kind of literature.

The expunging of Augustan by Romantic form was by no means an abandonment of form. Rather, there was a shifting of formal values and an invention of new types of patterning. More precisely, there was so profound an intensification and specialization of elements already present, in the way poems implicate the reader's cognitive powers, that there was developed a new manner of proceeding. Another principle of composition is either achieved or hinted. This is the principle of psychological process, of achieved surprise, of movement, of planned spontaneity. Nonetheless, while Coleridge and Wordsworth edged toward sprung rhythm, free verse, and the prose poem—when, for example, they spoke about the absence of an "essential difference" between the language of prose and the language of verse—neither of the two spelled out a poetics of the attempt to be unprecedented. A more radical theory of prosody was to be worked out fully by later generations of the avant-garde.

Augustan Form	Table 1. *Romantic Transformations of Augustan Poetic Premises*	Romantic Form
Augustan form rests on a concept of the unity of language—poetic language as referential prose modified by regulating conventions.	**1. Language**	Romantic and Modern form rests on a concept of the poet's own language within language.
Augustan poetry imitates Nature as the theoretical source of ancient art.	**2. Nature and Art**	Romantic and Modern poetry understands itself as but one conscious phase of the whole of creative activity going on in Nature.
Innovation is correction.	**3. Innovation**	Innovation is the wish to be or seem unprecedented.
Augustan genre theory is a fixed and unhistorical hierarchy.	**4. Genre Theory**	Romantic and Modern genre theory aims at the dissolution of genres—in practice this means mixing, reweighting, and occasionally inventing genres.
In large-scale organization, Augustan form employs the accretive method of antilogical impressionism, completing a fragment, filling a known pattern.	**5. Organization**	Romantic and Modern form typically employs the method of the "coalesced totality," order through "multeïty," a "fusion to force many into one."
In local deployment of devices, Augustan form tends to avoid effects that draw attention to the arbitrariness of language.	**6. The Device**	The device must, like language and meter, be reinvented from within by avoiding previous usage or exposing its deficiencies.
In the buildup of segment and line, Augustan form seeks to construct larger patterns out of exactly equal temporal units.	**7. Buildup of Line and Segment** (idea of meter and stanza)	Romantic and Modern form seeks intense differentiation of time into units of unexpected type and measure.

Augustan Form

Civil war and Commonwealth seared the minds of Englishmen of all factions in the seventeenth century. A period of revolution, confusion, and diversity generated after 1660 a ferocious and overcompensating return to orderly ways in all spheres of action and thought. An ethos of agreement, ratified in the formal arrangements for parliamentary democracy in 1689,

understandably becomes the expression of the politics of qualified monar-
chy, religious toleration, mercantile expansion, the sacredness of property.
Church and state, as Ian Watt has pointed out, "faced by religious and civil
dissension . . . had combined to set up more centralized and codified systems
of order," finding "a useful parallel in the political, social, and cultural life of
Augustan Rome."[5] The challenge of chaos and the mob was the same—in
their proper sphere—faced by Augustan poetry and Neo-Classical criticism,
as these pursuits mediated doctrines that were "the spirited rearguard action
in the retreat of Renaissance humanism before the march of science."[6] The
justifications for imaginative literature that emerge between 1660 and 1750
display "a strikingly diminished and nervous humanistic tradition,"[7] with
many of its emphases borrowed from a common European stock, especially
from France.

English Neo-Classicism was never so aggressive or inflexible as that in
France, yet in this case the plain facts of the matter are not so productive as
the way this period style was understood by the style that supplanted it. For
Neo-Classicism was surpassed earlier in England than it was in France—
Romanticism and revolution first becoming "one composite form"[8] in 1795,
in an England that had its revolution and regicide in the seventeenth century.
Roland Barthes and Pierre Sollers would date the coming of an uncom-
promising and Modern intelligence in the France of the 1840s; in England the
condemning and subsuming of the Enlightenment took place fifty years earlier in the practice and critical justification of poetry.[9] Walter Jackson Bate
remarks that the emergence of Romanticism was "slower and longer prepared for in the actual writing (as distinct from critical theory) that preceded
it" than the "brisk transition" to the previous, Neo-Classical period style.
"There is no other instance, after the invention of printing, where you find a
settled group of literary premises and aims imported almost bodily, adopted
with such dispatch, and then transformed into orthodoxy, or near-
orthodoxy, for so long a time (a full seventy or eighty years), despite a large
undercurrent that runs counter to it."[10] To produce such uniform agreement
so quickly, the need for codified systems of order must have been very great
in this age, as in every other area of human experience after the return of
Charles II. Augustan form does not scorch the earth of alternate modes; it
would be wrong, however, to discount the strength of centralizing forces in
this aesthetic: the dominance of the couplet, the hierarchy of the genres, the
strictness of syllable-count meters, and the legislative force of often-
reprinted regularizing manuals like Edward Bysshe's *Art of English Poetry*
(1702; going through nine editions by 1762).

The high Augustan period, down to 1750, is especially apt for the present
attempt to declare "how a poem . . . transfers the qualities of system from
the code of the message,"[11] from cultural premise to literary practice. Considering the underlying code of ideological and generic assumptions, for a
moment, we may specify for it a handful of pertinent tendencies expressed

as descriptive phrases, each of which may be considered as applying to all seven categories of Augustan form. Augustan form, then, *strives for authority.* This is a form drive that, especially in the couplet, has "promptings toward intellectual control and public articulation,"[12] and rhyme, metrics, and syntax in satirical couplets as in sublime blank verse display, as assumptions, an adequacy to pronounce upon all issues raised. Augustan form is *a clique or class phenomenon,* in a sense precisely opposite to the elitism of the avant-garde poetics. Norms were discovered by considering what gives pleasure to all men, or at least to all educated men; however, and crucially, "it little mattered to these critics that the educated readers were only a small part of human kind."[13] Augustan form is *overtly ethical.* A unified period style trades in familiar techniques and civic virtues (we *know* and will then *say*). In its heyday the closed couplet is an index of moral earnestness, not of ethical quest; a medium "for the definition of public concerns and the address to a publicly situated audience."[14] And Augustan form is *unhistorical,* taking historically evolved ideological and poetic modes as natural givens. These modes are considered to have come to something like final fixity and perfection in the eighteenth-century present, which in its highest forms recapitulates without distortion the normative thoughts of persons distant in space or time. Thus for John Dennis (ca. 1725), "there is for poetry no system of known rules but those which are in Aristotle and his interpreters, and therefore if they are not the rightful rules poetry is not an art."[15] The norms of politics, religion, and aesthetics show themselves, then, as separate but related features of the same historical moment, maintained somewhat perilously by certain fictions about the universality of human hopes and fears. The grandeur of generality for the Augustans meant not so much abstractness as ubiquity of application; but actually what was universal and cosmopolitan was so only for the class, sect, and style that happened to be in control. Roland Barthes's statement that Classical literature is class literature is an oversimplification; yet that Augustan form partakes and exhibits a historical ideology of strictly agreed, codified norms is as unquestionable as the unity, elegance, and rational imagination of Neo-Classical practice in all the arts.

Geoffrey Tillotson, James Sutherland, Reuben Brower, and others have ably shown how Augustan poetry transfers a narrowed range of technical devices, genre rankings, and themes to the texture and structure of individual poems.[16] Assuming that interpretive groundwork, it becomes pertinent to comment on the very strictness of Augustan premises that led Pope typically to write: "The wingèd Courser, like a gen'rous Horse, / Shows most true Mettle when you check his Course"—and that leads a modern admirer of Pope, W. K. Wimsatt in his essay on eighteenth-century poetry entitled "Imitation as Freedom," to praise "the enabling restraints of formal bondage."[17] In most artistic styles, in poetry and the other fine arts, the relation between theory and practice is not so sensitive, but normally somewhat loose and muddled. However, as Charles Rosen has remarked in his book on music, *The Classical Style:*

> Neoclassicism is aggressively doctrinaire: it is art with a thesis. . . . There is a conscious attempt on the part of the artist to make practice follow theory, even when this theory, professed and expounded, collides head on with artistic habits and with less conscious principles which only practice can gradually bring to light. In most neo-classic works, a considerable tension results from this conflict, a desire for theoretical coherence which leads paradoxically at moments to an incoherence within the artistic language, forced into contradiction with itself in order to conform to something exterior.[18]

What is at issue here is the kind of intelligence that requires, for its life and ordonnance, such strictness of aesthetic code, and that in its greatest works must permit into the code, as part of the total effect, "an explosive force that is in excess of the works' own pretensions."[19] W. K. Wimsatt has gone further than most writers on the Augustan Mode in English poetry to describe "a split in the Augustan ideal of eloquence—between a social side and a purely literary side," calling Pope and Swift "laughing poets of a heightened unreality," and noticing the curiosity "on the face of the matter, that the great age of classical order should be at ease only in the Gothic and mystical shackles of rhyme."[20] This other side of Augustan realism and sweet reasonableness, to be seen in the frequent Crazy or Cave-of-Spleen writing in Pope and Swift and their use of fools and lunatics as vehicles of literary speech, and to be coordinated with the reductive wit and paradox that is the major ethical-rhetorical medium, suggests that a desperation closely attends the Augustan confidence, limiting both the cogency and the nonsense.[21] Clearly we need to see complexities and vivacities of this sort beneath the definitive Augustan assertions. And with respect to details of technique, very likely Rosen's comment on the chastity of Gluck's music, "the refusal to permit vocal display, the absence of ornament, the endings of arias which leave no possibility for applause," applies with some accuracy to the verbal music of prosody: "The austerity is not only a form of stoicism, a holding back from pleasure, but one of the main sources of pleasure in itself."[22]

The ethos of vanquished difficulty, of Pegasus in check, is a stock premise of all Neo-Classic theories of poetic creation, so Rosen's usage is original only in the way repression is conceived as contradictory, "incomplete," and withal a term of highest commendation:

> The deliberate cult of the natural leads in neoclassicism to an effort of self-denial and repression which becomes indistinguishable from the "perverse": it gives the greatest neoclassic works—the operas of Gluck, the architecture of Ledoux, the paintings of David—an explosive force that is in excess of the works' own pretensions.
>
>   What this comes to, in fact, is that the greatness of so much of neoclassicism arises from the incomplete repression of instinct by doctrine (in-

stinct being here nothing more mystical than unformulated doctrine). It has, therefore, the curious result that the theory of neoclassicism is in a special sense built into the works themselves.[23]

In theories of culture, the value of this way of speaking is in its coordination of overt and unexpressed meanings in a given text or period style. With Rosen's help, I introduce it first to urge that studies of Augustan verse that concentrate mainly on the civic virtues of the "honest muse"[24] stay too much with the official meanings of the poetry. Also and primarily, it remains to point out with Coleridge, a Romantic, that suppression prepares for overthrow, and that often what is excluded from Augustan form returns after 1795, with a new access of intensity and detail, and with the insistence of an original discovery. I refer to cognitive and prosodic variety in the constitution of line and verse segment, the noncouplet forms of diverse or weakened shape that instance an era of stylistic pluralism; to the kind of poem that sounds in the ear by emphasizing accent rather than theoretical ictus; and to the larger, culminating stylistic-moral motive force of English Romanticism, the rapport (of admiration and aversion) with the achievement of Shakespeare and Milton. Let those two names stand, with some hyperbole, as icons for everything outside the categories of Neo-Classical aesthetics, for that is how the situation was understood by the emergent aesthetics of organic form.

Existing studies of Augustan verse emphasize the great satirical poems in couplets. Achievement in this format is by general agreement supremely distinguished and arresting. Yet there is perhaps a parti pris in such valuation of the satirical, related to the element of Neo-Classical revival René Wellek has noted in the New Criticism.[25] Representative of most studies in taking the satirical poetry as the fundamentally Augustan type, W. K. Wimsatt's essay, "The Augustan Mode in English Poetry," mentions the sublime or descriptive mode only to disparage it.[26] In an essay with the same title, Ralph Cohen undertakes a correction. Implicitly throughout, explicitly in a footnote, Cohen argues that the Augustan poetic mode must include the recognition of the two poetic genres, satire and the Georgic-descriptive poem, that share a body of common features, similarly used.[27] Moving from generic through technical-formal to religious contexts, Cohen lists ten "habits of expression and thought" to summarize his description of the Augustan mode, which term he takes to mean "no more than a range of specific uses of conventionalized figures, images, ideas, and syntactical, metrical, or organizational structure in the poetry of 1660–1750."[28] Very likely, in this encounter, Wimsatt undervalues the continued presence of descriptive poetry, while Cohen is mistaken in seeing this type as equal in achievement as well as tendency. The encounter itself illustrates what Claudio Guillén has said about the multiplicity of time—the combined presence in a single historical moment of a "cluster of durations."[29] Plainly the first order of business is to ascertain and to date the dominant type. In my reading the descriptive-sublime poem, which is secondary until 1750 despite the immense popularity of Thomson's *Seasons,* after that date becomes an insurgent type, and is eventually transcended by its heir, the greater Romantic lyric.[30]

Involved in the shift from Neo-Classic to Romantic is a change of the dominant, in the sense of a reigning form of thought or aspect of technical form in the work, from uniformity to diversity in all levels of aesthetic experience.[31] Until about 1750 satirical and sublime types partake of the same dominant, sharing (as Cohen convincingly demonstrates) a common way of posing technical and moral problems. I aim to particularize this Augustan dominant by developing the seven postulates already shown on my table on page 34. The action of these postulates may be imaged as a type of ideological DNA, which replicates everything essential for the life of Augustan form in particular poems. The breakdown, dispersion, or reversal of these matrices is the causal explanation at the level of literary ideology for the emergence of the Romantic concept of form; and that is why exposition of these same topics, in their Romantic transforms, must follow on after the end of the present section.

Since the first four postulates describe the cultural code behind Augustan form, they may be called postulates of system. The remaining three, describing more precisely the executive or formal code, may be termed postulates of structure. System and structure here separate out, for purposes of exposition, aspects that are united in the writing itself understood as act and as created text.

The postulates of system concern language, nature and art, innovation, and genre theory.

1. *Augustan form rests on a concept of the unity of language—poetic language as referential prose modified by regulating conventions.* Pope had written, in the *Essay on Criticism:*

> But true *Expression,* like th'unchanging Sun,
> *Clears,* and *improves* whate'er it shines upon,
> It *gilds* all Objects, but it *alters* none.
>
> (315–17)

That view of verbal art as expression, not invention, is perfectly matched and explicated by an Aristotelian critic, writing in a Neo-Classical spirit in 1952: "Words must be subordinate to their functions, for they are selected and arranged with a view to these."[32] Elder Olson shares with Pope a sense of division between subject and expression, and the wish narrowly to restrict the medium of language by the bounds of logic. In Pope's time, especially, there is little need for an evolutionary history of device and counterdevice, genre and countergenre that derives from a nuanced concept of convention, and from an appreciation of the materiality of the medium of language. The sensuous-selective aspects of literary function are decreased, in favor of the combinatory and rational-relational features of sheer grammar, which already has a system of rules. In addition, a rules system is imposed on the sensuous-selective function: a formulaic diction and syllable-count metric serve to routinize the language material, and to decrease the possibility of randomness. The Augustans, explains Rachel Trickett, "hesitated to play with language, because language is the common means of communicating truth, and it is dangerous to meddle with it. Instead they felt it their duty to fix and purify the literary language so that its precision and its clear referential qualities should be preserved."[33] Since by seeming to have independent life the sensuous, concrete, phonetic aspect of language jeopardizes this unity of language, it is not so much systematically combated as *left unrecognized.*

Accordingly, in Roland Barthes's phrasing, poetry is another prose with an extra dosage of equivalences. In the Classical period, "prose and poetry are quantities," says Barthes. "Their difference can be measured; they are neither more nor less separated than two different numbers, contiguous like them, but dissimilar because of the very difference in their magnitudes."[34] The difference between prose and poetry is one of sheer quantity, not of essence; poetry for the Augustan writer and reader does not evoke "any particular domain, any particular depth of feeling." Poetry and prose, literary and ordinary language, can be changed one into the other by addition or subtraction of a certain repertoire of sociable signs. Neo-Classical verbal art, created before a Romanticism's suspicious attitude toward literary language,

> could have no sense of being a language, for it *was* language . . . it was transparent, it flowed and left no deposit, it brought ideally together a universal Spirit and a decorative sign without substance or responsibility; it was a language "closed" by social and not natural bounds.

Surely Barthes overstates, in the urgency of opposing a Classical to his own avantgardist frame of mind. Yet as the next postulate tends to show, the broad opposition does not hold up, and whatever is debatable in his account of the "natural" cannot be discussed except with categories developed after the avant-garde fracture of the Augustan unity of language.

2. *Augustan poetry imitates Nature as the theoretical source of ancient art.* Again Pope is centrally characteristic:

> Those rules of old discovered, not devised,
> Are Nature Still, but Nature methodized.
> *(Essay on Criticism,* 1.88–89)

The belief that "Those rules" of artistic practice "Are Nature" derives from the standard-setting currency of ancient art, whose survival through many ages and climes is taken as the best evidence that the old works mirror nature, and that there exist universal standards of excellence. (It is important to remind ourselves that, excepting Perrault, all the major participants in the well-known Ancients-versus-Moderns dispute agreed that nothing could compare with the literary works of antiquity.) This postulate, like the other six, represents one aspect of the nonhistorical, nondevelopmental bias of the era.

The ordinary universe of life and detail is not to be abolished, for Augustan poetic theory does have a place for the particular and the normal; but, sieved for essentials, these elements are to be raised to a level of generality that dignifies them with the simplicity and probability of the normative works in Greek and Latin tradition. Action, characters, and diction are to stylize reality yet not to move so far from it as to evade plausibility. England adapted Neo-Classicism to its needs, and English critics allowed the poet greater freedom than in France, yet these are regional variations within a cohesive and supranational doctrine—maintaining the superiority of Classical-language poets to vernacular ones, and the consequent need for model-following modes of translation and of imitation as free-running parallel. Although the Classical theory of models "had a close bearing on the Augustan vogue of translations, paraphrases, and 'imitations,' "[35] clearly the last of these could include realistic description, compliment, and also personal reflection; and the other two types were not uninfluenced by contemporary feeling.

Pope's advice, "First follow Nature," makes the presumed nature being imitated in ancient poetry the test of Augustan form; thus identifying "Nature, the ancients, the rules, and sound reason, so that to follow any was to follow all."[36] So Nature was equal to Art, and yet also the test of Art. This involved a circular argument, whose construction helped to keep unrecognized an uncertainty at the center of the Augustan aesthetic system. One dilemma from many—the controversy carried by Dryden and Howard, on whether rhyme or blank verse was the better medium for drama, shows the imprecision of the fundamental assumption of Augustan criticism, the imitation of nature. For Howard the closeness to ordinary speech of blank verse was most natural, for Dryden the hieratic distancing effect of rhyming language; yet the way the argument is framed, neglecting that both types of poetry are products of art and convention and thus more alike than different, doomed the dispute to unreality, and at the end of his career Dryden is to be found arguing Howard's position. The Augustans, for reasons related to the coherences that define their civilization, are in their critical theory unable to perceive what is a commonplace after Kant and Coleridge: that the concept of Nature is itself a projection of the desired. Nature for the Augustans had a "strong social cast," was a nature of man's creations, including literature;

Romanticism changed all that. "The Nature of one age becomes the Art of the next."[37]

3. *Innovation is Correction.* In the 1690s and the first decade of the eighteenth century, Walsh, Congreve, and Garth—conscious heirs of Dryden—initiated a minor Classical revival. Formal odes, imitations, and translations rather than satire were their preferred vehicles, and it is under their glance that Pope begins as a writer—with the well-known advice of Walsh on the *"one way left of excelling;* for though we had several great poets, we never had any one great poet that was *correct;* and he desired me to make that my study and aim."[38] Innovation, the initiation of change in literary history, is by this and attendant premises defined as correction. Originality is welcome, provided that in all cases it includes its contrary, familiarity; so Samuel Johnson's definition of wit, as that "which is at once natural and new," typically understands verbal invention as a repatterning of existing counters. Ralph Cohen has called the "beginning of a change" in literary history " 'innovation,' its continuity, development, and extension . . . 'variation,' "[39] but that Modern distinction is overridden for the most part in Neo-Classical aesthetics, where innovation is most often a subset of variation. Partly, one imagines, this preoccupation with correctness is the result of rational pride in the taming of loose sound and meaning; but also, beneath this reason, the result of an uneasiness that such fixative measures should be required to prevent the decay of English. Pope's "envy of the adamant of Latin," says Tillotson, led him to "precise correctness" in choice of vocabulary, and to "close Latin-like packing of the line . . . Correctness was a likely preservative."[40] In Pope we are not to understand correctness of this sort as a general term of value, then, but "as a more specially descriptive term, meaning something like symmetry and something like restraint and precision."[41] As applying to fulfilled intentions, a decisive combination of rhetoric and meter, correctness is a term of the highest commendation.

Three phenomena of Augustan poetics derive from these assumptions about innovation: the vogue of translation and imitation and the refinement of fixed modes; the casting about to find founders of a period style in the "easy" yet strict couplets of Denham and Waller; and the specifying of "Rules for Making Verses" in the manual-poetics of such as Edward Bysshe, who could write of Chaucer, Spenser, and Shakespeare that "their Language is now become so antiquated and obsolete, that most Readers of our Age [1702] have no Ear for them."[42] Bysshe, finding that poetry is "very much polish'd and refin'd since" those days, sets out to provide "Rules which they neglected." By the time Johnson comes to write on Pope's perfection of Modern technique, three-quarters of a century after Bysshe, it is now "dangerous . . . to attempt any further improvement in versification": dangerous, that is, to define innovation in any way but as variation.

4. *Augustan genre theory is a fixed and unhistorical hierarchy.* Literary conventions, as Claudio Guillén has said, "are not only technical prerequisites but broader fields or systems resulting from earlier, singular, genetic influences. The goal of the impact is transferred, as it were, from the writer to the vehicle."[43] Augustan poetics gloried in that transference, wishing to subsume individual voice in the sociable dialogue of tradition; so genre theory was developed to an extent quite unparalleled in literary history since 1795. At best the elaboration of a descriptive-legislative genre theory, including structural and stylistic criteria, gave all readers a standard of judgment as to whether the poet had chosen adequate means for producing a certain effect; whether he had adopted the proper decorum. Yet at times the rules of the genres became "the rules of a game and in practice often a set of pedantries which allowed the unimaginative reader and critic to judge by a ready-made yardstick." In writing thus René Wellek summarizes the view not only of the English Romantics, but also the sly satire against an imaginary critic, Dick Minim, written by Samuel Johnson in two of his periodical essays.[44] Of course there were attacks on the rules during the Augustan era, directed not by writers who were rebels from Neo-Classicism, but by persons simply hoping to preserve its genuine humanistic basis.[45] Again, three notions—stereotyped as "poetic fury," "a poet is born not made," and "the grace beyond the reach of art"—were escape clauses, codicils permitting the careful percolation into theory of more transcendent views of poetry.[46]

Lack of a developed historical sense made any concept of dialectic between genre and countergenre unthinkable, and so there was the blind antihistorical trust that an ancient genre would have the same resonance in a Modern setting. The antidevelopmental bias could only create anxiety in a period most of whose epics and tragedies could muster but tatters of heroic idiom from Dryden's Vergil, and whose diminished humanism expressed itself (marvelously, but that is not what is in question here) in mock heroic, a form that depends on the absence of heroic values. Despite the prevalence of the "massive theory of epic,"[47] a poem like Pope's *Dunciad* imagines an environment that rebukes heroes and the possibility of the heroic; that is satire's way of rebuking not the heroic, but rather an age in which it seems irrelevant. We have, too, the curious phenomenon of one of the final fragments Pope drafted before his death: lines for the beginning of *Brutus,* a possible English epic, significantly in blank verse, very likely in a small way an admission of the lack of fit between the official couplet medium and the demands of epic.[48] Following after René Le Bossu's then-definitive *Traité du poème épique* (1675), John Sheffield, earl of Mulgrave, wrote in 1682 "An Essay upon Poetry," of no merit as a poem, but typical in setting out the range of literary types from lowly song to lofty epic:

> By painful steps we are at last got up
> Parnassus' hill, upon whose airy top

> The *Epic* poets so divinely show,
> And with just pride behold the rest below.[49]

Epic, Sheffield says, is "the chief effort of human sense." And yet Homer and Vergil are the only two exemplars; neither is exactly an eighteenth-century wit. A century later, after many such English efforts as Sir Richard Blackmore's *Prince Arthur* (1695), the theory of epic was extinct. Augustan poetics could not admit to itself what it knew, that loss of the epic is the price of civilization.

Despite the new interest in classifying genres, certain matters were never properly examined, among them the difference between essential principles and arbitrary rules, the distinction between the genres, and the manner in which, if at all, the ancient table of genres was to be increased. "It was rarely clear," says Wellek, "whether the table of genres was closed or whether new genres could be admitted."[50] Hybrids arose, like the successful innovation of the Georgic-descriptive poem in Sir John Denham's *Cooper's Hill* (1642), and for these rarities exceptions were made: Johnson's *Life of Denham* sensibly certifies this discovery, and Ralph Cohen has recently shown the poem's innovative quality to reside in a resolution of a seventeenth-century cultural crisis.[51] The Pindaric ode, against any rational expectation, was widely accepted after Cowley's versions in 1656—one suspects because the form, misunderstood from Greek, offered a plausible Classical cover for feelings and rhythms quite outside the Augustan agreements. Often, too, a form like the novel or the periodical essay had no contemporary justification beyond popular success, and this unreadiness of theory to keep step with practice tended to undermine the system of genres. (Henry Fielding's rationales for the novel as a comic epic in prose were the basis for such a justification; but how well were they known?) Finally, such genres toward the bottom of the traditional hierarchy as ballad, landscape description, and ode—minor precisely because personal in content and lyric in form—steadily gained throughout the century, so that between 1750 and 1830 the ranked schema of genres by and large reverses itself. Following the epic tradition of narrative discourse, Augustan form foregrounds the facts; Romantic form is more interested in bringing out how the facts feel.

In Augustan form regarded as a cultural system, at the highest as well as the lowest degree of sophistication,[52] critical thought thus equates literary and ordinary language, art and nature, innovation and variation, genre and immutable truth. Of course it is impossible for the writers to make admissions about this contradictory state of affairs, for the contradictions are the structure on which the period's civilization and literary style are based. (Romantic form, when it came, resolved many of these contradictions and went on to found itself on the basis of new ones!) With honesty, imagination, and a systematic thoroughness, Augustan poets and critics prevent the recognition of incipient Modernity, uniting, sometimes desperately, elements that must eventually come apart. Their achievement was very great; greater than they knew, for only after 1795 was it possible to suspect that the great formative premises of Classical civilization, which had conflated rhetoric and poetics since the time of Aristotle, were beginning to be challenged by the advance guard of an oppositional poetic system.

Augustan poetics gives very little latitude to the reader's chance thoughts or desires, stipulating as it does the poem as a plenitude that matches, and fills, the reader's mind. The Augustan poem, in Samuel Johnson's unintentionally dramatic phrase, will "shackle" the reader's attention by meter and other features, by regularizing, habit-dictating rhythms that convey ethical lessons through prosodic reinforcement. Eccentric versification can thereby become, and be called, irregular, idiosyncratic, chaotic, or vicious.[53] The data of aesthetics in such a scheme will reside in the formal quality of objects or in the constitution of the human mind, in either case a definition of data that excludes the subjective, historical response of readers. The poem is to have the ontological status of, say, a physical object. Affective stylistics, the process of response to the text's temporal movement, the "struggle for meaning," are outside such a definition, as is the post-Romantic idea of the poem itself, in Wallace Stevens's phrasing, as the "act of the mind." The poem, as instance of universal criteria of excellence, was freed from the pressure of fashion and personality, but at some hazard of losing its historicity, and of easing into a solely public mode of address, sonorous but hollow.[54]

The Neo-Classic wish to erect universally accepted standards of excellence has as one result an increased concern with the formal aspects of poetry. Augustan criticism, often to be found in justificatory contexts— Dryden's dedications and prefaces, Johnson's familiar essays and critical biographies—is surprisingly rich in descriptive content and highly conscious about questions of technique. The strongest criticism (usually by the leading poets of the age) shares with the pedestrian a taxonomic impulse to tick off stylistic devices, rhetorical figures, meters, but is at times able (with the finest Augustan poetry) to elude the worst faults of "a breakup of the work of art into categories viewed almost in isolation," and "the view of form as mere ornament [that] triumphed over older, more instinctively organic conceptions."[55] With Corneille as instance and in a European context, René Wellek speaks of the "cramping influence" of rules on practice; yet clearly English theory was less cramping than French—steering "a middle course between what in theory seems desirable and what in practice is found to work."[56] In fact, English poetry was more exuberant than even English criticism might rigorously expect:

The achievement of Dryden and Pope was that they used the guise of an apparently level and rationalized, even prosaic, discourse to accomplish poetic expression of a certain character. . . . The numerous and varied figures (mixed wit and false wit), anithesis, metaphor, pun and quasi-pun, Gothic rhyme, alliteration, turn, tranlacer, and agnomination, which actually mark the highly artful poetry of Alexander Pope, are scarcely alluded to in the reigning poetic treatise of his day, the *Art of Poetry* by Edward Bysshe.[57]

W. K. Wimsatt's implication in these sentences of his, that the success of Augustan poetry "consisted in its being a hundred years behind the most advanced theory," seems to involve an unnecessary anachronism. But the absence of a more complete cross-indexing of theory and practice in this most authoritative period style in all English literature must be a cause for wonder as we now study, at the intersection of poetics and metrics, how the official rules relate to the procedures that actually generate the Augustan text.

The postulates of structure concern overall organization, the concept of the poetic device, and the construction of segment and line.

5. *In large-scale poetic organization, Augustan form typically employs the accretive method of antilogical impressionism, completing a fragment, filling a known pattern.* The manuscript shows that the first sixty or so lines of Samuel Johnson's "Vanity of Human Wishes" are written in the same hand with two different types of ink, and divided not in the middle of the whole passage but always near the middle of *each line*. One surmises that the author, having in his head composed this much of his free-running imitation of Juvenal's tenth satire, dashed off the first half of each line to jog his memory—then, at another sitting with a different ink and pressure, filled in the other half-lines at his leisure. A similar case of verbal virtuosity, Johnson's occasional poem "To Mrs. Thrale, On Her Completing Her Thirty-fifth Year" (1776), a bagatelle of eighteen lines in octosyllabic couplets all on the same rhyme sound, was extemporaneous; these were, Mrs. Thrale said, "Verses which I wrote down from his Mouth as he made them." Johnson told her that this was dictionary maker's poetry: "You may observe that the rhymes run in alphabetical order exactly."[58] In both cases Johnson performs the feat of running division on the groundwork (as Dryden described the task of literary translation). In the "Vanity" instance his proactive and retroactive memory is helped, if not enabled, by the presence of Juvenal's matrix text; in the other instance, yet more schematic, the extra trammel of the alphabetical sequence of rhyming, from "alive" to "wive," is a program that, once exhausted, stops the machine. I take these to be somewhat extreme instances of a usual trait of Augustan poetry—its reliance on preexisting for-

mal conditions, its tendency, in plot as well as prosody, to work as narrative exposition rather than as freestanding lyric.

Johnson's constructive imagination, in prose and in verse seeming to move by sharp, calculated bursts rather than by immense traceries of ratiocination, illustrates the aspects of the Augustan mode Ralph Cohen has usefully generalized as: "composition . . . by accretion with revisions and additions, implying a view of knowledge as extended and detailed observation of experience"; "the organizational strategy of the inherited mixed form, with its varied tones or varied speakers . . . implying a social and natural world in exhilarating, anxious, or dangerous change"; and "the use of the heroic couplet and blank verse as preferred metres in the primary forms, containing subtle shadings and rhymings that imply harmonies and contrasts in these completed fragments."[59] In Johnson's "Vanity" as often in the curve of a poem by Dryden, Pope, or Swift, an initial variegation in the scene, literal or moral, is detailed descriptively by elaboration of shadings and instances, then gradually or finally harmonized. Writing on Dryden, Alan Roper has remarked how important it is that Neo-Classical poems "strike at once the note of a man of good sense speaking to his social equals or superiors,"[60] and indeed once the opening has made such a firm contract the poem can only with willful perversity go off the skids. These poems leave the impression of being stable shapes even if the harmonizing ending, to paraphrase the end of Johnson's "Vanity," tends to make the happiness it does not find.

Yet so far we have forgotten the middles, and middles in texts that are composed "by accretion" may tend to be so minutely partitioned that we find a certain loss of energetic sequacity in longer pieces. Roper, and Piper in his book on the couplet, do not find this to be the case in Dryden; they argue for his cohesiveness of metaphorical structure, his ability to unify great webs of argument, his dynamic devices of movement in the couplet as interspersed with triplets and alexandrines. Trickett and others argue similarly concerning Pope's use of *concordia discors* principles in the largest and smallest details of poetic construction. Geoffrey Tillotson says that Pope is "the most connectedly various of poets," offering "several effects simultaneously," so that he must be read "slowly enough for intentness": "Otherwise the poem may seem a series of small inadequate patches."[61]

But, as may be expected, there is not a word in Bysshe's handbook about poetic construction at a rank above stress or word, for the sentence, segment, or whole poem. Larger organizational structure plainly depended on basic but unformulated constraints in the fable, syntax, and prosody, such as the period style of phrasal or balanced syntax, the extreme prevalence of adjectives in relation to other parts of speech, which Josephine Miles has shown for 1700–1770. We have not yet arrived at a way of building up metrical theory to mark grammatical structure, yet Miles's comment on the Gothic, Greek Pindaric, and biblical sublime poem in blank verse or ode stanzas—which is as much an Augustan type as the couplet—contains metrical and cognitive explanations of why Augustan poems may appear to seize up in places: "Phrasal poems, and phrasal eras," Miles says, "emphasize line-by-line progression, and cumulative participial modification in description and invocation without stress on external rhyming and grouping."[62] Reuben Brower finds defect of form more often in the "arbitrary chaos" of Cowley's Pindaric followers, and in Thomson's *Seasons*, than in the Augustan writers of couplets.[63] But Donald J. Greene censures most critical estimates of the couplet poets' logical qualities and asks about their freedom from self-contradiction and digression, the grouping of subtopics, and the clear indication of transitions, as well as the need by authors to preface many of these poems with an outline or argument. Greene sees in Dryden "a pleasing sort of informal, almost anti-logical impressionism," and writes of Johnson's "London" and "Vanity": "The plan . . . could hardly be more jejune. It is simply that of enumeration."[64] Considered, that is, as pattern of statement and not of imagery, eighteenth-century poetry is not logical but impressionistic in its movement. It is beyond the scope of this section to ajudicate the argument about coherence just sketched, and my purpose will have been served if the notion of the ready-made poem, evoked at the outset with Johnson, has been put into a tension of qualification. For the Augustan form of implicative openings and maximal closure, in texts extended beyond epigram, is also at the local level a poetry of accretion and commonsense impressionism.

6. *In local deployment of poetic devices, Augustan form tends to avoid effects that draw attention to the arbitrariness of language.* Prosody in a broad definition includes all the poetic devices of equivalence and not only rhyme and meter. Working with large statistical samples, Josephine Miles has found that a survey of such equivalences is not by itself sufficient to mark literary change by a regular pattern, but that on the other hand diction and metrics "are closely involved with sentence structure, which does reveal a sequential pattern." There is, for example, a dramatic cutoff of clausal or embedded sentencing, with fewest adjectives per verbs, after 1670.[65] A phrasal or balanced phrasal-clausal poetry, with more adjectives per verbs, becomes normal until 1770: a poetry that, in both satirical and sublime types, reinforces sentence structure with the formulaic phrases of a poetic diction. If the equivalences cannot be said to mark change, they will in any event help to define, at the local level, a period style that conceives it has made progress, in Johnson's words, from "savageness" to "poetical prudence." I do not question whether the varieties of equivalence, listed above by W. K. Wimsatt, were in fact used—of course they were—but would press further to inquiry why, and in what spirit, these particular devices were selected. In this regard Johnson speaks the axiom of the whole historical style when he warns that words should not "draw that attention on themselves which they should transmit to things" (*Life of Dryden*). The materiality of language, the

scandal of form that becomes in the Modern period suspicion of the device, is something Augustan poetics willfully refuses to recognize.[66] By inheritance the Augustan poets had a range of equivalences of rhyme, meter, parallelism, metaphor, and the like, whose very literariness—in suggesting a second system within the medium itself, in addition to the God-created things of the world—jeopardized the unity of language. Their response was very sensible and systematic: first, to omit or severely reduce the incidence of these devices in their poetry, and this was the fate of some kinds of metaphorical language, especially punning; then, to circumscribe by strict redefinition equivalences like rhyme and meter, which were indispensable, producing among other fixative innovations an official line length and rhyme scheme.[67]

So the full range is not present (nor need it be for great poetry); and those permitted devices usually appeal to the short-term memory. Couplets, in particular, create a texture of continual but tiny discontinuities of perception, thus affirming social and aesthetic assumptions of offering the least possible unpredictability. Nonetheless, it is the variation and discontinuity within the predictable that is the genius of the form. The mirror-image syntax of parallelism, antithesis, and chiasmus, carrying half-line chunks of diction in the formula

article plus adjective plus noun,

will also warp language toward familiarity of sense and rhythm. Augustan readers loved those pleasure of recognition; the poetic diction that Wordsworth deplored in this poetic idiom "is in fact the source of its best qualities," though a proper reading of it "is a skill to be acquired."[68] A refined diction, in common order of syntax, and in combination with rhyme at line end, will keep present but not obtrusive the poetic aura—will keep verse out of prose. Here the dominant satirical poetry, in couplets, seems implicitly the antagonist of the blank-verse sublime writing, which also uses a formulaic diction but pointedly avoids the extra equivalence—what Johnson called in praise "the shakles [sic] and circumspection"—of rhyme. When Johnson, last of the great Augustan theorists and a man whose Classicism was hard earned rather than inherited, came to write his *Lives of the Poets,* he had to conquer his aversion to blank verse in order to praise Milton; and he saw nothing but asperity and fatuity in the blank verse of his own century, written by "candidates for fame" who seemed to think "that not to write prose is certainly to write poetry."[69] Prose is to be avoided, of course, but prose sense is to be embodied; and to compound the contradiction, this is to be accomplished in a construction that chimes with the ancient, irrational-seeming device wherein two meanings find the same sound. "One might have thought it curious, on the face of the matter, that the great age of classical order should be at ease only in the Gothic and mystical shackles of rhyme."[70] The curiosity noticed by W. K. Wimsatt has never been fully explained; the couplet regulates the device of rhyme as tightly as may be, but only serves to heighten its literariness while attempting to exterminate it. The more narrowly Augustan form seeks prose sense within a chosen set of conventions, the more successful it is in defining a certain poetic structure and texture. The effect is of forcing a tremendous head of pressure through tiny appertures.

7. *In the buildup of seqment and line, Augustan form seeks to construct larger patterns out of exactly equal temporal units.* There are, according to a famous passage in Roman Jakobson, two modes of arrangement used in verbal behavior: selection and combination.

> The selection is produced on the basis of equivalence, similarity and dissimilarity, synonymity and antonymity, while the combination, the buildup of the sequence, is based on contiguity. The poetic function projects the principle of equivalence from the axis of selection into the axis of combination. Equivalence is promoted to the constitutive device of the sequence.[71]

Selection entails choice, alternatives and open options, whereas combination obliges one to keep within the rules of English syntax, which amount to a massive system of constraints. It may be hazarded that in general Augustan form tends to avoid the activities of selection, and as an obvious body of evidence one might mention the presence of a fairly well developed poetic diction, admittedly a sort of precision, but purchased at the cost of prefabricating chunks of the line. Combination, linear stringing, is the preferred mode of this period style, the buildup of the sequence, rather than any emphasis on devices. (Even in the sphere of poetic treatises, the emphasis between Puttenham and Bysshe has changed from rhyme and stave batching to "numbers," the stringing of short and long syllables according to a terminology taken over *tout court* from Classical prosody.) In the larger pattern, we may remind ourselves, poetry for the Augustans meant not lyric but something that strings events, a narrative history (yet oddly they wrote few narrative poems). In the smaller pattern, the placing of the basic units one after another, we have Johnson's flat and precise phrasing under *poetry* in his *Dictionary:* "metrical composition," meaning that extraordinary legislative paradigm of syllabism, artificial scansion, and poetic contraction which Paul Fussell has so well described.[72] In the *Life of Pope* Johnson extends this definition, stating that "the essential constituent of metric composition [is] the stated recurrence of settled numbers," a syllable arithmetic, then, sequences of long and short syllables forming metrical feet solely by theoretical scansion, eliding those English words ("many a" typically becoming "man-ya") which do not fit the pattern. The metrical sequence becomes the dominant form of equivalence, equating all long and all short syllables, and making every long equal to two shorts.

Other devices are omitted or tailored to fit this prosody, which with its isochronous units prevents all "interruptions of that constancy to which science aspires" (Johnson, *Life of Dryden*). The rigor of the Augustan ideal of form is expressed in the poem's absence of harsh sounds, intercalary pauses, or unpredictabilities. This plenitude of prosodic sequence, at once cognitive, elocutionary, and ethical, is to fill and direct the mind of the reader. The perverse energy in many of these poems becomes a way of mocking an insane state of affairs, on the level of structure, by way of formal disruptions. Augustan lunatic writing is a highly conscious, scholarly use of moral-prosodic dishevelment for satiric purposes.

Syllable-count metrics dictated the making of blank verse as well as the couplet, but on a looser rein. To a defender of the couplet like Johnson, Milton's choice of blank verse could seem "disgusting," and the fact that Edward Young's blank-verse style "is his own" was a serious fault. Apparently blank verse had not enough literary signs for Johnson to think it a fully social form of utterance; he added rhyme to numbers as a necessary way of marking off lines for the ear, "a distinct system of sounds" (*Life of Milton*) that provides the larger pattern syllabic verse needs to get above the looser flow of prose. In fact, in couplet versification the verse line itself is only a marker on the way to the next major unit after the syllable, the rhyme-mated pair of lines; and beyond the line pair there is no next-larger unit but the whole segment or poem. After the equalized units of the syllables, the larger ones are variously equalized by types of contrast: "Phrase against phrase, line against line, couplet against couplet—the poem typically develops through statement and counter-statement, achieving a final effect of poise."[73] For optimal contrast it was important to eschew triplets and alexandrines, to conclude sense in couplets, and not to split a couplet between the end of one verse-paragraph and the beginning of the next. During the reign of Augustan form, as the schemas of Josephine Miles show, there are few stanzaic poems; then after 1800 the couplet virtually disappears. Another, more delicate evidence for the existence of a determinate period style is the way poets previous to Denham and Waller become, prosodically speaking, unreadable within a generation after they had written. For instance, Milton's blank verse became an anomaly, and Shakespeare was not intelligible by the Augustan mode of scansion, a situation calculated to induce profound uneasiness in a critic as great as Johnson, who required himself to praise their poetry and condemn their versification. Johnson, late in his own life and in the life of Augustan form, found himself in the awkward position of arguing that while prosody had reached its ultimate refinement, poetry had not.

Augustan form was consciously and proudly marshaled as a period style. The only thing it had not understood or planned in advance was its own overthrow.

Romantic Form as Proceeding

I began the previous section by giving four general qualities of Augustan form, calling it accepting of authority, the product of the norms of an educated class, ethical, and unhistorical. Here I would show the Romantic transformations of these large tendencies. Form as proceeding is *diversitarian,* in A. O. Lovejoy's sense of admitting the *genre mixte,* local color, imperfection as value, a style of many styles. Form as proceeding is *primitivist,* typically imagining, in Mallarmé's words, "la corrélation intime de la Poésie avec l'Univers," assimilating poetry to nature, childhood, the imagined inner life of peoples remote in time or space. Form as proceeding is *exploratory,* and thus suspicious of pronouncement and of neat endings; rather than rhetorically seeking to persuade, it is actively "pressing toward knowledge" (Earl Wasserman). And form as proceeding is *consciously historical in outlook,* refusing to take evolved modes of thinking and writing as natural growths, "for whether the romanticist projects himself into the past, nature, or another person, he never forgets that he is playing a role. The result is that the experience makes him more acutely aware than ever of his own modernity and his own distinctness from the external world."[74] The Augustan writer, if we may imagine his frame of mind, is buoyed and enabled by a preexisting repertoire of forms—social and literary—in which he may set his materials. He need not put (or anyway, show) personal stamp, hidden depths, subtler language within the received language, but rather proceeds as by a filling-in of slots, assuming not only the presence but also the approbation of the reader. In the forming process after 1795 the writer must—or must seem to—continually wrench, reinvent ordinary language as the means to rouse his and the reader's verbal behavior, creating interiority in a public medium, making "a monument to spontaneity, a poem that coincides with the act and passion of its utterance."[75] The writer is left to survive in the destructive element, in this case the institutional language and convention of a historical moment when the readership is distant and diverse.

The shift of dominants, in the sense of frames of reference and hierarchies of devices, is from a collective and ahistorical mode to an individualist, historicist one. The change will not be understood by the scrutiny of single poems; rather we require a revision of period concepts, aided by the idea of an epistemological-prosodic break. From a time when literature is assimilated to all other forms of learned discourse, we pass to a time when literature tends to isolate itself from general discourse, and as the quality of literariness comes more into history so too does an intense interest in the conventions that create but never fully circumscribe it—along with the suspicion of those conventions I have called the scandal of form. Precisely because it responds to an era that separates individuals more than ever before, the constitutive new dominant of post-Romantic style is cooperative behavior, taken first in the cognitive sense of the poem's internal unity, the coherence of the act of mind it represents, the act of mind it notates, and also in the sense that this unity persuades, implicates, indeed constitutes a reader, any reader, who works within the poem by imagining its rhetoric as personal speech. While the poem lasts this imaginary "true voice of feeling" (Keats) not only mediates a self—it also puts that self into touch with the trained and responding reader. Of course, the same had occurred, less programmatically, in previous literature; after 1795, it is especially those reader-implicative earlier works which are most imitated, prized, and taught.

It would be a mistake to shift all our concern from the message to its receiver, or to the historical determinants of its generation. The relationships that obtain within and between the components, the real and implied selves, are what interest us, and hence the reading experience becomes subsumed in the more general topic of the literary system. Those "mental codes" (Claudio Guillén) which make up the theoretical orders of poetics are partial and defective in the Romantic mode, "common laws, entirely empirical, that should not be hypostasized into a canon. The code, here, like the message, has its gaps, and its surprises" (Gérard Genette).[76] Yet it is a code. There is a schema of both structure and system for all seven Romantic transformations of the postulates numbered in my last section. As before, *system* is here taken to mean the conditioning set, the assumptions that direct poetic creation (now, after 1795); *structure* is the term referring to interrelations between constituent units. Both *system* and *structure* are historical categories, but in my usage serve to characterize a historical mode and not, as in Claudio Guillén, the continuous evolution of genres. I do, however, subscribe to Guillén's working principle that "a system always incloses a structure, but the opposite is not true."[77] *System,* as applied here to concepts of language, nature and art, innovation, and genre theory, is the broader term; it describes, by and large, the attitudes that determine the more precise aspects of structure, namely organization, the device, and the buildup of segment and line. Plainly system and structure are interfused at all levels of theory and practice, and between the first four and the last three postulates certain connections might be worked out both for Augustan and for Romantic form. For my purpose, these terms serve, very modestly, merely to specify further the list of seven postulates.

1. *Romantic and Modern poetic form rests on a concept of the poet's own language within language.* To avoid taking the hyperbole of the Romantic manifesto as achieved fact, it is well to speak of tendencies and limiting cases. The urge of Romantic language theory, as I have hinted, is to murder language by enacting a "regressive semiological system" (Roland Barthes), taking words and utterances back to their final validation in the world of

reference. Earl Wasserman writes of how our poets would create a "language within language": "Within itself the modern poem must both formulate its own cosmic syntax and shape the autonomous poetic reality that the cosmic syntax permits."[78] Repudiating eighteenth-century poetic diction, which was a language within language not without its precisions and even depths, Romantics achieved little or no advance on the front of lexis, but a tremendous if very vexed advance in the idea of a poetic language. The push for a cosmic syntax must remain stubbornly a tendency because of the utter impossibility of language's reinventing its own terms, and yet the resulting deflection of poetic practice is immense.

Coleridge and Wordsworth treat poetic language and poetic meter as integral elements of the text, separable for analysis, both of which should at best originate in immediate experience. "Every phrase," says Coleridge, "every metaphor, every personification, should have its justifying cause in some passion either of the poet's mind or of the characters described by the poet— but meter *itself* implies a passion, i.e., a state of excitement . . . in the poet's Mind."[79] Because it assimilates art language to brute fact of living organism, this controverts the premises of Augustan form. Without, however, going so far as Roland Barthes's puzzling statement that Modern poetry is opposed to Classical art "by a difference which involves the whole structure of language," we can at least affirm that on these grounds (for Romantic theory if not for ourselves) poetic diction is an abomination, and meters that preexist the poem are suspect. What must solely preexist are enduring objects in a real world, for language is permanent (so the theory runs) to the degree that it is anchored in these; their existence is the most crushing criticism of formulaic diction. Between mind and world, mind and itself, divisions create the reflexive identity of the self; similarly, divisions within language give personal stamp to speech acts and to their simulacra in the text.

The more intelligent of the English Romantic writers were intensely, if intermittently, aware of the difficulties arising from the arbitrariness of language as a medium for thinking and writing. Their various idealisms, including those in prosodic theory, were attempts to resolve what they knew about the perplexities of language as a product of consciousness.

For Romantic and Modern poetic theory, literary language is both actual and virtual; the word both is and does something, and theory knows but knowingly blurs the difference. *Passion* usually is employed as a resolving term that permits the writer to affirm both the materiality of the medium of language and its transparency to a world of reference. Without conscious contradiction, in the space of a single paragraph of 1800, Wordsworth can write that "words . . . ought to be weighed in the balance of feeling and not measured by the space which they occupy on paper. For the Reader cannot be too often reminded that Poetry is passion," and also that "the mind attaches to words [an interest], not only as symbols of the passion, but as *things*, active and efficient, which are themselves part of the passion."[80] This language in a state of excitement gains concretion, hidden depth, subjectivity; it becomes, in contradistinction to ordinary language, absolutely expendable and absolutely of the essence.

2. *Romantic and Modern poetry understands itself as but one conscious phase of the whole of creative activity going on in Nature.* Especially in the early phases of the Modern outlook, we are dealing with the volatile concept of organic vitalism—with the analogy between poetic language and a living organism. The best guide to the full complexity of Romantic thinking on this is Coleridge's essay "On Poesy or Art," where he says that the fullness of nature is "without character." Nature and art require each other to give mutual meaningfulness, the one giving reference and the other giving signs that make sense of it: "Art would or should be the abridgment of nature."[81] The poet, in Coleridge's wonderful neologism, "must eloign himself from nature in order to return to her with full effect."[82] The device both of eloigning and connecting is language. The poet will, for Coleridge, use the literariness of the medium to separate himself from ordinary language as a kind of nature.

In the way it contains a rapport within a difference, the Romantic theory of language is complementary to those weaker notions, poetry-as-nature and style-as-man. Analyzed into its final terms it is not an easy primitivism, despite Romanticism's symptomatic wind, water, and plant-growth analogies for mind and style; rather, at best, it is a complex tension maintained between cognitive and aesthetic modes, with the text as "a middle quality between a thought and a thing, or . . . the union and reconciliation of that which is nature with that which is exclusively human."[83] If we saw, in Pope, art as "Nature methodized" within the received traditions of writing, in Coleridge, we must understand perfect works as "nature humanized"[84] through the agency of coadunative language.

3. *Innovation is the wish to be or seem unprecedented.* Coleridge's discussion of form as proceeding is set in the context of remarks on the sort of artistic pleasure that arises from novelty. This pleasure, he says, derives from reconciling two opposite elements, sameness and variety. To extend this commonplace, we may say that pleasure in the text may change over time as does the level and type of the fusion of opposite elements. "The dialectic of innovation," John Hollander says, "is always a subtle one, and the very concept of *originality* has shifted its ground since the founding of the formal conventions of poetry in English, from being at the source of a stream of tradition to drilling one's own Helicon, wherever one may be standing in time or place."[85] After 1795 to be creative in the fullest sense is to be most oneself, without contingent dependence on other writers or existing

formal molds; *self-effecting* is Coleridge's term for the "sphere of agency" of this new form sense. The new balance redeems the insurgent nature of a mere variety of thoughts and rhetorics, after an Augustan period style that tended to define innovation as eliminating rough spots from previous writers. In theme and prosody, Romantic writers all share "an interest or hope in the hitherto unexplored" (Walter Jackson Bate);[86] the other face of this impulse, exhaustively detailed by Harold Bloom, is the defensive misreading of great predecessors in order to preserve an identity for oneself as poet.

The ideal scene of composition is the bare desk and blank page of unprecedented creation. But due to the conservative nature of the medium, the actual scene of warfare, agonism, perpetual changes of satiety and renewal is the more credible as it is the more easily described. We are familiar with the recurrent components of this scene: manifestos, stylistic pluralism, reshuffling of the hierarchy of genres, shifts in the dominant function of formal elements, and acceleration of stylistic dynamism and canon formation. Certain experiments emerge from this chaos as logical developments, highly intelligent and accomplished but doomed, however imitable, to be dead ends; I think particularly of Robert Bridges's turn-of-the-century quantitative efforts, and of the minor fiddling with concrete verse since 1945. Other methods, like the prose poem and especially free verse, justify themselves within the Modern tradition as open forms, endlessly renewable because they foster the development of a personal voice, of poetry as thinking and talking. (What these forms foster may be illusions from the point of view of modern philosophy; but such illusions are apparently necessities for poetry, even as late as the 1980s).

4. *Romantic and Modern genre theory aims at the dissolution of genres— in practice this means mixing, reweighting, and occasionally inventing genres.* The premises and analogies of organicist aesthetics are overcorrections, designed to reassert the priority of essential principles over arbitrary rules. That is the way form as proceeding attempts to resolve the divorce, which the Romantics saw widening in the period style just previous to their own, between theory and practice.

With a few notable exceptions, Modern critics have learned to read the anarchic overstatements of the Romantic tradition, sensibly unwilling to take this logic as a matter of actual intent or achievement. Admonishing American Modernism with the example of W. H. Auden's use of canonical forms, John Hollander says that the "effect" of making works that are identifiable only as "Poet X poems" is "to dissolve genre."[87] But that is a tendency, not an irreducible effect, and it is a tendency that does not exempt either Hollander himself (as a poet) or Auden. There is no post-Romantic writer of any stature who will defend, as a working principle rather than as a limiting case in manifestos, the notions of pristine beginnings, uninfluenced uniqueness, the poem as natural growth, or the abandonment of any idea of genre. Just as we require language and sequential thought, we require the concept of genre in order to write, read, and judge; it is an essential enabling condition of literary work. And yet something momentous happened to traditional genres at 1795, due to changes within the essence of meaning and interpretation traditionally defined. The "poetry of experience," as Robert Langbaum describes it, can now be

> understood as the instrument of an age which must venture a literature without objectively verifiable meaning. . . . Such a literature does not give us a meaning in the sense of a complete idea which can be abstracted and connected logically with other ideas. It resolves itself by immersing its uncompleted idea in an advancing stream of life—by shifting the whole argument into the context of a larger and intenser life, by shifting to a new perspective, a new phase of the speaker's career.[88]

Values are now turned "into biographical phenomena" (Langbaum's phrase), so that the poem's pronouns become more economical in the sense of containing richer implicitness: the "I" contains the whole earlier life of the speaker, but also the "I" of the reader; "you" includes not only the nominal auditor, as in the "Eolian Harp" utterance addressed to Coleridge's Sara, but also the actual reader. Of this profound deepening of intersubjectivity and implication, the rethinking of traditional genres is a symptom; but also, in respect of technique, the detailed figuration of the new interiority.

To turn to a more historical perspective, we might analyze the poetic work as a regularly ordered hierarchical set of artistic devices, showing how poetic evolution must come within the framework of the given genre, and within the hierarchy of all the genres. "Genres which were originally secondary paths, subsidiary variants, now come to the fore, whereas the canonical genres are pushed to the rear" (Roman Jakobson).[89] When the shift is within and among genres, involving the reconstitution of all devices and their redistribution among genres, then it may rightly be called a matter of quantum evolution. This happens but seldom in literary history, and when it does, as in 1795, it involves at the same moment the omission, reranking, mixing, and inventing of genres. Wordsworth in his 1815 preface lists the "moulds" into which poetic materials are traditionally cast, and these are Narrative or Epic, Dramatic, Lyrical, Idyllium or Descriptive, Didactic, and Philosophical satire; Wordsworth then turns immediately to add that his own collected poems will not be organized by these categories, but by faculties or psychological types, or by "the subjects to which they relate."[90] Here as elsewhere in Romantic theory, genre is not dissolved so much as reconstituted closer to the imagined curve of the experience. The lyrical type, third on Wordsworth's list, becomes the Romantic dominant and all the other types are either relegated, tailored, or reconstituted as autobiography (as narrative and descriptive in *The Prelude*). Especially through the subgroups of song, ballad, elegy, and ode, which were gaining ground throughout the eighteenth century as countercouplet conventions, the lyric is able to assert itself as the poetic norm.[91] Within a generation, Browning in the dramatic monologue makes of the speech or soliloquy a self-enclosed poem, redeeming or inventing a genre that had always been latent in theatrical literature. In this changeable climate of possibility, singable forms and metrics came from the underculture to the highest place; ballad structure, as Josephine Miles and others have shown, "became vehicle for new ideas and materials."[92] The point is that now, for the first time consciously in the writing itself, literary innovation is understood as debate between genre and countergenre. Moreover, for theory itself the break at 1795 prepared a truer understanding of the processes of literary change.

One deficiency of Classical poetics, which seems to be vocal about nearly everything else, is the lack of any mechanism for connecting genres and their appropriate meters. Alongside the formal poetics, there grows up an unwritten one that makes received or rule-of-thumb assumptions about the aptness of a specific meter or structure to a certain attitude, purpose, or tone. Impossible to routinize in a manual, all of Modern poetics has the status of this unwritten phase of Classical theory; even a provisional survey will not materially reduce the ad hoc nature of prosodic avantgardism.[93] Manifestos fill the absent place of the manual; form and prosody are now understood only in the plural, and justified only by ex post facto aptness; the link between poetics and metrics is no longer prescriptive. John Hollander has exclaimed that in "an eclectic, history-ridden age" like the present, "such stylistic anarchy prevails that one almost feels that a poem need be defined as any utterance that purports to be one."[94] And why not (so long as we have standards well enough developed to make commonsense judgments on the formality of the form chosen, its fit with the attitude expressed; so long as we remain willing to make statements about relative value)? There is no prima facie reason that, of two poems roughly similar in length and development on the same subject, the one in free verse or in prose is necessarily inferior to the one traditionally rhymed and metered.

5. *Romantic and Modern form typically employs the method of the "coalesced totality," order through "multeïty," a "fusion to force many into one"* (quotations from Coleridge). The definition of poetic structure, or the interrelationships between the poem's constituent units, must vary with each period's identification of those units. After 1795 the units tend to shift from being rhetorical or formal devices of equivalence that preexist the poem to being cognitive or grammatical measures. Rhetoric and meter do not disappear, but are deemphasized because of their priority to (and detachment from) the developing utterance. Art, for Coleridge, imitates not things, but

the processional changing relationships of things with other things, giving thereby an active representation and not a passive copy. Typically in his criticism Coleridge "begins with the product," according to M. H. Abrams, "but after a point, moves into the process"; and this elevation of imaginative fusion is the first instance of Modernity's "appeal to inclusiveness as the criterion of poetic excellence."[95] Praising Wordsworth, Coleridge spoke of the quality of *spreading the tone:* this later becomes the central strength of a whole poetic mode, whose best discoveries are structural, morphological, the building of verbal engines of perceptual and moral eventfulness.

Those who charge Romantic poetry with vagueness or formlessness usually, as Classical Moderns, appeal only to the static inclusiveness of imagery and diction—thus avoiding the other, wider senses of syntax, sentencing, forward movement of stanzas, and the constitution of a fictive voice. Antagonists of Romanticism attack just where the mode keeps its deepest assumptions implicit. Once these assumptions are unfolded, the disagreements disappear. Thus, and briefly: the identity of personal voice can be had only in relationship; the antirhetorical style is itself a rhetoric. These deep structures were formulated definitively over twenty years ago by Robert Langbaum, whose conclusion cannot be bettered: "The point . . . in understanding the form of romantic poetry is to understand how the sincere, unpremeditated effect is achieved."[96] Though no given forms will be canonic, some of the elements of that ideal of artlessness are specifiable as recurrent structures, devices, measures.

In his survey of prosody, George Saintsbury claims for the nineteenth century an "immense enlargement of the poetical dictionary," in all directions toward "plainness, archaism, familiarity, gorgeousness beside which the eighteenth-century conventional ornament grew pale, technicality, everything."[97] In Josephine Miles's admirable catalog, the compositional unity of this new kind of poem includes

> a sentence structure of dramatic confrontation, which employs more verbs that adjectives, more subordinate than serial constructions, more actions and arguments than descriptions and invocations. . . . At the same time, the meter breaks, to allow for the effects of silence as well as sound in the verse line. . . . By about 1820 most of the leading poets' work was stanzaic in structure, while a half century before it had been mostly linear; the measures were freely trisyllabic where they had been disyllabic; by about 1820 half the major terms, the nouns, adjectives, and verbs most used by the majority, were new terms, characteristically sensory, concrete, and thus often symbolic, while oblique metaphors had taken the place of explicit similes; by about 1820 the sentence structures were more narrative than descriptive, more complex than coordinate, using more verbs and sometimes only half as many adjectives as in the century before.[98]

With allowance made for the differential between 1820 and 1950, this technical description of Wordsworthian association of ideas in a state of excitement is still the way of Charles Olson as he urges, "Get on with it, keep moving, keep in, speed, the nerves, their speed, the perceptions, theirs, the acts, the split second acts."[99] In an organicist aesthetic, the poetic means are considered as parts rather than rules, with each unit at once end and means, position and trajectory. The organism-atomism dilemma is left unresolved in an organicist aesthetics, perhaps by design, perhaps by a historical necessity only partly conscious in practitioners. But apparently such an aesthetic theory phrases the terms of the dilemma in a productive way.

The ethos is well represented by elements other than devices of equivalence and formal meter. Punctuation, for instance, insofar as it hints the speaker's pauses, is for Coleridge "always prospective," its marks "dramatic directions for enabling the reader more easily to place himself in the state of the writer" (Coleridge).[100] In his own sentences, Coleridge favors long, hypotactic strings; he calls short periods asthmatic, or lacking in "the cement of thought as well as style, [lacking] . . . all the connections, and . . . all the hooks and eyes of the memory," thus easily forgotten. Wordsworth knows that to place the verb "hang" at the end of an enjambed line, or at the beginning of the next line, is to enact the word's meaning by its position.[101] The tactical use of blank spaces between lobes of the free-verse line or segments of the poem, like the nineteenth century's discovery of the kinds of transitions that can be effected by stanza break, argues the value of ellipses of thought. Such spaces, pauses bracketed by type, span and spur the reader's faculties of mental sight and hearing. Such instances hint that a sharp distinction between part and whole is not productive, for every isolate strand is also wound into the progressive transition, by the "hooks and eyes" of proactive and retroactive memory.

Faced with the task of making an associative poetry continuous, Romantic and Modern poets sometimes turn to music as an image of persuasive continuity. That is symptomatic, but also unfortunate because it postpones the inquiry as to what verbal means enable the poet to spread his tone. Coleridge's practical ideal—the fusion to force many into one, and the union of the shapely with the vital—is more often to be seen in actual poems than in suggestive analogies. Any full account will have to explain, with texts from Romantic to post-Modern, at least some basic effects that draw the reader into and through the poem: the title whose syntax is part of the poem; post-Romantic and free-verse enjambment; the coincidence and noncoincidence of line and sentence; implicative dialect, rhetorical figures, and points of view; the directional "out-in-out" epistemological reversals of the greater Romantic lyric and many poems since; the poem as tightly focused by a constituting metaphor, usually stated in the title. I am reminded, in this context, of Charles Tomlinson's poem of the 1960s, printed as short lines alternating in ordinary and italicized type, each typeface system containing its own statement of meaning. This is a "Three-Way Poem," to be read first all the way through in ordinary type only; then through in italics; then in the meshed sequence, which locks and reconciles the opposed syntaxes. Read rightly, the poem loses all its initial appearance of randomness. Such a seeming chaos, which falls into an inevitable gestalt upon performance, is the perfect counterinstance to Augustan form's poetry of accretion and commonsense impressionism.

6. *The device must, like language and meter, be reinvented from within by avoiding previous usage or exposing its deficiencies.* It seems sensible to argue that literary language is to ordinary language as literary history is to literary Modernity—the unprecedented spontaneity of the nonliterary and the Modern make of them unreachable ideals in an era of avantgardism. Into this situation enters the agent of marking off literary from nonliterary language, the device, whose calculated equivalences put words into a higher state of tension. For Romantic critical theory, the various devices for thus overdetermining language are strictly necessary, and yet however much they change the state of language they are not by themselves sufficient to create poems. Beyond the inventory of devices always moves the vital penumbra of the innovative, the poetic. And so, by implication, the idea of a poetic device is the dialectical counterpart of the idea of literary Modernity, the preexisting as against the seemingly unprecedented. The device calls into question the conventionality of conventions and the historicity of history, and that is why Romantic theory and practice must again and again meditate on its status.

Romanticism discovers that devices are necessary to make literature—but no single device is indispensable. No one form is essential, only formality itself, the detectable frame. Typically William Carlos Williams condemns the sonnet because "it is a form which does not admit of the slightest structural change in its composition."[102] The Romantic idea is to make an utterance wherein the relation of significant parts to the whole is not fixed or predetermined, but depends on the unfolding of the unique statement; as Alfred North Whitehead said, process and individuality require each other. This is why Coleridge could write, apropos of the device of meter, "since Dryden, the meter of our poets leads to the sense; in our older and more genuine poets, the sense, including the passion, leads to the meter." I have already considered this form-justified-by-passion argument, and remarked how the Romantic quarrel was with Neo-Classical poetics and not with the idea of convention. Coleridge himself resisted the easy opposition of passion or genius to rules, taking the view that "the comparative value of these rules is the very cause to be tried."[103] When he said that every phrase should have its justifying cause in some passion, he was implying for criticism the need to supplement every rhetorical analysis with reference to the powers of the human mind. Writing in the belief that Walt Whitman "can teach current American poets to destroy their own rhetoric and trust their own imagination," James A. Wright makes the Coleridgean statement that "it is difficult to distinguish between the delicacy of Whitman's diction and his sensitivity as a man. But that is just the point."[104] And it is the kind of point one feels disposed to make for many more poets than Whitman.

"The ideal," Coleridge wrote, "is a style defecated to a pure transparency," but of course the sound structure of language and the historical nature of its conventions oblige other metaphors for actual writing, like the stripping of veils or onionskins with always another, more diaphanous layer of style beneath the one just removed.[105] In practice, the transfer from Augustan form could not mean the abandonment of discourse and poetic convention. The idea seems to have been that certain, carefully chosen projects of "laying bare" the Augustan form of the device, can have telling results when they accumulate. For instance, the absence or unexpected placement of a rhyme, or a redefinition of the meaning of homophony as in Wilfred Owen's pararhymes, has an immediate effect on the structure of sound and meaning far out of proportion to the minor deflection of a single device. Paradoxically, the cognitive perceptibility of such devices as rhyme increases to the same extent that these forms of equivalence are wrenched or assimilated toward nonliterary language. Romantic poetry smashes the molds of Augustan lexis by risking a mixed, unsystematic diction; Romantic structure follows, so far as possible, the imagined plausibility of an act of mind, pushing the poem dialectically toward a recognition—"surprise into a perception," in Wordsworth's phrasing—and Romantic meter adds the sounding to the counting of measures, favoring insurgent stress, idiosyncratic and not mathematic elocution. For the most part the Romantic and Modern view requires the strategic laying bare and reranking of these prominent devices, adducing with Coleridge the principle that "*all* parts of an organized whole must be assimilated to the more *important* and *essential* parts."[106] Though punctuation, white spacing, and other elements come into the process, this is not, like the later movement calling itself affective stylistics, a theory that reduces received prominences to the same importance as other parts of the line.[107]

Introducing his translation of the *Anabasis* of St. Jean Perse, T. S. Eliot held that the sequencing of the imagery made the text poetic despite its format of justified margins. This is not to throw out meter and rhyme, merely to elevate, as does Eliot's original, one other prominence (emotional logic of the imagery) to their structuring role. Refusing to oppose poetry to prose, Eliot, like Wordsworth and Coleridge, provisionally resolved that choice into a question of far greater productive value: an opposition between literary language as palpability and as reference, here sketched by Roman Jakobson:

Poetic function is not the sole function of verbal art but only its dominant, determining function, whereas in all other verbal activities it acts as a subsidiary, accessory constituent. This function, by promoting the palpability of signs, deepens the fundamental dichotomy of signs and objects.[108]

Prosodic avantgardism acts as if this palpability, which it recognizes and salutes, might be reduced by subtraction or reemphasis. Generally speaking, there is an avoidance of devices that proclaim the virtuality of art language, and a preference for effects resembling the run of ordinary language. By means of devices, devices are hidden. Formal property and referential significance, concrete materiality and transparence of the sign, the marks of labor of text production and the easy naturalness of the speech act—the process of poetic language in its movement resolves all false oppositions, twisting the skein of form and sense.

7. *Romantic and Modern form seeks intense differentiation of time into units of unexpected type and measure.* As might be expected from all six earlier postulates and their explanations, the justification of meter is a topic occasioning intense concern for the Romantics. For (along with rhyme) meter is the most egregious type of equivalencing or overdetermination, a bold instance of the scandal of form. One phase of stylistic pluralism in the time just after 1795 was the invention of experimental schemes of rhyme and meter. Before touching on the most influential of these experiments, Coleridge's fragmentary (but not brief) poem "Christabel," it will be useful to glance at the central issues in Romantic metrical theory.

Typically, in this moment that overleaps the Augustan era to identify itself with massive early forerunners, Keats begins his address to Milton, "Chief of organic numbers!"[109] The oxymoron there, linking in one locution the spontaneous ("organic") and the voluntary ("numbers"), is not, for Keats, contradictory, for like the other Romantic writers he seeks a way to change traditional constraints for those which more closely adhere to experience. Even the most rigidly defined traditional forms are not exempt from this wish to throw everything into the crucible and burn away exteriority like "dead leaves in the bay leaf crown," as Keats urged in his sonnet "On the Sonnet" (1819):

> Let us find out, if we must be constrain'd,
> Sandals more interwoven and complete
> To fit the naked foot of Poesy:
> . . . .
> So, if we may not let the Muse be free,
> She will be bound with garlands of her own.[110]

The trope of covered nakedness occurs in Wordsworth, too, when in the 1800 preface he asks himself why he has written in verse when prose can also convey high subjects and vivid feelings. For paraphrasable content,

Wordsworth argues, there is "no essential difference between the language of prose and metrical composition," but he himself has attempted a medium "somewhat less naked" than prose in order, he says, to temper and restrain the poem's emotion by regularity, by "an intertexture of ordinary feeling."[111] Meter's expected recurrence makes it a more powerful form of equivalence than the possibly arbitrary associations of a poetic diction; meter reassures, and yet also carries a distinct pleasure in itself, "which the mind derives from the perception of similitude in dissimilitude." A "complex feeling of delight" derives from this different sameness, voluntary spontaneity, and estranging of the familiar. At best, meter is the motion of meaning.

In his contentious chaper 18 of *Biographia Literaria,* Coleridge takes issue with Wordsworth's arguments. By reference to the origins and effects of meter, Coleridge maintains that metrical conventions are what distinguish poetry from prose. Though Wordsworth never clearly shifted his discussion down from the subject of paraphrasable content to that of actual composition and reader reception, certainly he had implied the position Coleridge uses against him. It is possible to dramatize the many arguments and evidences in this collision as a debate, and by that means to rescue Wordsworth from an imaginary charge of revolting against the literary element in poetry, even to vindicate Wordsworth as "defender" of meter against Coleridge the "disparager";[112] but to my mind such emphasis is misplaced, for their sharing of the same problem is the great fact of their metrical theory. With both writers the exteriority of meter is a task and a problem; both argue sameness and progression, spontaneous impulse and voluntary purpose, the need to take meter inside the creative intention and vanquish its priority. By the end of his chapter Coleridge is himself using Wordsworth's word "superadded" for meter, showing how prosaic elements and gestures cannot be entirely excluded from the poem, and translating a stanza from Pindar into a medium "somewhat less naked" than prose and suspiciously like an early, awkward free verse. Do the first-generation Romantics, then, show an equivocation in their theory of meter? Yes; attempting to understand meter's precedence and to naturalize it in the kind of perfect poem whose "visionary state . . . spreads its influence and colouring over all,"[113] both writers took positions on both sides of the case, and their disagreement is a matter of nuance rather than of substantive division. Both dwell obsessively on the act of composition that integrates the metrical scheme with its meaning, and on the way the reader's acts of attention duplicate this sequential process of fusing sound and sense, "the quick reciprocations of curiosity still gratified and still re-excited." In Romantic and Modern critical theory, meter as measure is on the periphery or husk of the poem, while meter as meaning is in the very center; maddening and irresolvable, this outside/inside contradiction remains the condition of poetic production since Wordsworth.

In the prefatory materials to this *Dictionary,* Samuel Johnson had subsumed *prosody* as a minor subheading under *grammar.* The tendency, if not always the fact, of prosodic avantgardism is to reverse this priority and intrude grammatical categories into metrical ones. Walt Whitman developed a direction first enunciated for Modern literature by Wordsworth and Coleridge, and later called by Ezra Pound a "prose tradition" in English verse: "a practice of speech common to good prose and to good verse alike."[114] Pound called this antirhetorical method "presentative" and developed it in tandem with the prosodies of imagism and the ideogram, very Coleridgean in their attempt to "reduce succession to an instant."[115] Setting image against discourse, the innovative prosodies bring the poetry/prose opposition into the center of theory and practice, while they bring further into the light the importance of grammar and sentence-by-sentence construction. The post-1795 era of stylistic pluralism and metrical experiment shifts its dominants in such a way that elements other than meter come into much greater prominence, and among these, as I shall show in Part 2 below, the most significant is grammar itself.

If for now we consider meter apart from grammar, it seems plain that eighteenth-century theory and practice brought about a shift from quantity to accent. With notable exceptions like Samuel Say and Joshua Steele, eighteenth-century metrical theorists from Bysshe to Johnson had based their studies on a wholly theoretical scansion that abolished stressing and substituted counting; length and stress were considered identical, and the doctrine of elisions grew up to force the awkward elbows of language into the spaces available (elisions predate the year 1700; they begin to be crucial for a whole aesthetic, though, only after Bysshe's theory and Pope's practice). It is this system Coleridge wanted to overthrow by means of "a nobler, a freer and more powerful Versification." Whatever else it was at its inception in 1797, his meter in "Christabel"—"being founded on a new principle . . . of counting in each line the accents, not the syllables"—was certainly freer:

> "In the touch of this bosom there worketh a spell,
> Which is lord of thy utterance, Christabel!
> Thou knowest to-night, and wilt know to-morrow,
> This mark of my shame, this seal of my sorrow;
> But vainly thou warrest,
> For this is alone in
> Thy power to declare,
> That in the dim forest
> Thou heard'st a low moaning,
> And found'st a bright lady, surpassingly fair;
> And didst bring her home with thee in love and in charity,
> To shield her and shelter her from the damp air."[116]

The relative freedom of Geraldine's speech is in the position of the counted accents, the ability within limits to interpose variable numbers of syllables between the accents, thus cracking the molds of the traditional scansion by mixing trisyllabic feet into the same line as disyllabic ones. Coleridge explains in his famous preface:

> Though the [syllables] may vary from seven to twelve, yet in each line the accents will be found to be only four. Nevertheless, this occasional variation in number of syllables is not introduced wantonly, or for the mere ends of convenience, but in correspondence with some transition in the nature of the imagery or passion.

Thus in the line,

Which is lord of thy utterance, Christabel!

the two stresses (on "lord" and "ut-") require six surrounding scudded syllables, while the emotively spoken proper name after the comma comprises two accents in three syllables. Probably Coleridge would argue that this quoted personal speech, ending with an exclamation and charged with value by terms like "bosom" and "utterance" and the rhyming of "spell" with the name of the heroine, justifies the overleaping of traditional positions for strong stress, the more random placement of vocal emphasis, and also the contraction of lines in the middle of the quoted passage. How would he justify his own use of elisions ("heard'st"; "found'st")? Perhaps by saying that the imaginary speaker comes from an earlier era? The passage is a peculiar mélange of archaism and innovation.

Of a similar meter in Wordsworth's *White Doe of Rylstone,* Coleridge wrote that it was "rather dramatic than lyric, i.e., not such an arrangement of syllables, not such a meter, as acts a priori and with complete self-subsistence . . . but depending for its beauty always, and often even for its metrical existence, on the *sense* and *passion.*"[117] *The White Doe* is prolix, ruminative, prattling; the whole poem clings to moments when the doe makes its rare appearance, as animate emblem of kindly nature, and here the meter speeds and intensifies meaning:

> A moment ends the fervent din,
> And all is hushed, without and within;
> For though the priest, more tranquilly,
> Recites the holy liturgy,
> The only voice which you can hear
> Is the river murmuring near.
> —When soft!—the dusky trees between,
> And down the path through the open green,
> Where is no living thing to be seen;
> And through yon gateway, where is found,
> Beneath the arch with ivy bound,
> Free entrance to the church-yard ground—
> Comes gliding in serene and slow,

> Soft and silent as a dream,
> A solitary Doe![118]

In these lines we see a somewhat ungainly carrying metric transform itself by sheer intensity of concern, showing the flexibility of a prosodic method that can dart out of the a priori at will. About the many enabling details, I would remark only the way this meter gives full phonemic value to "solitary" (like "utterance," in the Coleridge line), with no need for a deforming elision; and the way the crucial term "soft" receives full stress in two entirely different functions of accented position—a repetition that is also a progressive deepening of sense. The nonappearance of expected stress emphasis or rhymes can have a cumulative effect of unsettling the reader, and predictably the early reviews of "Christabel" refuse the poem's method by saying that the writer "wants to teach the human ear a new and discordant system of harmony," or defying Coleridge "to show us *any* principle upon which his lines can be conceived to tally."[119] One reply to these objections is Josephine Miles's idea that "the meter breaks, to allow for the effects of silence as well as sound in the verse line," thereby differentiating the meter's time scheme by wedging pauses at irregular intervals.

> Coleridge sought, as his contemporaries sought, a varied and broken line pattern, the constant remission of four stresses to three, with consequent effects of easy repetition or wordlessness, the lightness of assonance as the shading of rhyme, feminine as the shading of masculine endings, shadings of echo and progression from stanza to stanza, and indeed in every new form of modification in sound, the quality of shadow, echo, or answer, rather than the massed and cumulative forces of the old pentameters.[120]

It does not take much, just a few extra unaccented syllables in every line, to expand the degree of metrical uncertainty to significant proportions, yet the effect will be great when the reader experiences and resolves these minor moments of ambiguity in series as cognitive tension and release. That implicates the reader in the meter's very gaps and irresolutions. "Coleridge," Angus Fletcher has written, "would dilate the prophetic moment." And later poets, too, in the minor details of metrical practice since the constitutive break of "Christabel," would explore the "betweenness of time-as-moment, pure thresholdness, barren liminality"[121] as the bard's version of the metaphysician's dilemma. In a direct line of inheritance from Coleridge, William Carlos Williams was later (1923) to hold that the meter should be "one of the words" of the poem—a perfect manifesto for the collapse of meter into grammar, trajectory into position.

It is hard to overestimate the importance of Coleridge's perception that smuggling but one extra syllable into the Augustan line, or taking accents seriously enough to count them not as numerical quantity but as vocal stress, could smash a whole prosodic system. The way was clear to sprung rhythm, alliterative revival, free verse, the prose poem, and more generally to form as proceeding, the technial inquiry of the avant-garde, which discriminates other linguistic features than the distribution of stress values. John Hollander's account of the visual format of William Carlos Williams's "By the road to the contagious hospital" is the sort of description that will become increasingly typical: "The meter here is a typographic strip about 30 ems wide with a general tendency to break syntax at tight points."[122] In direct line from Coleridge another Modern metrist, Harvey Gross, argues that we must "expand our concept of 'meaning' to include rhythmic cognition."[123] Poetic measuring, with Romanticism, had been recalibrated from chronological or clock time to human time. More than before in the history of English poetry, writers became aware that the phenomena that fill poem time are tensions both mental and physiological. The prosody that sounds in the ear measures but it does not count—it measures those parts of our lives when we are attending to the poem. The ordering is not of syllables but of perceptions.

There remains the question why the actual verse forms of the Romantic poets did not differ more sharply from those of their immediate predecessors. The usual explanation is that "a romanticization of subject matter long precedes the deliberate romanticization of the aesthetic medium,"[124] but though such an explanation itself suggests the detachability and scandal of form, the explanation is not sufficient. One cannot leave the subject by affirming that immediately after 1795 the inner form of texts changed while the outer form remained the same; the fact that prosody, of all elements in the poem, is the most resistant to style change seems pertinent but does not account for the quantum evolution of technique that we see at just this time. What changed was largely invisible, or visible only through unfamiliar lenses, as for instance by tracing the outline of the text as an act of the mind. Although it would be sixty years till the premises leaped into the metrics of avantgardism, the basis for the discoveries of Whitman and Hopkins was prepared in the generation of 1795. At this stage there was no thoroughgoing change in meter, rhyme, or stanza, but rather in the way these elements were regarded, in the concept of mind and of poetic form. There was the volatile new sense of the historical quality, the conventionality, of these prosodic devices of equivalence; the devices were not abandoned, but made relative. I have tried to show in some particularity why and how this took place.

After a certain point what Augustan form actually was, in its truest definition, did not matter; for the emergent Romantics what mattered was what it had become, what it represented, and therefore I have given selected attributes of that period style as logically contradictory injunctions. It is in this way that the formal premises behind Augustan poetry were regarded by the Romantic writers who, wishing to straighten out the logic, rejected or reversed or reinvented by distortion the entire list of postulates. So doing, they involved themselves in the new practice of a premeditated spontaneity that has not to this day been fully described, for if the new mode could be understood with any profound accuracy, we should already have our dwelling in yet another period style.

2
Form as Proceeding—Romantic Form in History and in Cognition

In History: Romanticism and Poetic Convention

In name and substance, Neo-Classicism is backward turning; its poetics are those of imitation, persuasion, the recognition of familiar gestures, the smallest possible disorientation whether cognitive or historical. By contrast the avant-garde has a poetics of the open margin, the unprecedented, the possible as well as the real. One of the avant-garde's subtypes, Futurism, may be taken as the extreme negation of the values of Neo-Classicism and as such a dramatic manifesto for all post-Romantic thought. Yet even Futurism is, like all such titles of movements and manifestos, a polemical exaggeration; the dominance of values and techniques *least like* those already existing might more accurately be called Presentism, but what bears emphasis is the direct fronting of experience that becomes the avant-garde program. This phase of post-Romantic thought becomes conscious in Russian Formalism's development, after 1916, of the notion of defamiliarization, a way of accounting for the evolution of devices, modes, and periods that strictly opposes the Classical aesthetics of recognition and least change.

One way, it would appear, of advancing into and beyond the present is to deny the reigning conventions of the past, for from the perspective of literary history this is what constitutes innovation. And again if, as Josephine Miles states, there is "a marvellously clean break" between Augustan and Romantic, involving "a new complex of attitude, terminology, and construction," nevertheless we must not, even here, "expect that the presence of a new style should immediately choke off an old one."[1] Where, in retrospect, Romanticism may appear to have closed off Augustan and late-Augustan ways of writing, what really happened in this process seems not to accord with any of the existing accounts, for this was not a warfare but a combination of durations, wherein avantgardist Romanticism allowed previous modes to coexist within the same stream as a group of innovative modes it had positively enabled.

Within this new ecology the older types became scarce, had not the right organs to survive. In context, between 1795 and 1810, the topographical or satiric couplets of Samuel Rogers, George Crabbe, and the early Byron are perfectly explainable as deferred Popian or late-Augustan phenomena; it is only our knowledge of the routes validated by major poetry that makes this work, or the isolated production of figures like Landor, Clough, or Bridges seem such curious, noble anomalies. And Popian personalities like Roy Campbell and Richard Wilbur, able in couplets, exist into the twentieth century as evidences that literary paradigms may be reborn, under pressure but technically perfect, in uncongenial periods.

Prosodic avantgardism is at one with Romanticism in looking beyond the device to the phrase; beyond the phrase to the line, segment, and text; beyond the text to the book; beyond the book to the mind and its operations; thence to reality and the future. Ultimately Romanticist poetics looks toward a poetry beyond the poem, or anterior to it, a disappearance of literature: "Modern Poetry, i.e., Poetry = Not Poetry" is Coleridge's equation, and the conditions have not since materially changed. Ideally poetry in this era will be closed by natural, not by social conventions; poetry is not illogical, yet neither is it bounded by logic. Romantic poetics thus becomes the meeting place, rich in contradictions, of an absolutist demand and a historical medium. After Coleridge, the most highly conscious theorists of this situation are preeminently Stéphane Mallarmé and his disciple in criticism, Maurice Blanchot, for both of whom poetry properly defined is hidden away in the future, round the next corner of nature and history. "The work is the waiting for the work," writes Blanchot in *The Book to Come.*[2] Literature is not an ensemble of forms, a graspable mode of activity, but it is rather something hidden from itself, "which one approaches by turning away from it," like Hölderlin or René Char, Blanchot's exemplary poets, in whom sings "the possibility and the impossibility of singing." Now art, truth, language are put into risk by an activity that depreciates itself; now poetry combats its oversimple identification with the subjective; now the poet becomes "bitter enemy of the figure of the poet." These contradictions take their origin in poetry itself considered, in Blanchot's terms, as "*a profundity, open onto the experience which makes it possible. . . .* Finally, every book pursues nonliterature as the essence it loves and wishes passionately to uncover." The avant-garde lacks that glory of Neo-Classicism, a fixed essential definition of literature as a discourse shorn of liberties, because the essential is always to be invented. Literariness leaps beyond the text, greater than the sum of the text's devices. As with other French commentators, Blanchot's presentation of the avant-garde involves a fiercer anti-Classicism than the critic in the Anglo-American tradition might need. To preserve the unity of language, and to "protect the common understanding against poetry," Classicism, for Blanchot, set out to render poetry "very visible, very particular, a realm cut off by high walls"; and poetry was also shielded from the realm of the poetic and its avantgardist recognitions, by highly determined sets of shared conventions.

Turning from Blanchot to Barthes to make a point that is implicit in the argument of my previous chapter, it is clear that by these assumptions Augustan form is a "strongly mythical system" because it innocently assumes that a historical array of literary conventions is a natural one. Augustan poetry "imposes on the meaning one extra signified, which is *regularity*,"[3] the one aspect Romanticism wishes not so much to obliterate as elegantly to hide, or deemphasize, or absorb. Literariness, as a result, becomes a scandal.

We have, then, the text that hopes to efface all the marks of the labor of its production. Poetry is precisely that which may not be identified with language, genre, or the prominent devices of equivalence whose repertoires, for the linguists, create literariness. To most poets of the avant-garde, poetry is elsewhere than in its formal conventions—"not just talking about life, but life itself," as Louis Simpson has written. "I think that the object of writing is to make words disappear."[4] Prior to the murder of poetic conventions must come the murder of language, the imagination that "if languages were perfect, verse would not exist because every word would be poetry; and thus no one would be" (Gérard Genette).[5] This imagining of a limiting case, and trying to think and write accordingly, leads on to attempts to discover styles that will so far as possible heal over the separation between *langue* and *parole,* the arbitrary conventional character of the liaison between signifier and signified, which linguistics after Ferdinand de Saussure assumes are working hypotheses. This tendency Modern poetics will describe variously as the assimilation of poetry to nature, an attempt "to overcome the secondary or elegiac aspect of language by making language coterminous with life," or as a "regressive semiological system" that "tries to transform the sign back into meaning."[6] Yet we must remember that however much these extremes are proposed as directive but unreachable models, it is the actual language, finite and historical and situated in relation to a writer, which is composed in the poem. Organic form in the language of poetry is neither more nor less than a powerful pretension.

Romantics, objecting to any conspicuous prior constraint upon their texts, take an extreme essentialist view of poetic devices. Like words devices must also, down to the most minute pauses and punctuation marks, be indexes of personality, symptoms of voice and feeling, and correlations between the work and the universe. Thus Mallarmé: "The orphic explanation of the earth, which is the only duty of the poet and the first-priority literary game: for the book's every rhythm, at once impersonal yet alive, even down to its pagination, correlates itself with this dream, or Ode." And Blanchot: "All that counts is the book, as is, far from genres, outside rubrics, poems, poetry, novel, testimony, under which it refuses to rank itself and whose power to fix its place, and determine its form, it denies."[7] The tendency, plainly, is to dissolve genre and technique into human faculties, bodily processes, and events in the natural world. Among faculties the most privileged is sincerity; among bodily processes, the breath; among natural events, the workings of wind or water and the growth of plants. Free verse and the prose poem have been taken as the shaping principles that display this concept of form, either caressed or battered according to the commentator's opinion about the innovative prosodies. But the debate should not be restricted to these special formats. Wallace Stevens's view of the matter, which includes on the same footing both the open and the traditional measures, is the only acceptable one: "The essential thing in form is to be free in whatever form is used."[8] The generation of 1795 enabled these new meanings of technique as sincerity, and of excellence as freedom.

Since the conventionality of language and of poetic forms is, however crucial a topic, strictly secondary, whether any particular text is in couplets or free verse is not material in post-Romantic writing. The identification of Romanticism with woolly or fluid forms, by rhetorical contrast with Augustan fixities, is an error. The quarrel with Augustan form was not about technical attributes at all; in fact, as Claudio Guillén points out, it was not even a quarrel.

> Poetic conventions were fully recognized for the first time by the cultural movement which had begun by estranging itself from them, namely the Romantic movement. . . . Poetry, considered as a triumph of the imagination, had no genuine quarrel with conventions, without which it would not be possible to draw the necessary line between the poetic and the natural. The revolt against conventions, in other words, had really been a reaction against neoclassical poetics. The rise of a new poetics stressing the power of the imagination would alter completely the terms of the problem.[9]

Guillén's point may be extended to explain what has so often puzzled students of Wordsworth and Coleridge, in their Romantic distinctions drawn between poetic essence and poetic medium. Coleridge distinguished between poetry and poems; Wordsworth drew his distinction not between poetry and prose, which would have been fruitless platitude, but between poetry and science. By such oppositions they preserve for poetry the idea of interiority, a special depth of substance that is independent of poetic devices. They never show themselves unaware of the difference between the ideal tendency or limit and the actual text, for it is the sparking between these two poles of energy that begins creation and that, as they know, makes of form both a scandal and a necessity.

But Romantic thinking about poetic form was not just a matter of pronouncement, for Wordsworth and Coleridge had both written poems that brought self, world, and language into persuasive unity. (Those unities will sometimes be assertive and precarious, as we will see.) One poem especially, Coleridge's "Eolian Harp" (1795), may be seen as marking off the epochal moment of Romantic poetics and the concepts of form I have been unfolding. The poem, with its subtitle "Composed at Clevedon, Somerset-

shire," may seem yet another late-Augustan topographical effort that separates out its syntaxes of description and meditation, but it redeems and
transcends that convention by turning the facets of a central symbol, the
wind harp of the title that "comprises within itself the blending of instrumen-
tal sound and outdoor noise of wind which was becoming, in later eighteenth-century England, the imagination's authentic music" (John
Hollander).[10] Coleridge's poem has five blank-verse paragraphs of irregular
length, punctuated by three direct addresses to his wife, Sara, as imagined
and internalized auditor (lines 1, 34, and 50 in the 1817 edition), and in
general arranged in sequence to work deeper into the subject: address to
Sara and setting, at evening when "The stilly murmur of the distant Sea /
Tells us of silence"; the lute as heard, with images of its power that make
plain that it is an emblem of writing; identification of the speaker with the
lute; expansive speculation that the whole of "animated nature" might be
"but organic Harps diversely fram'd"; and a closing that partly retracts the
utterance as "shapings of the unregenerate mind," showing the poet abasing
his own mental processes and expressing awe before God, "The Incompre-
hensible!" Though partly negated by the poem's ending, this identification of
the poet's art with the wind harp—outside language and conventions, non-
referential, aleatory—becomes a way of eluding so far as possible the
agonies of self-consciousness in the sphere of technique.

The harp's "long sequacious notes" (line 18), like the deep-breathed projection of phrase to line to verse-paragraph in Coleridge's processional syntax, become emblematic of a prosody opposed to Augustan form, a
celebration of natural sound, and of syntax as prosody:

> O! the one Life within us and abroad,
> Which meets all motion and becomes its soul,
> A light in sound, a sound-like power in light,
> Rhythm in all thought, and joyance everywhere—
> Methinks, it should have been impossible
> Not to love all things in a world so fill'd;
> Where the breeze warbles, and the mute still air
> Is Music slumbering on her instrument.[11]

The interfusions are richly worked in here: the poet in amity with his wife;
day meeting night and land meeting sea; the convergence of sound and light,
standing for feeling and thought; thought itself instinct with rhythmical measure; and the impalpable, multitudinous air "Is Music."[12] Yet if we weigh out
the ecstasies against the self-divisions in the poem as a whole, the ending
against the rest, the peculiarities of its negative affirmations ("it should have
been impossible / Not"), the animus that moves the exclamation points and
dashes, and the desperation suppressed by the "Methinks" convention, I
think we come to feel that the harp symbol is the meeting place for contrary
impulses. If we read for tone in the poem, it is clear that Coleridge both

indulges and chastises his wish to be *beguiled,* warily pursuing the same thesis that a later poet, Hayden Carruth, has expressed as "Freedom and discipline concur / only in ecstasy."[13] Because the harp's music is like a poetry without prosody, Coleridge luxuriates in its generation of "full chords of the fundamental, up to the dominant seventh, as a function of the strength of the wind," doubtless pleased that the instrument (to continue John Hollander's description) "does not play melodic lines nor does its fundamental pitch flatten."[14] But Coleridge is always aware that he is beguiled; the harp is the occasion both for expanding and for reprimanding the free consciousness.

In Cognition: Poem and Reader after 1795

Let us imagine a time that never was, when the world was an infinitude of things, ranged side by side. Language, in appropriating this plenitude, gestured "here," then "there"; or "if," then "then"; or language remarked "then it was that" and "now it is this." Sensation words, image words, dominated all the mind's procedures of exposition, for the major mode of perceiving the world was that of conjunction, addition, polarity, and analogy. Accordingly, art was perceived as catalog, and as "shape as superinduced." The poem, like the mind, imitated an autonomous, external order deployed horizontally like monuments in a field or like those old grammar books which listed and described in isolation the parts of speech, the diction as somehow separable from the predication. This was a bad time for poetry.

There were, in fact, two bad times: between Pope and Wordsworth, and between Whitman and Eliot. The disability shared by Hulme, H.D., Aldington, Flint, Fletcher, Amy Lowell, even Pound at times, with Thomson and Cowper and the versifying topographers, is this: however superb they may be at producing images, they have not the procedures to coordinate them. Though Imagism is a subtler, post-Romantic form of associationism, though Imagist poems are not as a rule barnacled over with poetic diction, the Imagist poem shares with the later-Augustan poem the lack of a principle of progression. *The Seasons* is flawed from first to last by its inept transitions, while *The Complete Poetical Works of T. E. Hulme* sets out systematically to suppress all transitions. Thomson like Hulme has no controlling concept, no syntax in the widest possible sense that will render perceptions fully significant.

Romantic and post-Imagist poets, beginning to write in the midst of this dilemma, required a causality that would prefigure in all its transitions the effect that was the poem. The need to convert a series of perceptions into a continuous poem, and to interrelate part and whole, description and discourse, obliged them entirely to rethink the question of poetic structure. Moreover, this strange project had to be accomplished in the process of

writing poems, a task clearly more formidable for English Romantic writers,
involving nothing less than a total crisis of personality in the poet as in his
readership. "I feel like the first men who read Wordsworth," Randall Jarrell
has said in a poem. "It's so simple I can't understand it." This difficult
simplicity is often discussed as one of diction, but the structural ensemble of
the continuous poem is far more important.

Wordsworth, Coleridge, Whitman, Wallace Stevens, William Carlos Williams, Charles Olson, Charles Tomlinson, and John Ashbery all write
meditative poems, in which internalized speech is designed to represent a
process of thought; and despite their differences from these and from each
other, one must also add Yeats, Eliot, and Thomas. The structure of extended lyrics in particular, of "The Eolian Harp," "Tintern Abbey," "The
Idea of Order at Key West," "The Kingfishers," or "Self Portrait in a Convex
Mirror," displays a track of feeling, a motion that if followed closely will
yield everything of importance for understanding the poet's habits of meditation. Such extended lyrics adopt the outer forms of logical discourse, advancing deliberately by devices that convey the fiction of spontaneous
ordering. At the same time that these poems appear to be destroying form
they are generating the form of a new and idiosyncratic utterance.

Even the finest of such poems might be misjudged by critics who, lacking
sympathy for the Romantic view of the self, would confuse mere volun-
tariness with creative freedom. Certainly the self of the writer is in this
poetry to be reckoned into the meaning in a different way than the Popian or
Johnsonian self. Think of the revealing pun in "The Eolian Harp," when
Coleridge writes that his own thoughts are "As wild and various as the
random gales / That swell and flutter on *this subject Lute!*" (lines 42–43). The
functional ambiguity of "subject" has the harp, as surrogate for the self, as
both the slavish register and the dominating organizer of its perceptions. In
fact, this minor effect may be taken as an instance of the perplexity at the
heart of the whole poem, and more generally as an instance of the Romantic
idea that the question of the self is a task to be provisionally answered within
the text. Whereas the Augustan self exists, fully chiseled, before the poem
begins, there is always a sense that the Romantic self is being modeled or
redefined as the poem unfolds.

Knowledge of the real, like poetry itself, is prospective in this mode, the
to-be-morally-individuated entity that pursues its nature in and through experience. This is why Wordsworth was able to call poetry "the breath and
finer spirit of knowledge." The historicity and extent of this knowledge,
gained as the coadunating imagination moves beyond Hartleyan associationism, are described by Earl Wasserman:

> No longer can a poem be conceived of as a reflection or imitation of an
> autonomous order outside itself. The creation of a poem is also the crea-
> tion of the cosmic wholeness that gives meaning to the poem, and each

poet must independently make his own world-picture, his own language within language.

The condition of man has not changed in this last century and a half, and Wordsworth's predicament is ours.[15]

The epistemology of this predicament is logically prior to the prosody, and though (as Wasserman has elsewhere shown) there were in England extremely diverse views of the grounds of knowledge, there was nonetheless as the common denominator a shared faith in the reconciling, synthetic imagination—and in poetry as the voice of humanity against oppression. Generalizing from a wide survey of studies of Romanticism, René Wellek shows the growing area of agreement in descriptions of this cultural mode; he finds that "the reconciliation of art and nature, language and reality, *is* the romantic ambition," and that belief in imagination, symbol, myth, and organic nature is part of a great, transnational endeavor to overcome the split between self and world, image and discourse, and poetry and prosody.[16] (That endeavor, through complex mediations, has its relationship to the political climate of a time midway between a Revolution in France and a Reform Bill in England.) A typically English empiricism, going from Hume through Kant to Coleridge, had returned from Germany enlarged and dignified in a theory of imagination not as accumulation but as interfusion of images, "Reason in her most exalted mood." In lyricized local poems, of which the first true exemplar is "The Eolian Harp," atomism is subsumed in and by structuralism through the repeated out-in-out process of mind in relation to world.

If the poetics of eolian harps is representative, the ultimate form of the ideal artwork must be the fullness of nature; and the object of the work is to take the plentitude and give it over with the least diminishing, embodied in motion. True art is a mediatress between universal and particular, nature and man. Coleridge's theory of imagination is in this context a faculty of immense powers of generalization, of accuracy, and of pertinence, connecting disparates and seizing wholes.[17] In *Modern Painters* Ruskin was later to term this tremendous aesthetic-moral-cognitive faculty "imagination penetrative." The Romantic theory of imagination makes sense only within this larger schema of the whole of creative activity going on in nature. The poet masters *natur naturans,* or at least some simulacrum of it in language, by imitating that which is within the outer thing, or, more accurately, by releasing materials into life. Hence the importance, in this theory, of the notions of progression: in, through, form as proceeding, the present participles of action-in-motion.

Coleridge's need to convey ad hominem what is in motion, to unify what is diverse, to correct toward spontaneity what is *voulu* and rule bound, makes him perceive the nature of reality, as of prosody, as a field in which opposites are unifying. According to M. H. Abrams, the same concept of "the dynamic

conflict of opposites and their reconciliation into a higher third," serves
Coleridge as "the root principle of his cosmogony, his epistemology, and his
theory of poetic creation alike."[18] Commentators from the great quarterlies
of Coleridge's time, their sensibilities formed in an Augustan climate, down
to those anti-Romantic Moderns, Irving Babbitt and T. S. Eliot, see only the
surface manifestations when they condemn the use of landscape, children,
or primitive states of consciousness as the expression of self-absorption, an
illicit "merging" of self and world. For in fact this form of thinking is a way of
postulating and enacting organic sensibility, a projection of self into things,
ideas, persons of value. It is a response in the imaginary to a permanent state
of separation from value. The act of philosophical reflection means a division within the self, just as, in the sphere of art, the poetic act, the writing, is
an admission of separation from ordinary speech and unmediated experience. There is no atonement. The poem, however, becomes a mechanism
that can push alienation to destroy itself, a device of anti-self-consciousness
that contains unitary solutions, unitary locutions, enactive reconciliations—
"never a completed act of integration," and conscious of deficiency, but
seeking to turn estrangement into self-instruction and knowledge, even in
the poems from this period that exist as created fragments ("Kubla Khan")
or as gigantic torsos ("Hyperion"). Alienation is the precondition for this
writing, and the final description both of its special success and of the social
condition from which it derives.

Yet another division-in-rapport, not the least essential, must be added in
the distance between writer and reader. If we proceed by logical rather than
temporal stages, the first tendency of the new poetic self was to exclude the
reader quite utterly. Only when this was recognized was there felt to be a
necessity of bringing the reader back; at that point, by overcompensation,
the reader's role was exaggerated and idealized. What emerged was a new
knowledge of the perplexity of the reader's role and new means to build the
reader into the discourse.

When Romanticism placed the author at the center of the poem, as the one
who forms and is formed by the text, the reader was also silently included
among the poem's several subjects. The reader's subjectivity became what
the poem was, in part, about, even as it was what the poem educed, ap-
pealed to, and played upon. This experience of the reader, one premise very
often lost in studies of Romanticism and of prosody, has been reckoned into
the interpretive process by Paul de Man's account of

> the question of the self in literature, which appears first of all . . . in the act
> of judgment that takes place in the mind of the reader; appears next in the
> apparently intersubjective relationships that are established between the
> author and the reader; it governs the intentional relationship that exists,
> within the work, between the constitutive subject and the constituted
> language; it can be sought, finally, in the relationship that the subject
> establishes, through the mediation of the work, within itself. . . . The

question of finding the common level on which all these selves meet and thus of establishing the unity of literary consciousness stands at the beginning of the main methodological difficulties that plague literary studies.[19]

Those are the factors which frustrate an interpretation; the Romantics themselves were far more interested in what enabled it. Do we find the post-1795 "level on which all these selves meet" in the cultural moment narrowly defined, or in the author's consciousness, or in the text considered as a clustering of certain ideas and forms, or in the reader's consciousness? Plainly all these variables are involved—and very likely others. Without pretending to settle the issue, perhaps I might advance a suggestion on a part of the larger difficulty, the relation of prosody to attention. In the large as well as in local detail, the technical features that help to create subjects in language during this era certainly implicate the reader in more and more dramatic ways than any previous poetry.

Reacting against a pragmatic poetics, Romantic criticism invests heavily in expressionist theories that focus on the figure of the poet, and as M. H. Abrams has said, this is "singularly fatal to the audience," as determinant of poetry and poetic value.[20] And yet what was being dismissed was not faith in the reader but in the more civic or Augustan view of poetry as eloquence, persuasion, a poetics of the recognition of fixed and familiar signs. What Abrams calls the "disappearance of a homogeneous and discriminating reading public" had been described by Wordsworth in 1815 as a division between "a small though loud portion of the community, ever governed by factitious influence, which, under the name of the PUBLIC, passes itself, upon the unthinking, for the PEOPLE."[21] Wordsworth gives his "devout respect, his reverence," to the people: "And how does ['good poetry'] survive but through the People? What preserves it but their intellect and wisdom?" In this setting his poetics becomes one of discovery, and he hopes, he says, "to extend the domain of sensibility." When Keats wrote in 1818 that he "never wrote one single line of Poetry with the least Shadow of public thought," he was similarly responding to the lack of fit between Augustan standards and Romantic production. Those standards had a kind of half-life in the great Regency quarterlies, despite the obliteration, over twenty years earlier, of the univocal aristocratic politics they stood for.

What was dying was the notion of the reader as an imagined single person (a social Being), and what was being born was the notion of a near infinity of readers, all somewhat different, so that after 1795 one might no longer assume so much about the reader. One had instead to face the fact that the writer speaks in vacuo but also to mankind—both.

In fact, then, in this crisis of readership that separated public opinion from the people, culture from society, the properly responding reader became all the more valuable because of his or her absence or distance. Such readers had to be reconstituted within the poem itself; their absence had to be turned into a presence within language. Prosody, in the broadest sense, was one means to that end.

What is absent and required is what is theorized and recreated. Alienation, the separation of the self from the self, is in this sense the instinct for life, the spur to creation. In practical terms in the poem, it meant inventing, by means of perspective and equivalence, the authorial self as a voice and the reader's presence as an implied collaboration. In *Lyrical Ballads,* according to Paul Sheats, the writer's role is the reverse of obtrusive in a vision that is "offered to the reader, not imposed upon him," by a poet who wants us to "see what he cannot tell us. These poems thus argue a trust in the capacities of the reader that is itself an act of charity, and what they offer is the sense that an exalted vision can be shared."[22] Wordsworth's prefaces of 1800 and 1815 display the seriousness of that trust in the people rather than the public, and in terms very like those of Edward Dorn's 1974 preface to his *Collected Poems:* "My true readers have known exactly what I have assumed. I am privileged to take this occasion to thank you for that exactitude, and to acknowledge the pleasure of such a relationship."[23] In their physiology as well as their moral sense, the true readers complete the work when it is regarded, now more than ever before, as a circuit of communication. A poetry that hopes to extend the domain of sensibility probably must expect to place trust only in a small readership—at least at first, while, in Wordsworth's avantgardist phrasing, it is creating the taste by which it is enjoyed. Such poetry, though, if it makes strong claims, also includes the imagination of a much more extensive readership in the future.

Coleridge described the four classes of readers as sponges, sand-glasses, straining bags—all incompetent—and "lastly, the Great Mogul's diamond, sieves. . . . these are the only good, and I fear the least numerous, who assuredly retain the good while the superfluous or impure passes away and leaves no trace."[24] The sieve and diamond metaphors, insofar as they consort together, combine the qualities of refinement and many-faceted reflection, the ability to bring to the foreground what is most precious. A reader with this skill would tend, in his activity, to associate himself with the author to a very great degree, becoming as much the second fabricator as the user of the text. A much more violent version of these ideas is the later view of Roland Barthes, who maintains that with certain types of work—avant-garde, writable *(scriptible)*—the reader is transformed from consumer to producer of the text, so to mend the "pitiless divorce which the institution of literature keeps between . . . maker and user."[25] For Barthes the Classical text is readable, linear, single in meaning, therefore exhaustible and passé; the writable text lives in the avant-garde's "perpetual present," totally transition and process, "a galaxy of signifiers . . . without beginning; reversible," and plural in meaning. This writable text, expressed as a compassable fact in Barthes but actually a theoretical limit, is "us as we write," or rather rewrite as Mogul-diamond readers in the vivid present: "The writeable text is not a thing; you search in vain for it in libraries. . . . The writeable is the novelistic without the novel, poetry without style, production without the finished product, structuration without structure." This is a stronger concept than those dim Romantic ideas for what the work enacts in the reader, suggestiveness and inspiration; nothing less than the idea of the scandal of form stated in terms of the reader's experience. The reader of the avant-garde text becomes, in theory, the writer's shadow or secret sharer, a co-creator, the one who completes the text.

So what is resolved in the poem is not (or not only) the poet's experience, but also the reader's experience—as foreseen and plotted by the poet and evoked by the poet's language. "The ultimate 'stability' of the work," as Barbara Herrnstein Smith has said, "refers not to a point at which the . . . reader's experience is 'finished,' but to a point at which, without residual expectations, he can experience the structure of the work as, at once, both dynamic and whole."[26] This is to understand texts from the gestaltist perspective that the Romantic tradition both proposes and enables.

Gerard Manley Hopkins called Parnassian those lesser works which, as reader, he could imagine himself writing. For him, as one of his century's great Mogul-diamond readers, this meant large portions of Wordsworth and Tennyson. He says in effect that the only truly readable works are those sublime and inimitable ones which strike wonder, those works which force readers to put on the stretch their imaginative and verbal competence. Even if, as with Mallarmé, the poet has proposed to himself his own elocutionary disappearance from the poem, the effective poem of experience yet builds the reader into its structures of implication. This is why poetry forces us, in Paul Valéry's phrase, to reproduce it exactly. Any reading that aspires even to moderate accuracy must thus rely upon astoundingly complex feats of attention, especially with the didactic qualities of post-Romantic writing. Whether it storms or cajoles the reader's defenses, this writing is trying to have a definite effect that is at once musical-prosodic, rhythmic, semantic, and moral. This poetry encourages the reader to know the world in a new way: see, hear, live, and know are the implied or stated imperatives, encouraging the readers to experience their experience.

By developing in poems the premise that a work of art is a structure of intention, Romantic writing anticipated the perception theory that, according to Morse Peckham, has helped to destroy the "entire psychological foundation" of existing aesthetic theory.[27] If works are viewed, that is, "not as artifacts, but as perceptual configurations" (Peckham), we will tend to think about them differently, needing now to account for the way they are both "dynamic and whole" (Barbara Herrnstein Smith). We will have to explore how, in a voice that implies and includes its auditor, the poem becomes a practice of memory. We have already seen Coleridge writing of the "hooks and eyes of memory," of the "quick reciprocation of curiosity still gratified and reexcited"; he also praised the "exertion of thought" called forth by long hypotactic sentences. Among Romantics, Coleridge was the most conscious practitioner of the psychology of expectation, aware that cognitive frustration keeps the mind working, seeking resolutions.[28] A shorthand writer at Coleridge's Shakespeare lectures found him different from all other speakers, for it was impossible to guess the latter part or apodosis of his sentences. "The conclusion of every one of Coleridge's sentences," runs the contemporary account, "was a *surprise* upon [the scribe]. He was obliged to listen to the last word."[29] Far from resting in stable or geometrical forms, the Romantic work in just this way makes language perceptible by rewarding the extension, contraction, reweighting, and continual readjustment of the reader's expectation. Moreover, successive readings, deepening understanding of structure and meaning, can only bring out more cognitive eventfulness and historical specificity. The initial discovery procedures are inalienable, for cognitive surprise is crafted into the acts of selection and combination performed by writer and constituted within the reader's own tensions of frustration and fulfillment. The poem, at any point in its movement, implicates the reader's prospective and retrospective memory.

Without wishing to stint either the text or the reader, as components of the literary process, I am bringing to bear on the Augustan-Romantic transition Kenneth Burke's postulate that "form in literature is an arousing and fulfillment of desires."[30] That position may be traced at least as far back as Romanticism itself, as I have suggested. It can usefully be developed further along both cognitive and historical lines, to reconstruct the limits within which a literary movement holds its knowledge of literary form. This has been done most notably by Josephine Miles in her long-term project of relating styles of sentences to styles of versification, over the whole range of English and American literature, and by Barbara Herrnstein Smith in her account of fashions in poetic closure.[31] Doubtless literature of any historical date manifests this traceable process of arousal and fulfillment as it directs the reader's developing sense of poetic form. To narrow the historical question, I would say the Augustan-Romantic shift is to be found in the degree of cognitive tension. Augustan form, with its rhetoric of precision, its special diction and regularized syllable-count scansion and cadential endings, more perhaps than any period style before or since emphasized the resolution of tension described by Morse Peckham as "the feeling that the situation matches the expectation of directive state."[32] Both the satirical and the sublime modes of the Enlightenment, according to Peckham, suppress "possible objections to a position by repeating the same idea in different words, over and over again, until the effect of the words blots out any threatening cognitive tension by a heavily enforced cognitive harmony." By contrast the Romantic mode increases dramatically the available discontinuities, and steps up cognitive tension to the point where, as we have seen, the earliest Romantic productions were barely readable by late-Augustan audiences. Indeed, to the degree that twentienth-century students have seen this writing mostly as a reconciliation and merging, apart from the deep divisions of alienation that poems recognize as their true subject matter and task, poetry from Coleridge to Ashbery has still not created the taste by which it is to be enjoyed.

One poem by Coleridge is especially striking for its knowledge of the perplexities of reading and its developed image of the competent reader: "To William Wordsworth: Composed on the Night after His Recitation of a Poem on the Growth of an Individual Mind" (1807). Over a period of almost two weeks, ending on the night of 7 January 1807, Wordsworth read to Coleridge the whole of *The Prelude* in the 1805 version; in Coleridge's poem to Wordsworth, we have a written response to an oral presentation of a written work, one important culminating moment in a cycle of communication that began over ten years earlier, with their personal friendship and collaboration. One way of reducing the distance between author and reader is to interpose a surrogate auditor, with whom the reader may identify. This Coleridge does in the present instance, as counterspeech to Wordsworth's gesture of addressing the long poem to him both within the text and in a private oral reading. Of course by naming the auditor (merely the world's greatest poet!) Coleridge also frustrated identification. At least the reader could eavesdrop.

The lines between speech act and written text are throughout these interchanges firmly drawn, and yet in the experience of the text they are continually overstepped as if to show, here as elsewhere, that we must distinguish without finally dividing. Coleridge begins with the invocation, "Friend of the wise! and Teacher of the Good!"—an awkward and abstract way of energizing Coleridge's verbal behavior, but we must remember the nature of the situation, "fraught with Coleridge's problematic, self-abnegating reverence for Wordsworth" (A. Reeve Parker).[33] The poem shows Coleridge fighting his way to identity as auditor, reader, and writer, and toward a handsome statement of praise for the one living writer whose talent oppressed his talent and judged his life and art more than any other. By line 11 Coleridge is quoting a whole line from the end of Wordsworth's "Intimations of Immortality," and he goes on in two verse-paragraphs (Lines 12–45) to summarize with penetration the leading ideas of Wordsworth's immense *Prelude*. After hearing thousands of lines of blank verse he is still able to think of Wordsworth as a writer without literature, author of

> An Orphic song indeed,
> A song divine of high and passionate thoughts
> To their own music chaunted!

(45–47)

Wordsworth's poem, he says,

> Makes audible a linked lay of Truth,

> Of Truth profound a sweet continuous lay,
> Not learnt, but native, her own natural notes!
>
> (58–60)

The sound of this discourse fascinates Coleridge, whose references to
music, bardic chaunting, and audibility are frequent, and who twice (lines 48
and 111) refers to the cessation of the utterance and the peculiar moral
resonance of the enchanting, oracular moment after the end. The sound in
this oral reading intensifies and transcends the discourse, and beyond the
sound is the enduring moral significance: reverberations of sound, feeling,
and meaning move out into the future, heightening consciousness as a mere
mental or visual reading could not.

The next lines show Coleridge turning inward; Coleridge is so oppressed
by Wordsworth's example that he must correct himself for imagining his own
corpse on his bier, during a complex moment of retrospective nostalgia in the
future. The poem ends with Coleridge absorbing Wordsworth's deep voice,
"In silence listening, like a devout child," but also like the archetypal Romantic reader and Wordsworth's only perfect auditor:

> My soul lay passive, by thy various strain
> Driven as in surges now beneath the stars,
> With momentary stars of my own birth,
> Fair constellated form, still darting off
> Into the darkness; now a tranquil sea,
> Outspread and bright, yet swelling to the moon.
>
> (96–101)

The poem ends in a verse-paragraph that is coincident with a long periodic
sentence, broken, indeed deeply wrenched, by problematic juncture and
reversal and reenergized statement. The passage is entirely characteristic of
the delaying procedures that create cognitive frustration in the Romantic
mode, but that also resolve that tension by hundreds of minute quasi-
prosodic devices like the resolving internal rhyme that the last line picks off
the end of two earlier blank-verse lines ("closed"/"close"/"rose"):

> And when—O Friend! my comforter and guide!
> Strong in thyself, and powerful to give strength!—
> Thy long sustained Song finally closed,
> And thy deep voice had ceased—yet thou thyself
> Wert still before my eyes, and round us both
> That happy vision of beloved faces—
> Scarce conscious, and yet conscious of its close
> I sate, my being blended in one thought
> (Thought was it? or aspiration? or resolve?)
> Absorbed, yet hanging still upon the sound—
> And when I rose I found myself in prayer.
>
> (102–12)

In an optimum situation of psychological threat, the proxy reader's selfhood is there fully engaged, asserting identity at the same time it is able to praise honestly for all it is worth. A. Reeve Parker convincingly argues that in the process of this poem Coleridge is able to define an image of himself toward which he can consciously aspire. "Not disavowing but recognizing the nature of his own ambivalent aspirations after Wordsworth's power, he turned 'personal' anguish into strenuous charity, and avenged himself on his friend by enriching their relationship with a poem that recorded his own egotistic and transcendent ideal."[34] Finally, if the last image of the poem is strictly blasphemous, in its use of the language of religious communion for the relation of writer and reader, that, too, is something the Romantic mode comprehends as an ideal.

3
The Crisis of Versification, 1855–1910

A General System of Relationships

Romanticism and its form as proceeding was the primary founding moment for a whole mode of poetry, or for a whole sequence of modes. Turning now to those times, closer to us in history, when the premises gave way to the metrics of Modernity, it is time to consider the era of Whitman and Hopkins and Mallarmé as a single, if always developing unit, which takes poetic theory and practice up to the threshold of the era of Imagism and a wider experimentation with free verse.

The pertinent questions are: How much pressure can be applied to one Romantic style before it gives way? What kinds of internal contradictions may coexist? Whitman, of course, as the most decisive of several post-Romantic inventors of radical styles, was working out the fullest implications of procedures developed by the first Romantic generation. However there is enough of the unprecedented in his overall achievement that Roy Harvey Pearce's claim for his priority may stand: "The 1855, 1856, and 1860 *Leaves of Grass* make a complete sequence—one in which the poet invents modern poetry, explores its possibility as an instrument for surveying the world at large and himself as somehow vitally constitutive of it, and comes finally to define, expound, and exemplify the poet's vocation in the modern world."[1] The idiosyncratic immensity of that invention may well have left Whitman, in our imaginations, a figure of loneliness until his vindication after 1910; but this chapter seeks to modify that impression by replacing the poet within the range of theories and practices that were current in his lifetime—and the next chapter finds for him a metrical comrade fully conscious of an affiliation with the American yawp and gab: Gerard Manley Hopkins.[2]

Before arguing that affinity I would like to show, by laying out a wide range of prosodic practice and theory, how this period manifests a crisis of versification. That crisis is by no means resolved even now, and the ensuing chapters will demonstrate some ways in which writers after 1910 have deepened the dilemmas of Whitman's period. (Acceptance of the prose poem and free verse have, for many writers and readers, resolved certain other prosodic impasses; yet we have hardly begun to explain to ourselves, with respect to poetic technique, just why we accept these innovative forms, or how we judge value in an era of stylistic pluralism.) The period from 1855 to 1910 is the precise time in which an ancient versification, believed by many to have its roots in Greek forms and practices, is weakened by the coming to consciousness of internal contradictions—and by defections from the ranks. The old versification is brought to the verge of a break, earthquake, or explosion; about 1910 that break occurs—yet, with a loss in prestige perhaps, that traditional way of writing is still possible. Indeed today it still has dominance over all other forms.

Though change occurs, nothing in versification is ever superseded, surpassed, for prosodies are preserved, or resurrected, in full strength if they have any foothold whatever in the language. They may return at any time in literary history when, for specific historical purposes, they sound well in a poet's ear.

Within the period from 1855 to 1910, there is a special relation of poetic practice to theory, which may be described as an array of competing possibilities. To describe the array calls for a rather rare type of presentation, which has been well characterized by Hans Robert Jauss when he spoke of criticism's need "to take a synchronic cross-section of a moment in the process, to arrange heterogeneous works into equivalent, opposing, and hierarchical groups, and thereby to discover a general system of relationships."[3] Such study is accomplished by inspecting a period wherein the older versification is being invaded, while at the same time it produces splendid poems as well as descriptions and justifications of itself that solidify its legitimate power.

The crisis of versification in the whole of the period since Wordsworth is that of stylistic pluralism, the absence of a period style that would permit an effortless choice of forms for certain subjects. The sense that we are as readers less helped by knowing determinate genres in all literature since 1795 is itself a crisis; and with respect to meter, this means we are less helped by our lacking, now, an institutional way of hearing and seeing the rhythms of the poem as we take it in orally or through the eye. Stylistic pluralism is not, fortunately, a matter of infinite variegation; several main types exist, and one of these is for the most part conserving, traditional, conspicuously the bearer of the main line of poetry since Chaucer. While, in theory and practice, this line is being praised and, from 1855 to 1910, actually given scholarly justification, simultaneously it is being undermined, or implicitly contradicted, by an insurgent prosody of the individual intonation.

Mallarmé, most conscious and articulate of the ushers of the Modern, traveled from Paris to Oxford in 1894 to bring news: "On a touché au vers," the poetic line has been touched. The "most surprising news" about poetic form will now be discussed at once, Mallarmé said, "just as an invited traveler unburdens himself, in a gasping way, from his witnessing an acci-

dent that preoccupies him." Traditional meter remains nearby, within reach
if one wants to use it; "very strict, numerical, direct, in combined play, the
meter, anterior, subsists." Yet this is the moment of a departure from meter,
of individual modulation, of the prose poem and free verse: "Thunderstorm,
purifying; and in the uproars . . . the act of writing scrutinized itself back to
its origins."[4] Verse waited until the death of the king of poetry, the French
Tennyson, Victor Hugo; whereby "the whole language, [heretofore] ad-
justed to [a] metric [prosody], recovered its vital beats, escaped, to a free
disjunction of a thousand simple elements." In this moment of incubation,
indefiniteness, free choice, and stylistic pluralism, of the crisis of the poetic
line, "for the first time in the course of the literary history of any people,"
every individual will organize a separate prosody. During such a "breakdown of the great literary rhythms" the measures of an individual's breathing, or their simulacrum in poetry, are as possible as the great institutional
rhythms of the alexandrine. "Whoever with his play and his individual ear
can compose himself an instrument will, as soon as he sounds, brush it or
strike it with science." Mallarmé speaks with a certain contempt for received
definitions in the versification treatise of, say, Théodore de Banville. His
"science" operates by the laws of *Pataphysics,* formulated as a joke by
Alfred Jarry a decade or so before the unfolding of the relativity principle in
physics: Pataphysics comprises those laws which comprise the exceptions
from all other laws.

The crisis of the poetic line *(crise de vers)* was its constitution by the
constructive powers inherent in the writer's own thought patterns, by the
writer's sense of line length at the moment of writing. This meant that
French syllable counting, or English stress-nonstress measurement, became
for some writers obsolete. The minimal shift that permitted, for instance,
one stress immediately to follow another, or a cluster of two to four unstressed syllables to accumulate, became over the course of the poem an
explosive charge, a prosodic revolution. This minimal shift introduced into
versification the possibility, if not yet the fact, of relativity, randomness,
entropy, and severely reduced predictability; thus it brought into the poem
the prose virtues of continuously new information, unimpeded by form and
unaided by it. It changed the proportions between the aesthetic and the
cognitive elements that must always compete in a work of literary art, placing a radically new emphasis on the cognitive mode. With the appearance of
speech stress, of syntactic measures instead of numerical ones, the nature,
function, and identification of the fundamental unit of versification became a
thoroughly vexed issue. Definition of the *foot,* the distinction between quantity and accent and stress, the role of timing and pausing in verse, the
relation of textbook metrical format to the actual meter, the relation of the
actual meter to rhyme and other nonmetrical effects of equivalence—these
are all inconclusively argued during the period from 1855 to 1910. Most often
the "debate" will, as here, be reconstructed as a fiction by the literary

historian; participants in the discussion do not, either directly or indirectly, respond to each other—prosody then as now being remarkable for the lack of logical contact between discussants.

In a major essay, "English Prosody and Modern Poetry," Karl Shapiro remarks that "if there is any one certainty in this field of study it is that dissension has been the rule from beginning to end," the reason perhaps being that "ours is not an exact but an approximate science."

> One assumes that the history of any science is continuous, at least in the sense that the classification of data leads to a statement of laws; and that as data are accumulated the laws are enlarged or changed. But in prosody the data are elusive and indistinct, the classifications are often arbitrary, and the laws resultantly narrow and one-sided. [Nevertheless,] were it not for the prosodic chaos of the present [1948], one could say with assurance that the science of our verse was definitely established between 1857 (the original date of Patmore's essay on English metrical law) and about 1910 (when Saintsbury finished his big history). For it had taken about five centuries to work out anything like a complete précis of English metrics, a period in which the richest body of poetry ever known flourished apparently with no more law than its own ear.[5]

Shapiro speaks of science as a monolithic solution, but does not do so with any confidence. The "laws" he sees being formulated between Patmore and Saintsbury were simply disregarded in the period after 1910, producing a situation of "chaos" in the late 1940s. Indeed Shapiro can go on to speak of "the emergence of a true English prosody and the accident of its eclipse by the new poetry," a statement that misrepresents the nature of an era of stylistic pluralism, where there is no longer any single "true" or standard prosodic theory, where with every element of the system complexly in rapport there is no room for "accidents," and where from the time of Whitman there is no eclipse but uneasy coexistence. Shapiro also neglects the presence of an eighteenth-century science of versification following the manual of Bysshe, formulated precisely to prevent a poet from following the law of his own ear. What is valuable in Shapiro's remarks is a perception that after the Romantic generation a prosodic system was evolved, on sophisticated models, based on a received body of prosodic scholarship whose line runs from Patmore through Bridges to Saintsbury, Verrier, and Schipper—thence to P. F. Baum, Omond, W. K. Wimsatt, and Monroe Beardsley, and even to linguists Morris Halle and Samuel Jay Keyser. In general, it is a Tennysonian prosodic theory that covers, describes, and supports a Tennysonian poetry, taking Tennyson somewhat unfairly as representing a dominant post-Romantic English prosodic tradition.

Despite the many differences of emphasis, which are sometimes extreme, I want to call this scanning prosody the normal science of the late-Victorian period. Despite Shapiro's sense that the received Patmore-Saintsbury prosody was flattened by the onset of Modernism, creating the "wounded prestige of our subject," or that free verse itself was an "accident," it does not appear that this cluster of attitudes has been dislodged as the reigning paradigm. Rather it remains valid, and in dialectical rapport with another sort of poetry, one that (in Shapiro's words) "sounds in the ear and therefore does not 'scan.'" There is not, as Shapiro seems to feel, one scientific prosody, but there are two or more, existing in relation with one another, and implicitly at war in their premises. This is the normal state of affairs in a period of prosodic avantgardism.

Following the definitions of scientific activity in the work of Thomas S. Kuhn, I propose that normal prosodic science in the post-Romantic period undertakes empirical work "to articulate the paradigm theory" that it supports.[6] Experiments, dummies, and selective quotations are deployed to articulate a paradigm, normal science assigning itself three classes of problem, namely, "detailing of significant fact, matching of facts with theory, and articulation of theory," operations engaged in on a vast scale from 1855 to 1910. "Rules," according to Kuhn, "derive from paradigms, but paradigms can guide research even in the absence of rules." Such work is scholarly and cumulative; there are no unanticipated novelties; operations and measurements are paradigm determined, and so are the choices of text for analysis. If an unsettlement in the table of prosodic forms took place in order to organize the current paradigm—as it did when Romantic writers overturned the measures and constraints of Bysshe—then that break between the former and the present style of thought is turned into a minor phase of development (as in Shapiro's "five centuries" concept, which hides a difficulty). By such convenient lapses of the historical sense, scientific revolutions, in prosody as in chemistry, have become so nearly invisible. Kuhn sees "scientific development as a succession of tradition-bound periods punctuated by non-cumulative breaks." Stylistic pluralism, in the sense developed in this book, would thus include the possibility that in a single period several possible paradigms would modify each other and struggle for dominance.

The period from 1855 to 1910 is a time of paradigm testing, of the sort that according to Kuhn "occurs only after persistent failure to solve a noteworthy puzzle." Such failures result in a crisis, which is itself "part of the competition between two rival paradigms." Sometimes a seemingly normal problem, something thought resolvable by known rules, resists the onslaught of ordinary criteria. The appearance of Hopkins was an anomaly in the Victorian poetic scene, even though his verse was rhymed and seemed to the eye to have the same internal structure as the line by Tennyson. In Hopkins himself, in Bridges to a lesser extent, "discovery begins with the awareness of anomaly" (Kuhn); but their contemporary Patmore was as poet and theorist scarcely aware of the anomalies—he did not hear them, had not the means to see them. "All crises begin with the blurring of a paradigm and the consequent loosening of the rules for normal research" (Kuhn), and indeed during this period the wild variation of the practice and the contradictory nature of the theory argues the blurring of a paradigm.

At the same time, and as a result of a perception of fragmentation, there takes place an attempt to get a purchase on theory. The paradigm is further elaborated, given more evidence, kept alive by injections of newly revised theory. Normal theory maintains that the fundamental entities that constitute the poetic work of art in English are syllables (stressed and unstressed) making feet, multiples of feet making lines, lines usually ending in rhymes, groups of lines making stanzas, and groups of stanzas making poems. Normal science is usually content to identify these stable entities, thinking that is in itself an interpretation of a sort. In this way, building up more and more detailed scientific evidence, mounting studies of great length with thousands of exemplary lines, using kymographs and oscilloscopes and multiple readers, the paradigm is spelled out (sometimes including its gaps and difficulties). A curious refinement is built into the normal theory, with the notions of foot equivalence and foot substitution—these are Saintsbury's two great laws, but both ideas are also prominent in the other normal-science prosodists of the period. Yet the efficiency of this scientific labor has a peculiarity that Kuhn covers in his account of "the completeness with which . . . traditional pursuit prepares the way for its own change." While every last embellishment of the one paradigm is worked out in detail, certain possibilities of the paradigm itself, and many possibilities within the language but outside the paradigm, are unseen; the less seen, perhaps, the more these possibilities become the nemesis of the reigning paradigm.

Thus do the experiments of the innovative poetries test the reigning paradigm. For example, certain poems of Whitman and Hopkins seem to seek out ways of magnifying the breakdown of normal prosody. Whitman and Hopkins are seeking to solve different problems than the normal writers and prosodists, so there is in this paradigm debate, as in those of physical science, that "incompleteness of logical contact" (Kuhn) mentioned before, a sense in the reader of poems and of prosodic theory that much is—as yet—obscure. The total picture is only partly available to the participants themselves. Such is the case with the paradigm debates of the late nineteenth century, when writers and proponents of the prosody that sounds in the ear seem shut out by the normal science that they sometimes consciously defy. Nonetheless, the fact is that these seemingly exclusive positions are in rapport one with the other. Whitman and Hopkins know exactly their relationship with the conventional versification; but the reverse is not true, for the reigning wisdom has little room for these poets.

A central phase of the debate is the mutual attraction and repulsion between two constructive principles, *stressing* and *timing*. The conventional, scanning paradigm wishes to bend speech to an abstract system; it tends to suppress, or anyway rearrange, the free stressing of speech. The insurgent paradigm wishes so far as possible to associate itself with speech rhythms, and thereby to avoid metronomic regularity. The one is formally a *meter,* the other only programmatically so, metaphorically so; what I have called insurgent stress creates a *rhythm,* which however involves the counting out of measures, wherein the counting and the measures are, within limits, regular. So, working from both ends of the conflict, the conventional paradigm would admit speech stressing and hope to include stressing as well as time, while the insurgent paradigm would admit measuring of some less rigid sort. But neither would permit mere metronomic regularity—even though insurgent manifesto writing would argue that the formal poetries and prosodies are legislative in just that disabling way. In the 1980s, *rhythm* has become an honorific, while *meter* is a pejorative; such the imprecision of our terms, such the libertarian triumph.

The broad difference I wish to emphasize is the going with or against the rhythms of speech—counterforces of a dialectical relationship. From 1855 to 1910, time-based theories will underestimate stress theories; and the opposite is also true. Stress theories will propose to affiliate with native English elements, and with speech; time theories will line up with Classical revivals, scholarly rule making, and musical analogues. Any one theory between 1855 and 1910 will emphasize one more than another of these biases, but neither will be exclusively correct—because, as I have shown, there is no success or error in such a conflict-in-rapport. Stress theory and time theory will alternate during the long term, and overlap during the short term, in the literary debates of such a period. And certain theories will arise to encompass both stress and time—Saintsbury perhaps goes furthest, after Patmore, to find an argument that includes both directions and summarizes and redeems the conventional theory. Hopkins, too, in theory and practice believes the two methods are compatible. His example is important for another reason; aside from metrical redefinition, there is also a marked development of other features in the poem, outside prosody in the strict sense but bearing on it: lineation, grammar, syntax, and rhyming.

The reigning and invaded system—which I have by crude shorthand called Tennysonian—preserves in this period an immense power, taking its force from the prestige of a great tradition that it consciously extends and develops, and from the innate capability of the system to develop capacities that palpably exist in the language. Alternate systems, as I have argued, arise that will be always to some extent invisible to the norms of the conventional wisdom. The newer form, of course, requires the other, feeds on it, deforms and omits elements of it. If the changes go beyond a certain point and are not merely reversals of easy logical projections of the first type, we call it originality. Innovation, regarded from close up, is in essence the restructuring of the hierarchy of forms, the filling of blank spaces on the table of forms. The "focussing component of a work of art," the dominant, is (in Roman Jakobson's words) that which "rules, determines, and transforms the remaining components."[7] In this period, we observe a shift of dominants in poetry. Jakobson shows how at various times between the fourteenth and twentieth centuries, rhyme, syllabic scheme, and intonational integrity were the dominants of Czech verse. In traditional English verse—in, say, Tennyson, whom I have called the godlike laureate antagonist of the writers to be discussed in this chapter—the dominant is rhyming accentual-syllabic pentameter. In the alternate, extreme, and anti-Tennysonian systems of Whitman and Hopkins, the dominant shifts to speech stressing, new emphasis on grammar and syntax (notably in Hopkins's hyperbaton), and absence of rhyme (Whitman), or extreme prominence of rhyme or rhymelike effects (Hopkins). Elements "which were originally secondary become essential and primary" (Jakobson). Whitman and Hopkins converge in the shiftings of the rhyme-meter dominant to a way of breaking up the exact regularity of the accentual-stress meter, allowing stresses and dips to come not randomly but less predictably. Through the displacement of a stress many times multiplied, they achieve a significant innovation. Once the mold was broken the possibilities were immediately limitless; that is what was learned earlier in the century, in "Christabel," a landmark poem to which all poets and prosodists return, the century's first indication of the meaning of a prosody that counts only stresses. Speech stressing is, on this model, the "science" of the individual ear composing itself as an instrument (Mallarmé anticipated by Coleridge).

Personal intonation tends to be substituted for counted stress pattern, with the attendant deemphasis (or overemphasis by comparison, in rare cases like Hopkins and Swinburne) on that heretofore central indicator of the poetic, rhyme. There may occur a "transfer of the verse-function in poetry from meter onto other features which are in part secondary and resultant" (Yuri Tynjanov).[8] In the period from 1855 to 1910, Robert Bridges estranges poetry toward a rigorous convention on the one side of Tennyson: quantity and syllable-count measures. Whitman and Hopkins estrange poetry on the other, more innovative and productive side of Tennyson: toward speech stressing and unpredictable accent. Other elements that gain importance once meter is deposed are rhyme, stress itself as opposed to counting, syntax, and other forms of equivalence and parallelism, including punning and alliteration. Especially important in relation to Whitman is Tynjanov's notion of the interconnectedness of prose and poetry as they change value in different eras: "The function of prose with regard to verse remains, but the formal elements fulfilling this function are different. . . . A period may come in which it will be unessential whether a work is written in prose or poetry." The emphasis on speech, edging the work toward prose discourse, seems to be the reason for certain technical innovations, for the prominence of certain devices and not others, for the interest in dialect as style, and it is also the connecting link to a social concept, to a view of an author in relation to a reader.

Speech stress seems to entail a view of the social function of poetry. It deemphasizes in the social realm, as well as the prosodic one, the institutionality of literature, pushing toward prose and conversation. The private voice is desired and glorified, all the more so just at the period of the emergence of modern cities, industrial factories, and the dirt language of newspapers—when the nervousness and personality of the voice, its very grain, is threatened with annihilation. The literary function changed in relation to the neighboring functions, but at a different rate and in different ways. The structural function of this avant-garde system worked itself out in further and further attempts to strip off the veil of form, further and further resolutions of verse line into grammar and into ordinary prose, the ceding of versification to grammar. There occurs a steady erosion of the principle of meter, and a broadening out into a principle of measure. Without these specific transformations in the attitude toward devices in the dominant, the subsequent formal ruptures after 1910—Modernist distortions and enrichments of prosody—would be unthinkable.

Paradigm testing and shifting of the dominant are the components of crisis in versification. Just at the time when prose poems and free verse are invented, the traditional versification is given what appears to be a definitive theory, a defense, and an illustration. The breaks, the divisions in literary history have remained hidden to us because of the tactical superiority of the reigning over the insurgent prosody. After all, the former now had a completely worked-out theory, whereas the insurgents have never yet had a full-scale justification. Are there, even a century later now, any valid terms within the reigning theory for the adequate description of technique in sprung rhythm, free verse, or the prose poem?

"Governments change," says Mallarmé, "poetry remains always intact." Or seems to. Prosodic revolutions usually go unnoticed because shifts of the hierarchy of the dominant rearrange existing elements, or add elements thought lost in history, or omit elements not considered as making language perceptible. Form does not disappear, merely certain forms or devices thought for the moment, or in special contexts, to be too familiar. Again, changes in stanzaic preference, in the definition of perfect rhyme sound, all the innumerable details of technique, fill the mind of the historian—tending to block the invention of an imaginative historical category to describe a shift so disruptive that it requires that "the act of writing scrutinize itself back to its origins" (Mallarmé). Yet this very emphasis on the structuralization of structure is what Mallarmé locates in the late nineteenth century: "On a touché au vers." Such revolutions are omitted from the story because it takes a Mallarméan act of perception to have seen them, to have known that they existed.

A Map of Poetic Practice

To sketch that body of assumptions already called Tennysonian is to identify the standard versification of English in the post-Romantic period, from

Wordsworth to the present day. There is, of course, a very great deal of variety within this set of norms, and yet this sort of poetry adheres to a fairly restricted self-definition based on the alternation of stressed and unstressed syllables; that is, on accentual-syllabic meter, usually rhymed and in stanzas. Strategic deviations are the sine qua non of the style, because these create that so-called bucking against the theoretical meter which keeps the verse interestingly out of jingle or doggerel. Yet the theoretical meter is absolutely essential, indispensable, lurking, and countable whenever one really wants to scan it out. Lines are divided into feet, feet into syllable stresses, with stresses arranged to come home every second or third syllable; syntax is determined by (and at times modifies) the requirements of the meter; and rhymes, in the same way, are separated into places in the line by numerical count. There is a pattern set up by the poem's beginning that the reader expects the writer to keep—a "metrical contract" (Hollander).

By far the greatest proportion of the verse written between Wordsworth and the present is Tennysonian in this general definition, and when the execution is impeccable the effect is at once reassuring and stunning:

> Old yew, which graspest at the stones
>   That name the underlying dead,
>   Thy fibres net the dreamless head,
> Thy roots are wrapt about the bones.
>
> The seasons bring the flower again,
>   And bring the firstling to the flock;
>   And in the dusk of thee the clock
> Beats out the little lives of men.
>
> O, not for thee, the glow, the bloom,
>   Who chantest not in any gale,
>   Nor branding summer suns avail
> To touch thy thousand years of gloom;
>
> And gazing on thee, sullen tree,
>   Sick for thy stubborn hardihood,
>   I seem to fail from out my blood
> And grow incorporate into thee.
>
> > (*In Memoriam*, 2)[9]

The strategic violations here are the production of—and draw attention to—immense skill, scholarly allocation, precise knowledge of what may be allowably deformed. "Flower" (line 5) and "incorporate" (line 16) add another syllable, or rather engage at once the convention of eliding words in order to fit the theoretical meter and the actual pronunciation convention, giving a sort of hovering stress that is one of the pleasures of such poetry. Similarly the "hardihood"/"blood" rhyme hovers between eye and ear identities, giving the pleasure of a slight wrongness that is nevertheless absorbed into the pattern of the whole. The overlay of speech tones and metrical-rhyming conventions, elements of strict equivalent tolerating violations of certain rules in chosen places to gain expressiveness, gives a specific recognition. Repeated many times in the quatrains of *In Memoriam,* with the slight but dramatic variations on the way elements are clustered within the little cage of the line, stanza, and segment, the prosody naturalizes the reader in a long carrying rhythm—which, in its sphere, corresponds to the emotional-logical intent of elegy.

It is not possible to know whether the more extreme versifications employed during the last half of the nineteenth century—free verse or the prose poem or sprung rhythm—had any direct bearing back on the conduct of the normal paradigm of poetic practice, and yet it seems clear that the traditional products themselves reflect the crisis of versification. I do not think one argues this by quoting single poems; the one poem, above, can hardly reflect a sense of disturbance by itself, in the slight disturbances of its local texture. One requires a panoramic vision here, to perceive the whole of *In Memoriam* in the first instance. The bravado of the one stanza used so consistently, over such a great distance, in a poem whose progress is not narrative, is sometimes forgotten. In 1855 Tennyson passes on to *Maud,* polymetric, extremely various in meters and rhymes, as apparently a change from the sameness of the patterns of his earlier long poem-in-segments. In both long poems the work is experimental in different, opposing ways, and both are part of a search for adequate, ever-new structures. One symptom of crisis, I am arguing, is a proliferation of line-and-stanza structures in Victorian poetry: in the very citadel of the traditional poetries, in Tennyson himself; very notably in Browning, whose *Sordello* is full of consciously odd patternings; in Arnold, Rossetti, Swinburne, and Bridges; and in a culminating way perhaps in Hardy, who could not write a new poem, it seems, without inventing a new stanza.

So the very virtuosity of Tennyson and others in this period is one expression of crisis. Most often the dissatisfaction manifests itself in the structure of the stanza, not the line; in such a thing as the making of microscopic or gargantuan texts; or in the revival of the sonnet sequence, the long idyll, the literary ballad, and the closet-drama-in-verse. The poetry of William Barnes is traditionally metered, yet in diction deeply innovative and related to the vernacular poems of Kipling later in the century. When the innovative effects in this traditional poetry are directly metrical, these are consciously undertaken as resurrections, as in Tennyson's few Anglo-Saxon alliterative poems, or in Swinburne's strongly stressed anapests and dactyls. When the innovative effects are not metrical, as in the flaccid free verse of Arnold and Henley, the results can be awful—symptoms of crisis rather than paths out of crisis. Within the probability system that is Tennysonian style, these indications of restlessness show that the central mode of the period is itself shaken, uncertain. A few of these central poets, notably Browning, Arnold, and Meredith, muzzle the tones of magniloquence. It was only Swinburne, whose work is the exaggeration of the singing-robes side of Tennyson, who could call Tennyson the master, "in the sunshine of whose noble genius the men of my generation grew up and took delight."

But Arnold, Clough, and especially Hopkins and Whitman, while they could recognize the reasons that the laureate's was the dominant style, and could salute its era-defining value, were to various degrees anti-Tennysonian in theme as well as form. Knowing that Tennyson was himself in his innovations driven by the same situation of crisis, they were able to understand his work as a major internalized influence; they were thereby able to cast out Tennyson, to engage in aversion tactics, to do otherwise on principle. In that way they could repress whatever in them was laureate or (in Hopkins's phrase) Parnassian. Their ethical and prosodic selfhood was always to some extent defined by reaction against Tennysonian norms. If the Hopkins-Whitman reaction may seem extreme, this innovative violence is due to the success of the model's own experimentalism; to outdo Tennyson, himself coping with an era of stylistic pluralism and avantgardism, they had to go very far, indeed they had to invent new spaces on the table of forms, or had to return to spaces, combinations never before occupied, or occupied long ago or elsewhere.

Tennyson himself, through his efforts in anglicizing Classical meters, partakes in the assault on the mode I have called Tennysonian. There are a few such poems, mostly with Classical subjects for which the meters are tailored (as in "Frater Ave atque Vale," 1880). Swinburne, Hopkins, and Bridges are all poets who also attempt either theory or practice of the Classical meters; and Arthur Hugh Clough's *Bothie* and *Amours de Voyage* are successful hexameter-dactyllic poems, using the Classical meters for narrative and comic purposes, deforming them by employing stress and not length as the principle of construction, yet clearly getting an extra reach by the reference to Classical tones and measures. In fact, this side of Clough is one of the central Victorian instances of an archaism that is not pious nostalgia or mere reconstruction but rather magnificent. *Amours de Voyage* is a major poem.

The whole process is taken a stage further later in the century in William J. Stone's treatise, published by Bridges in the 1901 edition of *Milton's Prosody*. Here it is hoped that English verse can actually be refounded, rethought on the principles of quantity taken over from Latin and Greek. Bridges toyed with the notion, wrote dull but not bad poems on the principle in the years just after 1900, and published this work under a title with avant-garde resonance, *New Poems*. Bridges and Stone, for that point in time, actually seemed to believe that quantity might be a way of making everything new, yet by the 1921 reedition of *Milton's Prosody*, Stone's treatise was dropped and unmentioned, and Bridges had moved from that sort of experiment to free verse ("Noël," 1913), syllabics, and was on the verge of the strange *Testament of Beauty* line. This Classicizing of the 1855–1910 period was somewhat productive of decent, viable poetry in English; it is one other symptom, if one is needed, to show that the reigning versification seems outworn. It was a solution, but an inimitable one; the solutions of Hopkins and Whitman were more workable, more capable of extension by others. Nearly every writer of those mentioned seems to think that his principle of construction is the successful innovation. Nevertheless there are at this moment several workable paradigms, some more valuable than others by virtue of their footing in the language and literary tradition; it is clear now, if it was not in their lifetimes, that Whitman and Hopkins had found such a footing.

Through hindsight we know that the insurgent stress prosodies are the victorious ones, and that what they win is a parity with the normative prosody. I have, on the previous pages, been able to sketch a map of the late-Victorian stylistic pluralism, by clustering a number of poets around Tennyson and showing in what ways these styles were normative. They were so even in their characteristic experiments, and Hopkins was accurate to call Tennyson's Classical experiments botches, and to praise rather the laureate's central creations within the accentual-syllabic line. Against the Tennysonian norm I have set the Classicizing poets and the speech-stress one on either side as distinctly minority verse. This spectrum validates Saintsbury's remark that there never was before a time "so knit, overlapped, latticed, cross-hatched, intertwined, as regards the style and characteristics"[10] of poetry, because both in theory and practice there were crossings from one cluster to another. Indeed in one poet especially—Bridges—we find a writer who tries all the possibilities from sprung rhythm to main-line accentualism to syllabics and quantitative counting. Browning's metrics, too, in their sheer oddity and multiplicity, might deserve a chapter of their own. Saintsbury has said, at the end of his long history, that "time will show" where "our rhymelessness, our discord-seeking, our stress-prosodies belong," doubtless feeling their presence as an irritation or anomaly. He finds Whitman and Hopkins unreadable. Of course, the history of poetry since 1910 has seen far more authentication of the discord-seeking prosodies than Saintsbury could have imagined or would have approved. These are no longer extreme or marginal but justified by a mass of worthy writing; nevertheless they remain strictly speaking anomalous because not yet explained in their artistic character.

A Map of Prosodic Theory

In his authoritative work on the theory of prosody in the eighteenth century, Paul Fussell maps treatise-and-manual prosody between 1660 and 1800, contrasting speech-stress scansion with a still more artificial numerical method. That demonstration affords crucial precedents for the terms and methods of the present chapter, but also gives clues that we may adopt as to the proper analysis of the conceptual situation just now in the study of the line of verse.

The same theory of ideality and the same practice of artificial scansion which flourished in the mid-eighteenth century thrust themselves anomalously into the world of Ezra Pound and E. E. Cummings, where they remain to this very day, visiting the brains of the most learned and sensitive critics. In fact, there is no better way to appreciate the power of eighteenth-century prosodic conventions to perpetuate themselves almost indefinitely than to contemplate the prescriptive "scansions" and regularistic exhortations which now and then offer themselves to the public view in various modern critical works and in the scholarly quarterlies. For historical reasons, verse composed syllabically should be so scanned; and verse composed accentually should be scanned according to true speech-stress. Nothing is gained by reading into eighteenth-century verse the modes of nineteenth-century verse construction, and a very great deal is lost by laying over modern accentual verse a prosodic "explanation" which is suited to dealing only with certain poems composed syllabically.[11]

All I would add is that something is lost, too, by giving metrical explanations to poems not composed metrically. Those who keep to the theory of ideality seem to overlook the change at 1795. In the prosodic realm the post-Romantic principle is preeminently that of English stressing, the simulacrum of speech stressing. Both free verse and accentual-syllabic verse are speech-stressing poetry in a broader definition and require measuring out by the new kind of reading whose elements I sketch in the second part of this book.

W. K. Wimsatt and Monroe Beardsley in their essay, "The Concept of Meter," have argued that quantitative versification is dead. This I would accept, but not their division into two kinds of stress verse: strong stress and syllable stress. For all verse after 1795 is strong-stress verse, only some kinds of strong-stress poetry have more definite shapes than others. So the irregular poetry of strong stress, particularly free verse, is more regular than most prosodists would accept; and the regular poetry of strong stress, counted out by feet, is less regular than its apologists would accept. The fact is that any poetry, Tennysonian by the definitions here advanced, which has as its rule the punctual unexpected breaking of a theoretical meter, is "regular" only by a reductive definition.

To prepare for explanations that map prosodic theory during the period between Whitman and Pound, it is well to situate this period historically by viewing Tennysonian as a period style. It is shared by a number of poets, and even its opponents have internalized its norms. Leonard Meyer has said, writing of music but with implications for poetry, that "a . . . style is a probability system . . . a finite array of interdependent melodic, rhythmic, harmonic, timbral, textural, and formal relationships and processes."[12] Literary change, when it comes, will revise the system and restructure the dominant. Josephine Miles has concerned herself with these shifts of proportion.

Change may be thought of as persistences through varying contexts, or as dominances from time to time, or as tendencies visible toward the future. Every poet and period shares in all three kinds, and so may be characterized by what he preserves from the past, or by what he chooses to stress in agreement with the present, or by what he suggests for the future.[13]

For Miles, the singularity of one poet's language does not "work in isolation" but is part "of the competence of poetry" in a given time. Even what is demonstrably singular must be defined, described, and analyzed within certain specifiable limits. Change, singularity, and innovation are to be seen against a background of the available literary stock of genres and the current language of literature. So, too, with the fiction I have called Tennysonian.

The actual mechanisms in the process of form shift and genre transition, the change of dominants, are difficult to describe. Consider that form as proceeding and its correlative prosody, strong stress, are the new rule. Progressively the definition of stress verse is refined and enhanced over the course of the nineteenth century, so that by 1910 the only true antagonist, quantitative verse and the temporal theory, is obliterated. The quantitative principle, however, lingers in our very terminology of prosody, our terms themselves for description of verse units, weights and measurements. The exceptions to the new rule forming are gradually eliminated, indeed, and yet these exceptions are not, even today, destroyed. Avant-garde writers and their prosodies are phenomena still to some extent peculiar, seen as unexplainable rather than as elements of the passage from the tenets to the metrics of a new prosody. In their own day, Whitman and the others were seen as exceptions to the Tennysonian rule system; but, by a shift of perspective, Tennysonian can itself be seen to be part of the same post-Romantic strong-stress rule system.

These conflicts are to be expected in a period of stylistic pluralism, where the coexistence of different and seemingly opposed styles is normal. As Renato Poggioli has said, such periods operate by other laws than those of chance. The evolving system of Romantic premises illustrates the necessity of Modernity to "break out of literature toward the reality of the moment" (Paul de Man). The substitution of speech molds for metrical molds is never entirely successful,[14] and thus Modernity folds back on itself, "engenders the repetititon and continuation of literature. Thus modernity, which is fundamentally a falling away from literature and a rejection of history, also acts as the principle that gives literature duration and historical existence."[15] Strong stress—metrics of a paradoxical Modernity. This "inherent conflict," as de Man says, in fact "determines the structure of literary language."

From 1855 to 1910 is one period in the life of this self-contradictory entity. My description of the structure of the line in this period is led, by the nature of the materials, into the field defined by conventional metrics. And yet this is from the outset seen to be an insufficient arena; the terminology is, as always, imprecise, and the limits of the discussion are entered only to force them wider. Prosody, in the definitions scholarship ought to foster, includes not only the specifying and repeating of the smallest unit; it involves grammar, syntax, rhyme, stanza making, webs of imagery, and the form of the whole poem. W. K. Wimsatt speaks of the end-of-the-range definition of versification where it "vaporizes into cognition"; if the phrase is meant as condemnation it seems to miss its mark, for precisely the task of the post-Romantic writer is this subsuming of prosody in thought, in speech, in event, and in the activities of the apprehending mind and self of the reader. The narrow, scientific end of the spectrum, taken strictly, will no longer yield to us the power of explanatory adequacy.

Until 1910 the central type in English, normative Tennysonian, is accentual-syllabic, "foot verse" in the usual description.[16] And yet after 1855 the dominant is beginning to shift, in what H. R. Jauss calls "the evolutionary give and take of function and form," and the native roots of an accentual prosody come more into the open. This is presumably because the only direction of discovery, the only open space of the table of forms that may be used to estrange the normative versification, is for English the stress verse that has some footing in this and related northern-European languages. One remembers Hopkins's innovation in his scholarly return to Anglo-Saxon, Middle English, and Welsh words and devices.

During the period from 1855 to 1910, and especially after, the two principles of accent and number of syllables begin to lose their previous proportion. Accent becomes more emphatic, and number of syllables becomes less predictable. Such a change is clearly related to the poets' perception that Tennysonian can no longer carry so much meaning, that it must be shaken roughly into perceptibility by making random the number of syllables between speech stresses. This is the historical moment when the new phrasal verse can violently force the old foot verse into perceptibility. But afterward the two types can be blended—or foot verse may actually come to be used to defamiliarize phrasal verse—there are hundreds of examples of that since 1910.

Metrical theory in this period has been described somewhat hastily by Karl Shapiro. In his essay and his *Bibliography of Modern Prosody* (both 1948), Shapiro sees two "major traditions" of theory, and a third that has "sprung" out of the "conjunction of the other two." These three are: (1) stress prosody, comprising the systems that emphasize accent not time, and divide the line into feet (Saintsbury the best representative); (2) temporal prosody, emphasizing time not accent, dividing the line into "measures" as in music (Sidney Lanier the example); and (3) mixed prosody, "all systems of metric which alternate between stress prosody and temporal prosody" (no important apologist here). The contrast or dialectic of stress and time should not be dismissed as a prosodic construct; and yet here it seems necessary to note the inadequacy of simply posing these as binary opposites with a muddy middle ground betwen them, entirely undefined in its relation to the two extreme types. Shapiro's schema begins to want a greater delicacy, when we remember the complexity of the argument in the books by Saintsbury and Lanier, neither of whom are purely in the categories he proposes for them. The plan he proposes turns up a vacant category, mixed prosodies, and it mislabels the major theorists; it shows no room on the table for the innovative prosodies that are coming onto the scene after 1855. In fact, it is to dignify the accentual and syllabic tendencies or principles to call them, or their prosodists, systematic; the real system to be understood is the rapport between types, the interrelated and fated unaccidental irreconcilable connections.

In my own range of theories, spread out in Table 2, there are three types of writing with their attendant treatises of justification. The table must include

Table 2. *Map of Prosodic Theory, 1885–1910*

Base Verse		Rule Verse
Phrasal Verse	**Foot Verse**	**Syllable Verse**
Attributes: optional stress; accentual; assimilating poetry toward speech; on the rise as sprung rhythm and free verse from 1855 to 1910.	*Attributes:* determinate stress; accentual-syllabic; overwhelmingly the standard form and theory before, during, and after the 1855–1910 period.	*Attributes:* no stress; syllable count; assimilates poetry toward the measures of music; declining as Classical quantity from 1855 to 1910, on the rise as syllabics after 1910.
Theorists: Coleridge's note on "Christabel"; Guest (1838); Whitman (1855); Hopkins, author's preface, letters.	*Theorists:* C. Patmore (1857); J. Ruskin (1880); J. Schipper (ca. 1890); R. Bridges in *Milton's Prosody* (1887, 1901, 1921); R. M. Alden; G. Saintsbury (1910); T. S. Omond (1903, 1920); P. Verrier (1909); and, later, P. F. Baum, L. Abercrombie, W. K. Wimsatt, M. Beardsley, and S. J. Keyser and M. Halle.	*Theorists:* E. A. Poe (1848); S. Lanier (1880); W. J. Stone (1901); W. Thomson (1904).

a range of possibilities, with foot prosodies in the center as the Tennysonian norm. The norm is criticized from the left by the phrasal prosodies that assimilate poetry to speech, from the right by the syllable-count prosodies that assimilate poetry to music. To the left, again, the tendency is to a programmatic irregularity, an unpredictability (within limits) that is the principle of the text. To the right, the tendency is to greater and greater regularity of a metronomic, counting sort in the rhythm of the Classicizing syllable count; those who count syllables alone and not accents, like

Elizabeth Daryush and Marianne Moore, have predictable line-length, but not predictable rhythm. In general, foot prosodies and syllable-count prosodies are regularity theories, and that is why Pallister Barkas (1934) has termed works written under their impress as "rule verse" in his array of theory.

There is no position on the range that is untouched by avantgardist concerns and consciousness. Even the central Tennysonian norms are, as I have said, attempts within strenuous limits to find a personal voice within the metrical pattern. But the positions on the range that are most powerfully original are the two extremes. By emphasizing one or the other element in the combined term *accentual-syllabic,* and restructuring the dominant, theories on either side of the norm act as destroyers of the norm (upon which they depend). With the exception of Bridges, who in his long career assumes various positions within the norm and on either side of it, most theorists are consistently identified with one of the three positions, and by far the greatest number are developers of the central foot-verse paradigm.

To move from right to left across the spectrum of theories: Stone and Thomson examine the question "whether classical metres might find a place in our language not merely distantly similar to that which they held in Latin and Greek, but really and actually the same, governed by rules equally strict and perfect, and producing on the ear the same pure delight" (Stone).[17] Their position is unambiguously quantitative with a radical deemphasis of accent and a principled objection (whether openly admitted or merely implied) to Edwin Guest and other phrasal-verse theorists. They share this position with a writer who does not use the terminology of quantity, Classically derived, but rather prefers to see poetic time as analogous to musical measures. Sidney Lanier's *Science of English Verse* tries to live up to its positivist title by inventing a musical notation and applying it to differently constituted lines in English: full notes and half notes, measures and proportions, and so on. Like his American predecessor in this line, Edgar Allan Poe, Lanier is a believer in isochrony, or the equal timing of measures, in this case, rather confusedly, feet; and to this extent Lanier is a quantitative theorizer who adheres to an inflexible predictability. (But his musical knowledge is brought in, at times, for subsidiary points about rests and cross rhythms; he speaks of Negro drumming in the American South, the overlay of rhythms.) These portions of the book, plus the long section at the end that takes up the nonmetrical prosodic elements including rhyme, seem to force the "musical form" of quantity theory in the direction of phrasal verse.

The emphasis on measure and proportion that Lanier takes over from musical analogues may be the one portion of his theory that catches the interest of William Carlos Williams as he writes to justify free verse, saying in admiration of Lanier that although he "developed his findings only to a pitifully ineffective degree," he "at least recognizes that it is the question of time in the make-up of the modern line that has to be wrestled with." Williams likes Lanier's avantgardist recognition of the tunes of speech, which might help us to remake "our stalled sentences." He quotes this from Lanier: "I am strongly inclined to believe that English poetry might be a great gainer if we would at once frankly recognize this rhythmic but unmetric verse as strictly rhythmized prose and print it as such without the deceptive line-division. . . . A development of English rhythm lies, I am sure, in that way." Williams comments, "A development of English rhythm!" and goes on to suggest that original movement will enter English only through intrusive application of rhythms from "the common usage of our prose," even news-paper prose. "Lanier discovered the bar. . . . But he never got the inclusion in the bar of the pure time element, the lag and rush of words, of measured pauses which are the essentials of our speech."[18] In another place Williams wrote, "The passage of time (not stress) is the proper (democratic) key to the foot (approaching Athens)—and music."[19] Thus does a free-verse theorist, needing in 1946 "a line loose as Whitman's but measured as his was not," seek to estrange and extend free rhythms by the help of the opposed theory understood as a measuring system, something in rapport with stressing but able to batch the accents, a principle outside stressing that superintends it. (In 1855, Whitman requires a phrasal principle that is outside the timing of syllables, and that can defamiliarize and superintend timing, or anyway take precedence over it for expressive purposes.) Williams uses Lanier to refine Whitman, but at both moments, different in theory and in history, the stress-ing and timing principles require each other.

Insofar as the syllabic principle is quantitative and not musical (that is, Classical in its definition), it is phased out between 1855 and 1910. Most historians of metrical scholarship are in agreement that the quantitative hypothesis is once and for all demolished in the years that bracket this chapter. By the mass of this period's treatises, English prosody is formalized as accentual-syllabic for the first time in literary history. Yet, no longer confused with quantity, metrics is in the same period challenged by the poetics and prosodies of insistent accent. With its double rule of accent and syllable count as embodied in the concept of the foot, this reigning prosodic theory seems designed to overturn the regularizing artificial scansion of the eighteenth-century writers (always excluding Say and Steele), but also and more directly seems a justification of the practice of the writers between Wordsworth and Tennyson. There is in Patmore's essay (1857) a survey of past prosodists, including Steele, Guest, and the early proponents of strong stress, and also a recognition of the likeness of poetry and music in their shared preoccupation with the measuring of time. The regularity and mag-niloquence of the Tennysonian line is the norm to be justified, and Patmore's own poems exhibit the same preference; but Hopkins in his letters effec-tively demolishes the linguistics and logic of Patmore's quantitative urges. A better account of the combined operation of accent and syllable count is given by Bridges in *Milton's Prosody* (1887; 1901; 1921), a book that, with

Jespersen's essay of 1900, best develops the body of assumptions that is the received orthodoxy in prosodic theory today. The book is a catalog of syllabic-accentual effects, where Bridges shows how vexed lines are not anomalies but quite metrical (spelling, contractions, and ellipses are all factors; even the lines in *Samson Agonistes* are shown to be fully deliberate in their explainable effects).

All the writers in the foot-verse column believe in counting feet, in the existence of real stress and real time, in scansion, and in the greatness of the English central tradition. Their heirs are such as Wimsatt and Seymour Chatman, recent explicators of a received paradigm. There is growing sophistication in the deployment of this theory, in the way deviations are accepted into the system, in the way competing theories are omitted or debated, in the way models and dummies are used—and especially, I should say, in the development by Trager and Smith of four levels of stress. But the tendency of the whole reigning-paradigm enterprise is to forget that feet are theoretical entities, so that feet are somehow found, reified, and believed in—and once exceptions and anomalies are reduced, prosody's work is done. Though this theory is strong, and within its limitations does not require a great deal of modification, we must finally say that these limits are unacceptably narrow and are deliberately placed that way in order to avoid certain other issues that, as it happens, are of the highest difficulty and importance.

Passage from right to left on the spectrum of theories brings us from Rule Verse to the Base Verse, which is less predictable. Rule Verse wishes to bend speech to an abstract system, to suppress the free stressing of speech and to develop an order by that suppression. The Base Verse wishes so far as possible to associate itself with speech rhythms, thereby to avoid metronomic regularity while it preserves an intrinsic rhythm. One goes with, the other against, the rhythms of speech; one is oratorical, the other metronomic in tendency. Remembering the points made by Williams against Whitman, it is necessary to remind ourselves also that Base or phrasal verse does want to count out measures, but that the counting and the measures are only within limits regular. For example, it is a high-level regularity in free verse if all the lines are either long or short, for this affects the minutest elements of rhythm and weight in the poem's movement.

With the 1855 publication of *Leaves of Grass* begins a process of abductive change or innovation in English metrics. A new rule is enunciated, and the curve of literary history is deflected as this rule strives to perfect itself and to eliminate exceptions. Since the accentual-syllabic versification, with its dominant history of great poetic monuments, is the major "exception," the process is protracted and formidable, involving internal modification and development within the phrasal-verse system itself as well as modifications of the syllable-stress verse of the central tradition. Most major poets after 1910 have used the one sort, at various points in their careers, to criticize the other, thus embodying the debate in their own careers and in the weave of poetry. Such is the case on a large scale, before 1910, with only Whitman and Hopkins.

As poet-theorists, Whitman and Hopkins are within the same column as Edwin Guest, an Anglo-Saxon scholar whose obsession with English intonation seeks to justify his field of scholarly interest, but also to find a way to speak about the poets of his generation, Wordsworth, Shelley, and Keats. Guest's deemphasis of temporal matters places him squarely in the post-Romantic frame of mind, and the reedition of his work in the 1880s, with W. W. Skeat as editor, brings his theory to the attention of the maturity of the Hopkins-Whitman generation. Anglo-Saxon rhythms Guest understands as "that main stock, from which have branched almost all of the later rhythms of the language."[20] The relative, mobile measures of alliterative verse recommend themselves to Guest: "Of all the metres known to our poetry, that which has best succeeded in reconciling the poet's freedom with the demands of science, is the alliterative system of our Anglo-Saxon ancestors. . . . Its verses admitted from four to six accents, and each verse contained two, and the longer verses three alliterative syllables. A metre thus definite might be made to include almost every rhythm that has been used in our poetry. . . . But where shall we find the men, that would use these opportunities without abusing them?—where mental vigour to resist the temptations, which extreme facility holds out, and at the same time capacity large enough, to fill up an outline thus varied and extensive?" Whitman and Hopkins were those men.

Hopkins began as a Tennysonian poet but soon enough came to feel that Tennyson was the prime contemporary example of a writing technically impeccable but without personal stamp, a writing anybody could do if he made himself expert. Hopkins wanted the impossible avantgardist quality in language, inscape, or personal pattern. He wrote to Bridges: "The effect of studying masterpieces is to make me admire and do otherwise. So it must be on every original artist to some degree, on me to a marked degree. Perhaps then more reading would only *refine my singularity,* which is not what you want."[21] Bridges wanted something more conventionally like Tennyson, something more intelligible; Hopkins resists: "The sonnet [on St. Alphonsus Rodriguez] (I say it snorting) aims at being intelligible." So Hopkins is a strong poet in the sense we have from Harold Bloom, a writer whose selfhood is so distinctive that it must distort received information, received language and tradition, turning the product into a powerfully original statement. Hopkins bends accentual-syllabic versification into a new, perhaps finally inimitable, direction for the purposes of the major writing of his career. Sprung rhythm prises open the foot, makes the stress "more *of a* stress" (Hopkins), and slips in scudded unstressed syllables, thus disturbing the iambic run of the line and making what he in his author's preface calls "the so-called accentual Trochee and Dactyl." This depends on the idea of a foot, but so redefines it as to make it outrageous, anomalous: "Sprung Rhythm, as used in this book, is measured by feet of from one to four syllables, regularly, and for particular effects any number of weak or slack syllables may be used." So Hopkins in practice radically revises such concepts as *rhythm, measure, regularity, weak,* and also by implication, *stress.* Elsewhere Hopkins writes: "Nominally the feet are mixed and any one may follow any other." This, the central body of rules in Hopkins's system, is in fact a set of procedures neither more nor less artificial than the Tennysonian accentual-syllabic system; but it is different, giving other tones and senses, raising new expectations and satisfying them. Bridges thought the innovations extreme and often said so, while in his own verse he modified and used what he could from Hopkins's discoveries.

Where Hopkins retains a sort of scansion, more random and less ideal than in the Tennysonian norm, Whitman largely abandons it, using the line and part line as the variable unit. Hopkins goes to Middle English alliterative examples in the native language, but Whitman, for precedents, employs mostly biblical-Hebraic models. However Whitman's parallelism is never so syntactically restricted as the Hebrew types, and extends often over many lines.[22] Whitman knew and revered the poetry of Tennyson and Longfellow, traditional prosodists, and could himself write in the forms of the contemporary masters. But he preferred the "metrical laws" of his own form: "The rhythm and uniformity of perfect poems show the free growth of metrical laws, and bud from them as unerring and loosely as lilacs and roses on a bush, and take shapes as compact as the shapes of chestnuts and oranges" (1855 preface). His manifesto calls for an impossible language, assimilating the poem to nature. Such manifestos are strategic overstatements, important if we can winnow from them the innovative tendency, the wish to sink the iambic pentameter. Nearly every commentator on Whitman attempts to show how lines are covertly metrical, how they can be parceled into measures with the terminology and knife of the traditional prosody. But how much of value can such a method yield?

The case is similar when prosodists like P. F. Baum can scorch Hopkins for his prosodic theory and the mysteries of his radical practice, on the grounds that Hopkins did not know what he was saying and doing. Conservative prosodists, as late as Baum's article of 1959, were absolutely incapable of seeing other paradigms than the acentual-syllabic norm. The weight of theory in prescriptive prosody is still brought behind the paradigm norm, outlawing other rhythms, sometimes on grounds unambiguously ethical. One lingering tentacle of Neo-Classicism's idealist prosodies is the position that random effects are less moral than regular effects. Many of the prescriptive positions of current prosodic theory are rewritings of idealist rules of an earlier moment, current and still viable into the midst of an avant-garde era that knows linguistics. The scandal of form, and of theories of form, is that form is not altogether congruent with other historical progressions, at least not in any single or easily describable way. Literary paradigms are unlike scientific ones, because the process of weeding out dead pattern concepts is endless in literature, where there are no adequate falsification procedures short of burial of the texts themselves. Incommensurate viewpoints, texts, and techniques habitually coexist.

However, during the period in question one set of theory and its terminology seems effectively ruled out, namely the Classical quantitative poetry written on the long-short system. A consistent area of disagreement may be discriminated within the period as between the two ends of our range map of theory. The broad distinction between temporal and nontemporal theory is accurate enough, though some theories, as in Lanier, while emphasizing one aspect also at least include and acknowledge the other. Musical meter, though there are periodic attempts to revive it,[23] seems unworkable now (but a change in popular music might suddenly bring it to life again); and very likely English poetry will see very few Classical revivals in poetic technique. But phrasal verse, associated with native English and Anglo-Saxon or balladic resurgency, has made itself the major alternative way of writing. Traditional accentual-syllabic verse has been deposed as a norm, and since 1910 has been one of several possible options. After 1910, as Wimsatt notes, we see especially in Eliot the coalescing in a single poem of strong-stress and syllable-stress meters. We do not have, then, an opposition between temporal and nontemporal, but rather a relation wherein each is necessary to the other, may substitute or estrange the other, may in fact split the other. One thinks of the drugged cadences of Tennyson, Swinburne, the early Yeats, and of how (sometimes by the later Yeats) these rhythms of lassitude are split or recharged by proselike gusto, speech reality, especially in Hopkins, Whitman, the poets after 1910. The Imagists, Pound, even Eliot, all wish to punctuate the poem, cut it into odd assortments of pieces and lengths, cut up the flow of time by insistent stressing and effects of juncture. Quite specifically the post-1910 decades discover, for the first time in literary history in a conscious way, the revolutionary avantgardist concept that "a new cadence means a new idea" (Pound).

That axiom confounds the traditional apologies for foot prosody. Pound's statement implicates a parallel morphology of meaning and prosody, of two systems as wholes. The prosody becomes more closely associated with the meaning, the speech value of the poem, the personal relationship implied in the poem between writer and auditor. Accentual-syllabic verse becomes in this process also susceptible to theories that would relate sound to sense directly in even the minutest elements of the reader's unfolding attention; a new style-language enters, and the traditional norm of versification is not so much abandoned as placed in a new field of force, unharmed in everything but its prestige. What has occurred? I should say, the deposition of regularity as a definite signified. Curiously the foot hypothesis is dethroned at the same time it is given its most detailed defense in the theorists between Patmore and Saintsbury.

In Mallarmé and then Imagism, there also develops now a visual poetics, wherein the whole page becomes part of the poem's form, the relation of type to white spaces one of several constructive factors. This too dislocates a normative metrics, whose rigidity till now has blocked any such evolution. The techniques include use of the visual prosodies, miniaturization (Hopkins), gigantism (Whitman), polymetrism, the exaltation of juncture and line punctuation, and the opposite strategy of continuity where (as Hopkins says) "the scanning runs on without break from the beginning, say, of a stanza to the end and all the stanza is one long strain, though written in lines asunder" (preface). The Bible, Ossian, Welsh, and Anglo-Saxon precedents are all harnessed and their formal suggestions adapted in order to elude the stale language of Parnassian. The intent seems to have been to smuggle a speech orientation within a print-soaked tradition, and to enable a clearer dialectical relation with the medium of prose. There is an intense, driving wish to obscure the form of the poem in order to prolong the perception of it. As in that "eye-wandering" technique in certain Modern paintings, the reader's attention is kept frustrated and unsatisfied by the prevention of a final focus. Literary form is here used to contravene the gestalt postulate that the most satisfactory forms are those which result from simple, stable commands.

So the period from 1855 to 1910 affords remarkable instances of how "minor usages become major for a few poets," and then become, when successful, determinative for later "vogues of choice" (Josephine Miles). This is a process accompanied by the rise to prominence of nonmetrical prosodic features. The accentual-syllabic dominant is deemphasized, and other categories gain a parity with it—notions of word juncture, syntax, line, rhyme, and the like are sound-sense patterns other than meter that begin to emerge, insistently.

The history of this period's contentious and incomplete scholarship on prosody may serve as a reminder that, even today, we lack a general principle of equivalence, which will subsume meter and all other equivalence patterns, putting each in its place. To my mind Jiří Levý's "Meanings of Form and the Forms of Meaning" is the crucial study. His discussion of three principles of linear arrangement is working at the proper level of generality; he avoids any easy or univocal identification of meter, by testing the proportions of three sets of opposed qualities: "continuity (coherence) vs. discontinuity; equivalence (lack of intensity) vs. hierarchy; regularity (predictability) vs. irregularity."[24] These conditions are possible to trace with some assurance because, as Levý says, "the relations between the acoustic and semantic levels consist not in a one-to-one relation between segments of both levels, but in a parallel morphology of the two systems as wholes." The human meanings of the text are not unrelated to the metrical meanings, and the role of poetics in relation to metrics is to interconnect a historical system of literary genres with a parallel system of verse forms, and to make the forms clear as communication channels that shape, and implicate, their own messages.

No doubt difficulties lie in the path of inquiry into the meanings of form and the forms of meaning. Paul de Man has questioned the legitimacy of criticism's reduction of rhetoric to figure of grammar.[25] The same objection is phrased differently in W. K. Wimsatt's position on meter when, speaking of "the ever-present, the ever-different disparities and tensions between formal meter and the linguistic totality," he affirms: "You can't write a grammar of the meter's interaction with the sense." The reminders in both de Man and Wimsatt are apt, and yet the poets of prosodic avantgardism—all our poets since Wordsworth—are writing as if it is possible to draft such a grammar. These writers wish radically to deemphasize the disparities and tensions between "formal meter and the linguistic totality," to transform the sign back into meaning. The project, essentially the Romanticist one announced by Coleridge in the idea of form as proceeding, is impossible of completion and known to be a theoretical limit by the writers themselves. Nevertheless these writers persist in their wish to collapse poetry back into speech, rhetoric into grammar. That is the mission of the writer in an avant-garde era, a task that, while it can never be adequately fulfilled, can at best constantly redefine the canons of literature and literary success.

Part Two: *The Innovative Poetries*

4
Sprung Rhythm and the Figure of Grammar

The Subjective Counterparts of Linguistic and Prosodic Pattern

Aristotelian logic, the reigning mode until the time of Coleridge and Hegel, analyzes the forms of coherence found in completed acts of thought.[1] What Coleridge proposed as a dynamic supplement, in his idea of method as "progressive transition," is a logic of the activity of thinking. That is, form as proceeding proposes another perspective on the text: in addition to the observation of the whole as a spatial entity rounded and complete, there would be a linear tracing of the work from its beginning point, a miming of the writer's choices at transition points and of the reader's shifting attention. There is in Coleridge's thought no special valuation of process over product as a method of regard; each way of reading shows a different aspect, each logic is necessary to the other, and together they contribute to the adequate interpretation. Simply, for Coleridge, it was necessary to put a highlight on proceeding because it brought into view neglected elements of earlier works (such as the plot of *Tom Jones,* which he thought perfect)—and tended to explain, and even justify, certain aspects of Coleridge's own poems and of Wordsworth's. What is historically new is the extraordinary interest in thinking, in energies of consciousness previous to genre, grammar, and literary structure that yet have some bearing on those systems of signs.

What bearing? The disciplines of psychology, linguistics, and literature have not adequate explanations of thinking in writing or in the making of art. While new theories of grammar and text grammar offer the promise of more powerful explanation, the current moment seems contradictory. The manifestos and poems of Romanticism and after would banish genre, rhyme, meter, stanzas, and other forms of anteriority—systems existing before the making of the poem—while the practice and theory of this writing reinstate anteriority in other places, in categories and inner rhythms of thought. (For instance, by what logic do readers use implicit schemas to make a narrative out of a string of sentences?) The intent to bring out an inner rhythm by making poetry's language transparent is typical.[2] That intent, expressed as an attitude toward form that might condition the making of the poem, apparently runs counter to the reigning tenet of post-Structuralist criticism, which says, No psychologizing reduction brought about by blurring the boundaries between rhetoric and grammar, prosody and cognition, art and non-art. Though some of the manifestos for this poetry do indeed blur the boundaries, most of the poems themselves rather redefine them. So the aim of a book on the logic of form as proceeding must be to show that there is no necessary conflict between the innovative poetries and contemporary criticism's dismissal of the speaking subject and its questioning of the essential structure of the sign. Nonetheless, when conflict occurs, usually the limitation is on the side of the criticism and not of the poetry, which criticism will overread as attacking its own discursive category, attacking even the canonical structure of the language itself.

Emily Dickinson and Gerard Manley Hopkins, for example, fully recognize the insufficiencies of human words as vehicles of divine and secular-temporal presence, so their works center on language itself as well as on Christian revelation. However, it is well to remember that the religious overthought dominates and uses to its ironic advantage the linguistic underthought.[3] It could not be otherwise with devotional poets of profundity, even though religious discourse in poetry has neither logical nor chronological priority. Like other modes, religious ones are formed at the same time as the literary language that carries them. The priority is of investment in a metaphysical institution.

As devotional poets, Dickinson and Hopkins are in their different ways both despairing and singular personalities, isolated, without audience in their time, strikingly innovative in their use of language and prosody. Isolation doubtless gave a permission to remake poetic convention—something impossible for lesser contemporary writers (Longfellow, Swinburne) who were relatively closer to the center of society and publication. But the truest permission was faith commensurate with doubt, which required literary forms intricate enough to express the struggle of belief. As devotional writers, both rework two quite different types of orthodox belief, in two styles radically rebellious—styles so unfamiliar and seemingly barbarous as to make them all but unreadable to contemporaries. Dickinson in her dash-punctuated, off-rhymed hymn or ballad stanzas modifies traditional metric, but not so severely, I think, as to require treatment in this book's survey of nonmetrical prosody. As sole proprietor of a new type of form as proceeding, foreshadowed but never delivered by Coleridge, Hopkins belongs.[4]

This book's argument has been that Romanticism stated the promise of an avant-garde poetry in Coleridge's form-as-proceeding axiom; and that the nonmetrical prosodies that exemplify such a form arrived somewhat later, in the middle of Victoria's reign, with sprung rhythm, free verse—and the prose poem, that French import. These three major nonmetrical prosodies were in place more than a hundred years ago, and none of the newer developments in syllabics, visual or sound poetry, have come along with claims large enough to increase the set. The extent to which the three major insurgent forms are still insurgent is open to question, especially with sprung rhythm, which, despite the interest it evoked in the 1930s and the revival in works by writers like C. Day Lewis, Stanley Kunitz, and John Berryman, has not traveled widely or well outside the nineteenth century.

There were two strict constraints on whatever new prosodies emerged in the nineteenth century: the new forms had to be in agreement with the facts of the language and with the dominant, namely Romantic, aesthetic premises. Because the Stone-Bridges attempt to revive Classical prosody ran counter to both these laws, it was stillborn. Given the inability of more than a few generations of brilliant poets to create a major new way of writing, perhaps what places were left open on the table of prosodic forms have now been filled by the three nineteenth-century discoveries.[5]

It is the business of the poet to find (or create) open places on the table of forms. Here I reconstruct, after the fact, what might have been the available poetic resources within a reigning period style. From the perspective of literary history, it is obvious that sprung rhythm, free verse, and the prose poem were either emergent or archaizing versions of existent traditional forms. They clear spaces for themselves by canceling meter, or line, or rhyme, or stanza, or some or all of these, or by distorting or reweighting some or all.

As Harvey Gross has shown by selecting for quotation Hopkins passages from a twenty-year period, syllable-stress metric gradually disintegrated as Hopkins developed. Hopkins came to identify and isolate his own form by stressing the stress and exaggerating the principle of rhyme, and by coordinating with these effects the nonlogical syntax of hyperbaton. One might well say of Hopkins, in his relation to accentual-syllabic meters and their rhythms, what Charles Rosen writes of a composer of the period before 1910, a period of crisis in all the arts: "The saturation of musical space is Schoenberg's substitute for the tonic chord of the traditional musical language."[6] In Hopkins, the analogous saturation of the verbal space means the use of a special syntax inside, and against, a special construction on the rhythm of the line, stanza, and poem. His specialty is the simultaneous overlay of grammatical and prosodic systems of segmenting discourse.

All the accounts of sprung rhythm known to me follow the habit of traditional versification theory, and stop when the strictly prosodic features have been described. If grammatical features are described, this is done in a separate chapter. My own inquiry will follow Hopkins's own elaboration of the notion of form as proceeding, as found in a sentence from the *Notebooks* that contains his whole poetics:

> The further in anything, as a work of art, the organisation is carried out, the deeper the form penetrates, the prepossession flushes the matter, the more effort will be required in apprehension, the more power of compari-

son, the more capacity for receiving that synthesis of (either successive or spatially distinct) impressions which gives us the unity with the prepossession conveyed by it.[7]

This gives warrant for our considering prosody the scissors of grammar, grammar the scissors of prosody. Hopkins saw that the figure of grammar in a poem occupies the same poetic space as the figure of rhythmic sound, and he determined to segment the reader's acts of attention so as to make every syllable count, every smallest unit unpredictable and thereby forceful. He proposed to draw out in response to patterned language the reader's energies of intellection, seeking "the more effort . . . the more power . . . the more capacity." By "prepossession" he meant the inner rhythm of thought, a pulsion and a compulsion that is, for him, Christ. When the prepossession flushes the matter, grammar is prosody, and prosody is praise.

The Word itself cannot be said in words of human language, but this need not mean that, for a Christian poet, intimations of divinity are prevented from shining through the grillwork of language. Hopkins, concerned for what he called the selving of things and beings in the world, the self-taste of perceptions and words, was able to develop as a poet by arguing that self-taste of personal style (variously called by him inscape, singularity, and emphasis) was the means by which divinity shone through the grillwork. A personal construction upon the line was the means of bringing together his roles as poet and priest, though not without unceasing anguish that he had used himself and his style for purposes contrary to a religious vocation. When a recent Deconstructionist reading insists that Hopkins's poetry is bound within the prison house of language, and that no account of the poet can neglect to explore this place of confinement, it overcorrects the many previous studies that dwell on the sacramental function. A more balanced, if unfashionable, statement would hold that the stronger Hopkins's scholarly and poetic understanding of linguistic limits, the stronger will be his attempt to see behind, around, and with the grillwork of language. As several of the commentators have argued very finely, "stress" is the crucial concept of Hopkins's sprung rhythm, because gathering rhythmic and lexical power in a single word makes meaning burst forth: "Brute beauty and act, oh, air, pride, plume here / Buckle!"; "it will flame out, like shining from shook foil; / It gathers to a greatness, like the ooze of oil / Crushed"; "Gush!—flush the man, the being with it, sour or sweet, / Brim, in a flash, full!" If the meanings had been restricted to being allegories of the writing process, Hopkins's poetry would never have been written. He could not be so self-indulgent in these matters as a nonreligious poet.

Sprung rhythm probably has one origin in Coleridge's poem "Christabel," and in Coleridge's brief note on that poem. Hopkins was certainly conscious of Coleridge's priority. He was also aware that the new rhythm that haunted his ear was both in theory and practice largely his own invention; he named the rhythm, he defended it, and he embodied it in poem after poem. Hopkins wanted heavier and more frequent stress than is prescribed by accentual-syllabic metric, and this he achieved by springing the stresses from their mathematical preordained slots in the line. He attained a certain freedom, within limits, by counting only stresses—each was followed by a variable number of unstressed syllables or, on occasion, by another stress. As an example, the first four lines of "The Caged Skylark" (1877), a poem Hopkins classified as being in falling paeonic rhythm, sprung and outriding:

> Aš ă dáre-găle skýlaȑk scántĕd ĭn ă dúll cáge
>
> Măn's móuntĭng spíriȋ iñ hiš bóne-hoǔse, méan hǒuse, dwélls—
>
> Thăt biȑd bĕyónd tȟe rĕmémbĕrĭng ȟis fȓee félls;
>
> Thiš iñ drúdgerȳ, dáy-lábouȓrĭng-oút lifě's áge.[8]

Line 2, with "spirit in his" has the first paeon, a scatter of scudded syllables before the heavily rocking end of the line, "bone-house, mean house, dwells." Line 4 puts two stresses up against one another in "day-labouring-out," giving a lurching or rubato effect. In developed sprung rhythm the foot always begins with the stress, and so may continue to the beginning of the next line, as between lines 2 and 3 here. Line 1, with "scanted in a dull cage," combines both these effects, which in Hopkins are quite different matters, worth distinguishing. For rare occasions, like the last line of "Spring and Fall," one notable effect of sprung rhythm is to compel stress onto almost every syllable. "It is Margaret you mourn for." Here are, possibly, eight stressed syllables, for how can we dare ignore any one of them? Even "Margaret," normally a trochee, now gets stretched out into three almost equal sounds. Mar—gar—et: a new name. Thus Hopkins counted only the number of bold stresses in the line, and he bunched or spaced his stresses, dropping or adding unstressed syllables according to the needs of local sense.

Hopkins also used alliteration, rhyming, punctuation, and especially syntax to make the stresses bolder and more frequent yet. Sprung rhythm, he insisted, was "the nearest to the rhythm of prose, that is the native and natural rhythm of speech, the least forced, the most rhetorical and emphatic of all possible rhythms, combining . . . opposite, and one wd. have thought, incompatible excellences, markedness of rhythm—that is rhythm's self—and naturalness of expression."[9] To many readers, beginning with his friend Robert Bridges, the expression has not seemed natural, but naturalness in literary language is always a category of prejudice, and what one begins with, here, is Hopkins's own belief that his expression could be taken as related to a kind of ordinary speaking.

The poet who could use and extend our ordinary knowledge of adjectives in a phrase like "the rolling level underneath him steady air," or who could embed, extend, and interlink genitive nouns in Chinese boxes in a line like "Our hearts' charity's hearth's fire, our thoughts' chivalry's throng's Lord," certainly knew that his meter was demanding. He also had faith that his readers would meet the challenge, and to help them hear the rhythm he supplied his famous author's preface, his diacritical marks on the poems themselves, and his indentations of lines to give visual cues to their sounded structure. He himself must have seen the likely contradiction between the claim for "naturalness of expression" and the need for a notation, but here as in his letters to Bridges he is willing to sacrifice a measure of theoretical rigor in order to be understood. He might well have reasoned that the poems would scarcely have a chance to show their naturalness if they went unread.

"Binsey Poplars, Felled 1879" uses this auxiliary system of markings and indentations in its second stanza:

> My aspens dear, whose airy cages quelled,
> Quelled or quenched in leaves the leaping sun,
> All felled, felled, are all felled;
>   Of a fresh and following folded rank
>   Not spared, nor one
>   That dandled a sandalled
>   Shadow that swam or sank
> On meadow and river and wind-wandering weed-winding bank.
>
> O if we but knew what we do
>   When we delve or hew—
> Hack and rack the growing green!
>   Since country is so tender
> To touch, her being só slender
> That, like this sleek and seeing ball
> But a prick will make no eye at all,
> Where we, even where we mean
>   to mend her we end her,
> When we hew or delve:
> After-comers cannot guess the beauty been,
>   Ten or twelve, only ten or twelve
>   Strokes of havoc unselve
>   The sweet espècial scene,
> Rural scene, a rural scene,
> Sweet espècial rural scene.[10]
>
> Sweet especial rural scene.[10]

Indentation indicates the number of stresses to the line, the most interesting line coming at line 8 with its six stresses and "outrides" (one, two, or three "slack syllables added to a foot and not counting in the nominal scanning": Hopkins in his preface) at "wandering" and "winding." Sprung rhythm has as one of its primary effects the juxtaposition of stresses, as here in "felled, felled" and in "wind-wandering." The selving or inscape of the scene is so important that its destruction disturbs the fourth-from-the-last line, where "un"—receiving a stress though it goes against the grain of any normative versification to accent such prefixes—gains very great prosodic (and ethical) weight through the deviance. We would not hear or understand this if Hopkins had not marked the word with his own accent. Such accent marks, on the outrides and stresses here and elsewhere, have the same motive as Hopkins's summaries and headnotes to difficult poems. Hopkins knew these devices were, strictly speaking, unpoetic, yet he felt the reader needed help—especially a reader who would take in the poem by the eye. (Taken in by the ear, he said, the poems come out all right.)

By its relentless emphasis on the emphatic, sprung rhythm clearly encourages a tendency to omit constructional syllables. Thus at the beginning of line 3 the poet banishes "Are" and at the sixth-from-the-last line he rewrites and shortens "those who come after cannot guess the beauty that has been." (The word "been" is also notable for its compression of senses: it seems to be on its way from past participle to plain adjective.) At the same time, in the same short poem, we get at other places an "oftening" (Hopkins's term) of syntax: "All felled, felled, are all felled," and—most remarkably—the elegiac refrain of the ending, with so many words repeating with slight change for theatrical emphasis. The unexpectedness of syntax, diction, line length, and rhyme is a stylistic signature for a poet who wants to go a good distance to separate himself from everything Parnassian, everything Tennysonian.

Hopkins wrote in his last poem, a sonnet "To R[obert] B[ridges]," of his hope for an expressiveness that would come through the grillwork of language, "the strong / Spur, live and lancing like the blowpipe flame." Bridges himself, the weaker artist, recoiled from Hopkins's assertions of expressive and prosodic strength, and none too politely. But Hopkins is strange, as Father Ong once said, "only to those not used to this strength of emotion in verse."[11] The concept that relates strength of emotion to strictness of form, in Hopkins, is one we might call sense stressing. Hopkins was right to respond to Bridges's critique of sprung rhythm with the stubborn words "With all my licences, or rather laws, I am stricter than you and I might say than anybody I know."[12] Stress, he said, "is the life of it," and "the stress is more *of* a stress." It is more of a stress, because more sharply calibrated against the syntactic and lexical divisions of the sentence. The insurgent principle of sense stressing has the effect of forcing more attention on the constituent elements of the word, phrase, line, sentence, and stanza, rather than suppressing awareness of them, as in traditional running rhythm. With Hopkins there is no mere libertarian desire to unregularize, to prise apart the iamb, but rather a desire also to look at the grammatic-prosodic parts more closely. Far beyond even Coleridge, Hopkins exhibits a new fascination with the minutiae of poetic language. In this he joins with nineteenth-century inventors of free verse and the prose poem, innovators who want to get closer and closer to the details of language.

The Figure of Grammar

In the historical unfolding of Romantic premises, a number of procedures become optional when poetry is seen to be synonymous with the act of the mind. Rhyme, meter, line, and stanza become expendable; cognition does not need them. The more daring formulation seems to come somewhat later—for by these premises sentence and phrase and word and syllable are also expendable, since meaning is stored over time and, from the reader's or listener's perspective on ordinary prose discourse, what is stored is not linguistic form but semantic content. Unlike ordinary discourse, however, verse obliges us to recover the linguistic form as well; but a literature that assimilates itself to ordinary discourse will seek out pulsions or surds, ever more basic notations of the activity of thinking. The history of the avant-garde prosodies is a relentless stripping away of artistic and grammatical codes to lay bare the operations of thought. The next step is to question whether predication, modification, and connection can be separated from their origin, if they have one.

Not many writers arrive at that next and possibly last-imaginable step; like Hopkins, they rest content with wrenching the received device and idea of the sentence. From the perspective of what might be possible in the stripping of literary-grammatical signs from the work, Hopkins's experiments may appear rather modest. After all, he retained the categories of rhyme, foot, line, stanza, and sentence. For sprung rhythm, it was sufficient to redefine and intermesh these categories. In a famous essay, "Poetry and Verse" (ca. 1873–74), Hopkins defined *verse* as "speech wholly or partially repeating the same figure of sound. . . . the same figure of grammar."[13] The passage has influenced Roman Jakobson, who considers the figure of grammar "an area within the problems of language and verbal art which has, until recently, remained virtually unexplored."[14] Yet Jakobson's own several studies of the subject have emphasized the repeated figure of grammar, as in anaphora, thus leaving aside the other possibility Hopkins presents in the same place, that "*once* of the inscape [can] be enough for art and beauty." The linear directionality of syntax can also constitute an inscape for Hopkins, indeed for any poetry. Hopkins wrote in another place that "metre, rhythm, rhyme, and the structure which is called verse both necessitate and engender a difference in diction and in thought."[15] Once the poem has been written, the figure of grammar may just as easily be taken as engendering a difference in the figure of sound. The engendering is mutual as between sound and grammar. Sprung rhythm segments the attentional space of the reader, by asking arabesques of sound and grammar to scissor each other. This is a more narrowly technical way of describing the saturation of poetic space in Hopkins, alluded to above. The effect cannot be understood by scansion alone, though Hopkins does condescend to count feet in a line. Rather, we require a method of reading that can show how sentence and line occupy the same quadrant of poetic space.

The author's preface and other statements have been criticized for deriving arguments from a foot-based system but warring peculiarly against it. Hopkins combines a preference for accentual meter with an isochronous prosody built up of measures as in music, and to these adds a foot system appropriate to neither.[16] Insofar as he attempts to think stress and time in the same thought, he tries to perform what is very likely impossible. He does seem to use the terms *meter* and *measure* interchangeably, but might that mistake not also have its productive side for a prosodic innovator? In his early Platonic dialogue, "On the Origin of Beauty," Hopkins describes meter as "the combination of pieces of rhythm of certain lengths, equal or unequal."[17] Inevitably, the unequal and equal lengths of sound sequence are also lengths of syntax, which will break either with or against pauses of sound within the line or from line to line. For example, in a final revision the poet changed

Brute beauty and valour and act, oh, air, pride, plume, here
   Buckle!

by dropping the comma after "plume"; he wanted to stitch the last word, "here," back further into its line, so that the abrupt turn onto "Buckle!" would be even more energetic, delivering even more stress to "Buckle!" as the word that oddly imitates the stoop of Hopkins's Windhover-God. This slight deflection of grammar, eliminating a mental pause and introducing a new perplexity (is "plume" a new active verb?—no; or is it the third noun of the series?—yes) has no effect on the pattern of heavy stresses in a row, but it does increase the degree of cognitive tension in the line. Such effects and the sprung rhythm they derive from might not have been created if Hopkins as a good Modern metrist had been able to avoid confusing cadence, grouping, and measure as the three factors involved in rhythm. If he had not set out to form abrupt irregular clumpings by the mutual partitioning of grammar and prosody, if theory impinged more completely on practice, literary history might have taken another route.

It was by virtue of sprung rhythm that he distinguished himself from the grand master of the Victorian verse period, Tennyson. To R. W. Dixon, who had written disparaging Tennyson as the "great outsider," Hopkins responded warmly by reasserting the centrality of the laureate, despite the "loss of relish for what once charmed us."[18] He acknowledges the "boyish stress of enchantment" of his first response to Tennyson, and also a certain deadening of response that comes from familiarity with Tennyson's effects.

The objection to Tennyson was nothing to do with his "mental material" but rather with a form "not equal to the material." Three days after he was writing on Tennyson's "technical faults" he was still writing to the same correspondent, Dixon, on the role of stress in sprung rhythm ("more *of* a stress"). But already by 1864, in a brilliant undergraduate letter to A. W. M. Bailie, he is turning Tennyson into an adjective: "He is, one must see it, what we used to call Tennysonian."[19] This letter's splendid account of the type of writing Hopkins calls Parnassian ("spoken *on and from the level* of a poet's mind"; "beautiful and unexceptional, but it does not touch you"), uses Tennyson as the main exemplar, and notably these lines from *Enoch Arden:*

> The slender coco's drooping crown of plumes,
> The lightning flash of insect and of bird.

These lines, Hopkins says, are "pure Parnassian," where we "seem to have found out [the writer's] secret." But why do the lines not "touch"? Hopkins does not say, but we may safely judge the difficulty to be metrical and grammatical at once, metrical because grammatical. It all goes too liquidly: adjective + noun + adjective + noun + preposition + noun in the first line; a pattern begun and then feebly disrupted in the second: adjective + noun + preposition + noun + conjunction + preposition + noun. The second preposition in the second line is unnecessary to the grammar or sense—there just because the line needs a slack syllable. Lack of abrupt turns in the syntax leads to a sequence of words and thereby of rhythms entirely too predictable (Parnassian, to Hopkins, is a poetry that "palls"). What the two lines lack is the torsion that springs stresses out of a repeatable pattern, words out of logical order.[20]

After dissecting the lines from *Enoch Arden*, Hopkins goes on to quote from memory a quatrain from *In Memoriam* that he not only approves but finds "divine, terribly beautiful":

> O Hesper o'er the buried sun,
>   And ready thou to die with him,
>   Thou watchest all things ever dim
> And dimmer, and a glory done.

Hopkins admires the poet's projection into the perspective of the evening star, above the sinking sun, but much more he admires the handling of the last line—especially the last clause and word. The energy of that last phrase, "and a glory done," comes from the mind's being set into a fury of pattern hunting atypical of Tennyson. One of the patterns that operates is substitution, when in lines 2 and 3 "thou" stands in for Hesper; then at the next stage the pronoun is itself deleted and left to be implied, as in "[Thou Hesper watchest] a glory done"; and "done" as past participle is itself a condensa-

tion for a whole relative clause that might read "which has been completed."
There is even the absurd lure of a false pattern, if it is possible to think of
"dimmer"/"done" as comparative and superlative of the adjective "dim."
These readings do not exhaust the possibilities, but are sufficient to show the
final phrase as—at first—a kind of nonsense, perpendicular to the meanings
and grammar of the earlier parts of the sentence. But it is not nonsense, but
rather the nonlogical syntax of the figure hyperbaton or transposition, which
Hopkins uses, in conjunction with overdetermined speech stressing, to imitate the way the perceiving mind works.[21] What he saw in the last stage of
Tennyson's sunset—in the emphatic participle "done," used like an adjective
to modify a noun and to substitute for an implied relative clause—was himself.

The conceptual foundations of grammar have not been excavated to the
point where the analyses of Part 2 of the present book can adopt and turn to
use any one theory of grammar. Anomalies in the paradigm of generative
grammar are now so numerous as to make it questionable to linguists and to
the literary critics who borrow and, no doubt, distort and embroider the
linguists' formulations. No persuasive new paradigm has asserted itself to
take the place of generative grammar.[22]

Criticism, as semantic, requires a reading that establishes that the exact
sequence of words is part of their collective meaning. The spatial qualities of
literary style are well known, but the sequential qualities need to be brought
to equal prominence. Accordingly, in my study of the verse period, I rely on
these working premises.

1. In the verse period (or the sentence within the poem), the cognitive and
   the aesthetic structures of a poetic text are in a condition of mutual
   interference. Each requires the other, each attempts to reduce the other
   to the minimum. Hopkins saw this when he wrote of the "oftening, over-
   and-overing, aftering of the inscape," and Jan M. Meijer has recently
   posed the same in another idiom: "Dynamics in verbal art is a matter of
   the number of systems involved and of the number and variety of their
   intersections."[23] Grammar is the cognitive, meter is the aesthetic, and the
   two systems occupy the very same words. While the line is scissoring the
   sentence, the sentence is scissoring the line.
2. Forms of arrangement in the poem are related to forms of meaning in the
   poem along a linear continuum, since the poem carves a shape in time.
   The meanings and their arrangements are in a special fraternity of interference (see # 1). The meaings of form and the forms of meaning are, as
   Jiří Levý says, "not in a one to one relation between segments of both

levels, but in a parallel morphology of the two systems as wholes." Forms of arrangement relate to forms of meaning in this fashion, as three pairs of oppositions:

Continuity————————Discontinuity
(Coherence————————Incoherence)
Equivalence————————Hierarchy
(Lack of intensity————————Intensity)
Regularity————————Irregularity
(Predictability————————Unexpectedness)

This is a simple set of proportions, in which, for example, semantic prominence (what Hopkins calls emphasis) takes the word out of context, creating a degree of incoherence, a decrease in predictability, and an increase in intensity ("And dimmer, and a glory done"). Intensity, as Hopkins well knew, is the dominant function.[24]

3. In order to account both for the eventfulness of the detail and the continuity of the whole, prosody requires at the very least the following scale of poetic elements, which borrows and modifies M. A. K. Halliday's model for English grammar.[25]

    The scale is:

    Poem
    Stanza
    Sentence
    Line
    Phrase
    Word
    Foot
    Syllable

As in the theory of grammar one moves down the scale of comprehensiveness from sentence to morpheme to study syntax, and up the scale to characterize the whole utterance, so in the criticism of sprung rhythm and free verse one moves down the scale of units to study local effects of movement or diction or sound, up the scale to study line, stanza, poem. (Halliday's scale of large up, small down, is perhaps too strongly visual for complete clarity. By larger and smaller he means more and less *comprehensive*.) Here, no unit is honored by absolute independence of the others; "criteria of any given unit always involve reference to others, and therefore indirectly to all the others"; "each place and each element in the structure of a given unit is defined with reference to the next below"; and "the smallest unit has no structure." Finally, for the description of particular effects of grammatical measure in the verse period, the best

method is to shunt up and down the scale as required. The scale's delicacy of description even permits it to include an adequate treatment of meter and rhyme, should a given text warrant such treatment.
4. Intersections of measure and grammar in the middle of the scale will usually be the most productive subject for inquiry. My focus in this chapter and the next will be the relation between the line and the larger units of grammar—specifically, the coincidence and noncoincidence of line and sentence. For hints as to method, I draw upon P. J. Wexler's notion of the grammetrical, a hybridization of grammar and metrics "whose key hypothesis is that the interplay of sentence-structure and line-structure can be accounted for more economically by simultaneous than by successive analysis."[26] Wexler's ideas have been developed for intensive analysis of the French Classical alexandrine, where "sentences and lines generally have coincident boundaries," but the ideas can also be applied, with appropriate reservations, to other forms of verse. That Wexler must rely for his analysis "on categories which it is one object of the analysis to change" is an equal challenge for the critic of sprung rhythm and free verse.

A grammetrical reading cannot consist of a set of *identifications* grammatical and prosodic; nor can it consist of an assertion that forms of arrangement are forms of meaning, even though, as in the case of Hopkins, the poet himself seemed to believe in a mimetic syntax and rhythm. In the pages to follow I attempt to interpret a poem and to describe the peculiarities of its sequential figures of grammar, touching as well on the poem's central metaphors; my purpose in hazarding an interpretation has been only to prepare a semantic ground for my more technical account. Grammetrics is inescapably interpretive, though the reading may be more selective and economical than this example. Certain lines and sequences of lines will be more productive than others in showing the mutual interference of syntax and prosody; but once grammar is brought in as a variable, the meaning of sentence and poem must be confronted.[27]

"Carrion Comfort," the sonnet in alexandrines chosen for description according to these premises of an emergent grammetrics, dates from 1885. Hopkins had begun as a traditional poet but even as an undergraduate in the early 1860s, as we have seen, was restless within the Tennysonian norms and anxious to be better than Parnassian. "The Wreck of the Deutschland" in 1875 was his first poem in (he said) "the new rhythm which now I realized on paper." There followed a number of poems some of which used sprung rhythm, such as the masterful sonnet, "The Windhover," and some of which kept and counterpointed the standard rhythm ("God's Grandeur" is one example). Certain poems of the 1880s lengthen the line and push as far as sprung rhythm can to a nonmetrical poetry, as in these lines from "Spelt from Sybil's Leaves" (1885):

Earnest, earthless, equal, attuneable, vaulty, voluminous, . . . stupendous
Evening strains to be tíme's vást, 'womb-of-all, home-of-all, hearse-of-all
    night.

"Carrion Comfort," from the same year, is demonstrably nonmetrical but not
so daring an experiment. Nonetheless, it represents sprung rhythm in its
typical and developed state. Like many of Hopkins's best poems it shows
sprung rhythm inseparable from a certain kind of sentence, inseparable from
Hopkins's anguished self-questioning of his double vocation of poet and
priest.

"Carrion Comfort" is Robert Bridges's title, not the poet's. It is not a very
exact title, because it derives from a passing image in the first line, a
metaphor in apposition to a personified Despair, to whom the poet speaks:

Not, I'll not, carrion comfort, Despair, not feast on thee;
Not untwist—slack they may be—these last strands of man
In me ór, most weary, cry *I can no more.* I can;
Can something, hope, wish day come, not choose not to be.
But ah, but O thou terrible, why wouldst thou rude on me
Thy wring-world right foot rock? lay a lionlimb against me? scan
With darksome devouring eyes my bruised bones? and fan,
O in turns of tempest, me heaped there; me frantic to avoid thee and flee?

Why? That my chaff might fly; my grain lie, sheer and clear.
Nay in all that toil, that coil, since (seems) I kissed the rod,
Hand rather, my heart lo! lapped strength, stole joy, would laugh, cheer.
Cheer whom though? the hero whose heaven-handling flung me, foot trod
Me? or me that fought him? O which one? is it each one? That night, that
    year
Of now done darkness I wretch lay wrestling with (my God!) my God.[28]

Part of the self is dead, and the speaker refuses to indulge himself by feeding
it, refuses to give in to suicidal Despair. The method of placement of the
metaphor "carrion comfort" in this first line is typical of many other effects:
violence of feeling puts the metaphor before the thing it refers to, just as in
the next line the pronoun "they" occurs, out of logical order, before its
referent, "these last strands of man."

I shall return to the reason that the term "Despair" is, in the syntax of
line 1, both an active verb and a proper noun in the vocative case—because,
as it seems to me, that is the indeterminacy the whole poem sets out not to
resolve but to understand. In the deictic structure of the poem, these first
four lines are addressed to Despair, the dead self. The next four are addressed to God, with four of the poem's ten question marks and no less than
three exclamations. These images of struggle with a massive antagonist are
tropes for the pain of religious conversion, something literature can only, at
best, urgently suggest. Here Hopkins's metaphor of struggle is manifested in
his use of the present tense and his special saturation of the figures of sound

and grammar. The first eight lines attempt to recreate for the reader, in the reader, the dark night of the soul that is the experience of conversion.

The "why" of line 5 is taken up again as the first word of the sestet. It is typical of Hopkins to push the questioning past the poem's major break, into the citadel where the answer will come—if there is an answer. Line 9 is also continuous and transitional in its use of the verb form "might," which by offering reasons for the necessary passage through despair opens the way for the relative security of the past tense in lines 10 to the end. After the refusal to despair in lines 1 through 4, the questions of lines 5 through 9, and the answers in lines 9 through 11, lines 12 and 13 raise more questions about God's paradoxical victory in the contest for the convert's soul. Again an answer is reached, so that it is possible in lines 13 and 14 to return to the original scene of the contest with greater understanding. In the sestet, remembering the soul-wrestling has its own urgency of intellection—and of awe at the sudden access of the scene of conversion's full meaning.

So the poem has a strict plot. In refusing to accept the comfort of Despair, that personification of the dead self, and thus in allowing God to throw him, the vanquished narrator was victorious. The time of conversion was a night that seemed a year, a year that seemed a long night, for the syntax of line 13 is reversible; but the match is over, the darkness "now done" (line 14), except as the anguish is recreated in the present tense in severely wrenched rhythms and sentences. The last line, by making the metaphor of wrestling explicit and naming the antagonist for the first time, throws all the previous images into a religious perspective. It answers all questions. It does so by overing and aftering the modest shifter, "my": "I wretch lay wrestling with (my God!) my God." The spring of the line and of the poem is the disproportion between the narrator-wretch (who yet creates the poem) and his God, and his amazement that God would stoop to wrestle for so insignificant a soul. The amazement is that God should be his God, internalized, possessed, vivid, palpable as a "lionlimb" physically pressed against him. Without God, one fights one's worst impulses without hope or resources, and that is why Despair in the syntax of line 1 is both self and other, both verb and noun; but with a personal God's immense power brought into the struggle, it becomes possible continually to defeat rather than feed on the dead part of the self, "carrion comfort, Despair." The parenthetical "my God!" is thus a reinvigorated dead metaphor, a piece of familiar speech taken back to its first and fully religious meaning, and immediately followed by the same phrase restored.

By that turn upon English colloquial speech, and by the related use in line 3 where stating "I'll not cry *I can no more*" he momentarily does cry out those very words in vivid self-quotation, we are reminded of two of Hopkins's repeated assertions that sprung rhythm is closer to spoken language than standard rhythm, and that his poems come right only in oral performance. There are, of course, deceptions of logic in all such assimilations of poetry to speech, but whether Hopkins eludes the difficulties cannot be settled here. Also the claims contradict common sense when we have just come away from the overdetermined artificiality of sound and syntax in a poem like this. What he meant, I think, was that for all their artifice, poems in sprung rhythm come much closer than other poems of his era to the way the mind works on its chosen or given materials, thus closer to the procedures that underly ordinary speaking. As in the structure of many of his sentences and phrases here, and the structure of the poem as a whole (enactive octave, reflective sestet), something is delivered in the mode of enactment and then, once uttered, delivered again as specification and definition. The method of presentation is calculated to give the highest acceptable degree of incoherence, unexpectedness, and intensity. By these means the poet seeks to recreate in the mind of the reader the breakdown of reality. To ask that it try to mime the immediacy of events was a great deal to require from a patched and changing language, a mere human instrument, but if he did not believe that language could carry at least a residual self-presence of the writer and the writer's God, experiments with the figure of grammar would hardly have been undertaken.

The poem exercises a reader's faculty of attention with many different figures of grammar. The principal procedures, I should say, are: subordinating several clauses under one main verb (lines 3–4, 5–8, 9, 12–13); apposition ("carrion comfort, Despair"; "that toil, that coil"; "That night, that year"; "I wretch"); sequence of tenses from present to past; multiple questioning; correction of first formulation, on a large scale; deletion of unnecessary words on a large scale; and transposition. Only the last three of these procedures require further comment because of their prosodic implications, but their context deserves prior mention. The larger figures of the separate sentences are linked and blended to baffle the reader's sentence sense. Continuity, and saturation of attentional space, are gained by intense division upon the groundwork of the syntax. Either, as with the first sentence, embedded parenthetical remarks turn and extend the utterance so that it is difficult to know when it stops; or the ends of sentences are feathered into new clauses by the device of the question mark followed by a lowercase letter and another questioning clause, as in:

> Cheer whom though? the hero whose heaven-handling flung me, foot trod
> Me? or me that fought him?

I count nine sentences, but with little assurance that I have segmented the text correctly. Is "Why?" in line 9 a one-word sentence? Or connected back—or connected forward? Is "That night, that year / Of now done darkness I wretch lay wrestling with (my God!) my God" a sentence by itself, or part of the previous sentence—and if related backward, what are the boundaries of the previous verse period? And so on. Such sentencing tends to make of the poem one long grammatical strain, as Hopkins hoped. It deemphasizes sentence ends in order to expand and diversify their middles, their divisions into segments of irregular lengths. Inevitably such sentencing has its effect on the rhythm of the line.

Self-correction in midsentence is a signature of active thought. The dash structure in line 2 and the parentheses in lines 10 ("seems") and 14 ("my God!") are examples, but there are many others less obvious:

—"they . . . these last strands"—specification, line 2
—"I can no more. I can"—reversal, line 3
—"Can something, hope"—specification, line 4
—"my chaff might fly; my grain lie"—expansion, line 9
—"I kissed the rod, / hand rather"—expansion, lines 10–11
—"cheer. / Cheer whom though?"—specification, lines 11–12
—"the hero . . . or me that fought him?"—alternatives, lines 12–13
—"O which one? is it each one?"—specification, line 13
—"That night, that year"—alternatives, line 13

Operating in conjunction with the files of question sets in both octave and sestet, these are devices of expansion, taking space to show that the mind in the midst of the profoundest disturbance can shift to wider contexts, make sense of its own doings. A countermovement that cuts across this impetuous, expansive procedure is the deletion of purely constructive words—on a scale so massive that the poem would be a quarter again as large if these words were replaced. If relationships between and within sentences were made explicit, if auxiliary verbs were added, lines 9 through 11 would read: "Why did God do this? He did it so that my chaff might fly and so that my grain might lie, both sheer and clear. Indeed, in all that toil, in all that coil, since (it seems) I kissed the rod, or rather the hand, my heart (lo) lapped up strength, it stole joy, it would laugh, and it would cheer." Hopkins anticipates Modern poetry by omitting these words and forcing the reader to leap what has been elided, making connections, filling in blanks with what is known about the cohesion of English sentences. The leaps of thought required are also, inevitably, pouncings of rhythm, as phrases get clumped:

Hand rather, my heart lo! lapped strength, stole joy, would laugh, cheer.

This leaping forces greater stress on syllables usually stressed anyway and already.

Most characteristic because most frequent and dramatic of these procedures is hyperbaton, or transposition, a change from the logical order of ideas that Hopkins uses both to enact and evoke strong feelings in his narrator and reader. The most powerful instance is the arresting first line, with its early displacement of the crucial negative, first challenge in the wrestling match of conscience.

> Not, I'll not, carrion comfort, Despair, not feast on thee . . .

The word ought to be "no," as "not" is an adverb, requiring another part of speech (verb, adjective) to negate. Here there *is* nothing, there is no *thing,* to negate—it is not negation negating itself but negation suspended, alienated. You could write it out "Not/I will not/I will not feast"—finally in the third gasp we get the full verb blurted forth.[29]

When it brings to the front of the sentence the most important words and deictic gestures, the "But ah, but O" in line 5 uses the same feature. "Why?" beginning line 9 and "Me?" beginning line 13 are postponed interrogatives. Meaning is also withheld when logically cohering words are separated:

>   why wouldst thou rude on me
> Thy wring-world right foot rock?

Since this separates noun from adjective, and puts prepositional phrase and sentence object in front of the verb "rock," we have here a triple transposition. Less strenuous separation occurs sometimes by virtue of interposed exclamatory cries (e.g., "lo!"; "fan / O in turns of tempest, me"). The culmination of the method of interposition is, appropriately, the last line with its three insertions, crucial for meaning and tone:

> Of *now done* darkness I *wretch* lay wrestling with *(my God!)* my God.

Transposition with its other, related, and congruent effects of grammar interrupts the logic of the lines they form, and contributes to nonlogical patterns of association. In this poem these effects relate the structure of the syntax to the psychology of conversion, which must pass through the phase of anguished, even suicidal despair reimagined here in lines 1 through 8 and 13 through 14. What is enacted in the poem is this reimagining.

Similar effects are used elsewhere in Hopkins for similar purposes, and, by contrast, hyperbaton and inversion are usually absent in those poems, like "The Windhover," where the keynote is unambiguous praise, the subject a vivid imagining of God's grandeur, not of man's weakness. Hopkins is logocentric enough to wish for a syntax and prosody parallel to the thought of the poem. In fact, "Carrion Comfort" is probably the sonnet he referred to in a letter as "written in blood."

The poem's first line is typical of developed sprung rhythm, and is especially interesting for grammetrical analysis because it shows the complete

nonconvergence of grammatical and rhythmical breaks. In this notation, let
the asterisk (*) mark a break in syntax and the slash (/) a break between
separate measures (we can no longer say "feet" with such a line). I scan in
the falling rhythm Hopkins's later theoretical statements ·called for, and
below the line I number the syllables.

Measure #: 1   2   3   4   5   6
       Nót,* I'll / not,* cărriŏn / cómfort,* Dĕs / páir,* nŏt / féast ŏn / thee
Syllables: 1   2   3   4 5 6   7   8   9   10   11   12 13   14

None of the measure breaks corresponds with a syntactic segment, so the
line falters from one kind of division to another, alternately, sound and sense
never coinciding; so nearly every syllable (9 of 14) is isolated and therefore
emphasized. It is the pauses themselves that betray the line's anxiety. However, the internal relationships between the words are as disrupted as the
pauses created by grammar and prosody partitioning each other. Not till the
last word of the line is "Despair" known to be a noun, rather than a verb
modified by the initial "Not"—so that the withholding of meaning by hyperbaton appears to yield a semantic incoherence. Incoherence of the meaning
is morphologically parallel to discontinuity in the form of arrangement. Hopkins throws the reader into the midst of his discourse, but without familiar
sound patterns or single meanings. The reality breakdown of conversion is
shown with materials at hand—words, their stresses, the pauses between
their larger grammatical groupings, and the arabesque of meaning they
make.

One figure of grammar is the four instances of "not," three with hammered
stresses, in the first eleven words. This "overs" and "afters" the main theme
of negative affirmation, the struggle to accept God's authority and thus
snatch victory from defeat. The many breaks in line and sentence, so evident
at the start, by these and other means begin to be overridden by figures of
continuity. Where the first line had four major breaks of syntax, the second
has only two that surround the dash construction; where the first line had
emphatic ending, the second carries its measure on to the first two syllables
of the third—syllables Hopkins considered "outriders," outside the prosody
(as if they could be; he meant they were to be given little phonetic or
semantic emphasis).

Measure #:

       1   2   3   4   5   6
    Nót ŭn / twíst /* — slăck thĕy măy bĕ* — thĕse / lást / stŕands ŏf / man
              1   2   3   4   5   6
    Iň mĕ /* ór,* mŏst / wéar/y, /* cŕy I / cań nŏ / móre.* I / căn;
            1   2   3   4   5   6
    Căn / sómethiňg, /* hópe, /* wísh dăy cŏme, /* nót choŏse / nót tŏ / bé.

I have avoided the term *foot,* because sprung rhythm proper uses measures composed of varying numbers of syllables, from as few as one stressed syllable ("-twist") to as many as five ("slack they may be—these" has one stressed and four unstressed syllables). My scansion uses stress to emphasize emphasis wherever possible, as in the two-stress clusters ("hope, wish"), the rove-over scansion of lines 2 and 3 (lines that pick up unstressed syllables to attach to their line-end stresses), and the foregrounding of a pattern in:

    strands/man (rhyme)
    or/more (rhyme)
    can/can (repetition)
    not/not (repetition)

When measures cut with or against clumps of grammar, the line strains the reader's tolerance for cohesion, producing a search for relations, and thus eventfulness, intensity.

Grammetrics notices effects invisible to ordinary scansion, such as the peculiar ending of the first sentence of the poem, which falls in the middle of a falling measure: "more.* I . . .." The snatch of speech that the poem quotes, *I can no more,* is by these means, though the ending of a sentence, open prosodically on both ends, one syllable in each of the bracketing measures. By this we see the cry is not a final cry. Its use of an auxiliary verb with no main verb and object is immediately, in the next sentence, shown to be incomplete, when possible actions and objects are brought in. That constitutes a negative definition of despair as self-regarding, lacking objects. Such a reading is inseparable from the grammetrical noticing in which it originates.

The vocation of poet was always, in Hopkins, opposed in some degree to the vocation of the priest, and unquestionably this poem struggles against a self-indulgence that is, for this poet, related to artistic creation.[30] But for Hopkins from the start there is no hesitation about Christ as the true object of his poetry, the one authority whose mastery he resists or celebrates. The resistance is no place more violently self-destructive than the scene of conversion that the octave of this sonnet reimagines. The return to that scene in the last lines certainly admits that the religious life is wrestled for every day, but verb tense, syntax, measure, and tone, as well as overt statement ("*now done* darkness"), all situate the conversion struggle in the past.

The previous thirteen lines have been broken with twisting, wrestling, toiling, threshing, questioning. But the last line, where the poet twice specifies the identity of his divine antagonist, is physically broken once only, by the exclamation that is also an address. The doubled phrase shows him able to treat God as both internal to himself and an objective force in the world. Finally, explosively, he admits that God is his God, God's strength his

strength. He has had to get to that point by working through the previous
lines' debate on the meaning of God's victory over him in his night-year of
conversion. After the unbunched measures and noncaesural stringing of
words that open line 14, the exclamation leaps out from the rhythms of
descriptive drone, a final flash the more vivid because of its background,
"like shining from shook foil." As the word "God" twice receives the
strongest stresses in the poem, Hopkins not only identifies his antagonist but
also a singular relation to His authority.

To my mind Hopkins's major follower in sprung rhythm is John Berryman, who also combines heavy lurching stress with distortions of normal
grammar and syntax. Berryman's intent is the same: to rearrange words to
produce in the reader the flash of feeling, to convey to the reader the speaker's state of agitation. *Homage to Mistress Bradstreet* (1956), a fairly long
poem that is Berryman's first important work, uses Hopkins's methods and
measures to enter the mind of a Christian believer and poet. A connected
series of later books takes Hopkins's measures but apply them to a nonreligious subject matter, sometimes political, academic, erotic, even chatty, as
in lines on his former student:

> I think of the junior: once my advanced élève,
> sweetnatured, slack a little, never perhaps to make,
> in my opinion then, it.[31]

It is possible to trace the history of the measure by comparing with "Carrion
Comfort" Berryman's decidedly more colloquial (and mainly comic) meditation on untwisting the last strands of man:

> Anarchic Henry thought of laying hands
> on Henry: Haw! but the blood & the disgrace,
> no, no, that's out.
> They cut off, in Attic law, that hand from the body
> and burying it elsewhere. That I understands,
> but the destruction of the face
>
> quickly is what leaves this avenue unused
> and I have never discussed with anyone amused
> this, which has filled out many conversaziones
> on several continents: relevant experts
> say the wounds to the survivors is
>
> the worst of the Act, the worst of the Act! Sit still,
> maybe the goblins will go away, leaving you free,
> your breath coming normally,
> all quarrels made up, say it took twenty letters
> some to his inferiors, two to his betters
> so-called, pal.

The reading of Hopkins has already given most of the terms we need to analyze the sounds and the comic disjunctions of grammar in Berryman's *Dream Songs.* Because he was employing a kind of construction already in existence, Berryman's figures of sound and grammar are rather predictable. Comparison with "Carrion Comfort" may suggest an affinity between sprung rhythm and the more violent human emotions, but energetic thinking and (especially in Berryman) wit are within the likely range of this medium. Sprung rhythm is adaptable to joy and awe and praise as well as to self-loathing. Hopkins's hope for a personal language of belief, the religious basis of sprung rhythm, has disappeared; the legacy is a freestanding method, capable of several uses. Not many have, since 1930 when Hopkins came to be known more widely, taken up the legacy; by then, free verse was already established as the most versatile insurgent style.

Hopkins, Bridges, and the Internal Construction of the Line

"In a sense," according to a recent anthology presentation, Hopkins is a twentieth-century poet "born out of his time who had to wait until the present century for posthumous appreciation and influence."[32] Such an account moves Hopkins from the crisis of versification of his moment, and is thus unhistorical. I prefer the judgment of Robert Bridges, which comes from within the crisis and expresses the reservations of a reigning prosody. Bridges especially dislikes the metrical licence, the density of the rhyme, the notations for performance in Hopkins's scansion. Bridges's expressions of pique, distaste, and condescension recognize something crucial about Hopkins's relation to the normative prosody; and his cautious delay in publishing Hopkins's manuscripts is, stylistically if not morally, entirely appropriate, for Hopkins's Modernity, like Blake's Romanticism, forces a redefinition of the historical period both in concept and in chronology.

Bridges too shares the moment of nascent Modernity, and he is hardly the Classical poet of hard-edged forms who has visited the imagination of Yvor Winters, Albert J. Guérard, John Sparrow, and Donald E. Stanford. Neither is he in his prosodic writings merely the expositor of the normative science of verse. His poetry and theory move across the whole spectrum of possibility from quantity counting to a quasi-randomized stressing. That he occupies at one time or another every space on the table of forms except free verse, that he is at once attracted and repelled by Hopkins's daring in prosody, all this makes his career in itself an expression of this period's crisis of paradigms. In his penetration as in his folly he is a writer centrally characteristic.

Bridges in the 1870s imitated Hopkins in the use of a "mitigated" (Hopkins) sprung rhythm, and in the collection of his shorter poems he was to include two of his experiments in the section (Book 2) dedicated "To the

Memory of GMH." Here are the first stanzas of "A Passer-By" and "The Downs":

> Whither, O splendid ship, thy white sails crowding,
>   Leaning across the bosom of the urgent West,
> That fearest not sea rising, nor sky clouding,
>   Whither away, fair rover, and what thy quest?
>   Ah! soon, when Winter has all our vales opprest,
> When skies are cold and misty, and hail is hurling,
>   Wilt thóu glíde on the blue Pacific, or rest
> In a summer haven asleep, thy white sails furling.

*   *   *

> O bold majestic downs, smooth, fair, and lonely;
> O still solitude, only matched in the skies:
>   Perilous in steep places,
>   Soft in the level races,
> Where sweeping in phantom silence the cloudland flies;
> With lovely undulation of fall and rise;
>   Entrenched with thickets thorned,
> By delicate miniature dainty flowers adorned![33]

Here, as in "London Snow," the rhythm is unpredictable, with interchange of iambs with anapests, preserving a fixed number of stresses in each line. This is precisely what Hopkins called "mixed rhythms," and as both Hopkins and Bridges knew, the major precedent in their century was "Christabel." The lines are animated by stress, and this style is opposed by and large to the kind of counted rhythm Hopkins saw as the Neo-Classical mode of the previous century.[34] The five-stress line is here the norm; Bridges engages in the stress marking he condemned in Hopkins—drawing attention to the obsolete personal pronoun "thou," which might have had its emphasis muffled without extra pointing. These are by comparison with Hopkins very pallid experiments.

In 1913 Bridges wrote unrhymed syllabic verse of the sort his daughter, Elizabeth Daryush, was to imitate and Marianne Moore to perfect in the next generation of writers. "Noel: Christmas Eve, 1913," counts out six syllables per line, indenting every other line for visual effect but with no metrical aim whatever beyond the suggestion of a brokenness of movement:

> A frosty Christmas Eve
>   when the stars were shining
> Fared I forth alone
>   where westward falls the hill
> And from many a village
>   in the water'd valley
> Distant music reach'd me
>   peals of bells aringing:
> The constellated sounds

ran sprinkling on earth's floor
As the dark vault above
with stars was spangled o'er.[35]

This is the first of four twelve-line stanzas. It is counted out in syllabics, except for line 3, which is short one syllable—perhaps made up by giving "fared" an extra syllable as a fiction; it is not spelled with an apostrophe for elision or suppression of the "-ed" as in "water'd"; and except for line 7, which is long one syllable. The daring new technique of syllabics is itself undercut by devices from another prosodic-poetic mode: "many a," the famous phrase from eighteenth-century poetry designed to ram three syllables into two for a fictional elision; "aringing," an extra ornamental syllable of the prefix, a poeticism that ekes out the line by a syllable; and finally, the piece of archaic diction that conflates the two syllables of "over" to "o'er." Bridges has got his syllable count, but not thereby naturalness of utterance.

More natural yet in diction and movement are the poems in "Neo-Miltonic Syllabics," which Bridges thought capable of offering "their true desideratum to the advocates of Free Verse" (preface to *New Poems,* 1925). Here are two examples:

Mid the squander'd colour
idling as I lay
Reading the Odyssey
in my rock-garden
I espied the cluster'd
tufts of Cheddar pinks
Burgeoning with promise
of their scented bloom
All the modish motley
of their bloom-to-be.

* * *

A blazing afternoon in splendor of mid-July
Kate and my elder sister and I trudged down the street
Past village and pond and church, and up the winding lane
came out beside the windmill on the high cornland
where my new world began.[36]

The lines are either six or twelve syllables long, with elisions making the count come right: as in "splendor of" in the second passage, which preserves the count when read "splen-druv." (Yet in a format so like prose, who would think to elide, or even count syllables?) Bridges called his book of Neo-Miltonic poems *New Verse,* meaning to assert that the work there was a contribution to the free-verse movement. In the 1925 preface to this book, Bridges apologizes for a "distracting variety" of moods and measures:

He has . . . grouped his incongruities into four sections, so as to avoid mixing different versifications. This arrangement is in a backward order of time: Part I is in the writer's latest manner and still peculiar to himself: it may be styled *Neo-Miltonic syllabics.* . . . It pretends to offer their true desideratum to the advocates of Free Verse. The poems in Part II are in Accentual measures: the reproaches against this manner having been launched fifty years ago may be considered obsolete; Part III is all in recognizable old styles; and Part IV is of the most ancient facture, in William Stone's (somewhat amended) quantitative prosody: this is still in full taboo, but the hitherto unpublished specimens here included are of the date of the writer's earlier delinquencies.

The book is a conspectus of what Bridges thought possible in the 1920s. The poems represent nearly every possible method of constituting the line (except Whitmanesque free verse). With the Neo-Miltonic syllabics that are the prominent part of this volume, Bridges clearly thought he was rescuing free verse from the imputation of being formless.

With these intentions, *New Poems* is a further elaboration of cogent principles Bridges had formulated slightly earlier in "Humdrum and Harum-Scarum: A Lecture on Free Verse."[37] By this time, after World War I, Bridges was aware of French vers libre, and quotes R. W. Flint on rhyme and meter as "artificial and external additions to Poetry," now proposing to go still further and define a "positive quality" for free verse "bi which it will be distinguishable from prose" (Bridges's spelling). He aligns himself with Flint's search for poetic beauty in speech rhythms, for he had himself written on that subject in *Milton's Prosody;* and he cites Dujardin on the validity of the prose poem but on its separation from free verse as a technique—adding that Hebrew parallelism is not free verse either, nor is "irregular accentual verse" on the English model. A line of free verse is a "grammatical unit or unity," it may be of various length, it has no syllable counting as theoretical matrix, and it lacks all other "metrical obligations" such as caesura and hiatus. The free-verse line "is made up of short sections or lines which are in themselves accentual and grammatical unities," and somehow (he is not clear) this is its differentiating distinction from ordinary prose and from the prose poem.

The constitution of the line, however variously, however randomly, with every line different in itself, is taken as the crucial factor and positive definition of verse. Bridges writes, in his own cranky phonetic spelling:

However irregular the lines be, they are conscious of their length; they pose with a sort of independence and self-sufficiency: and where the verse is most successful its cadences provoke too much of the expectancy of verse to appear so wholly free from restreint as the best prose can: and it is right enough to call it verse rather than prose. And if it is quite satisfactory—as in short poems it very well may be—it is so bi virtue of the poet's sensibility to rhythmical form, and bi his mastery of it; and he will so combine his rhythms that they do create expectancy as they proceed: indeed I do not doubt that a free-verse poet would regard the pleasure which accompanies this satisfi'd expectancy, as a note of his success.

Now in so far as this free verse (or cadenced prose) actually creates this expectancy, its rhythms can no doubt be analiz'd and reduced to rule.

Again, and splendidly:

Free verse is good and theoretically defensible only in so far as it can create expectancy without the old metrical devices.

Expectancy is thus "the force which will hold . . . free verse together," as I, too, would argue. Bridges perhaps exaggerates the difficulties that attend the rejection of metrical systems ("loss of carrying power, self-consciousness; sameness of line structure; indetermination of subsidiary 'accent'"; later Yvor Winters had similar complaints), but Bridges rightly says that one difficulty of writing good free verse "of any kind is to escape from the tyranny of recurrent speech-forms, and the restriction imposed bi the rules of free verse must make that difficulty immeasurably greater." To avoid monotony free verse will have to give language perceptibility, to force "the hidden possibilities of speech" into a kind of measure, and to develop a "more exacting" diction than the diction of metrical verse (and here Bridges sounds like William Carlos Williams). The essay ends by affirming that there remains a "wide field for exploration in the metrical prosody," by proposing Neo-Miltonic syllabics as one workable restriction upon the freedom of free verse, and by welcoming the new subversive influences: "I have miself made so meny experiments that I cannot be suspected of wishing to discourag others. No art can flourish that is not alive and growing, and it can only grow bi invention of new methods or bi discovery of new material."

That Bridges tried everything, even quantitative poems "of the most ancient facture," is one index of crisis. "Now in wintry delights" dates from 1903:

> Now in wintry delights, and long fireside meditation
> 'Twixt studies and routine paying due court to the Muses,
> My solace in solitude, when broken roads barricade me
> Mudbound, unvisited for months with my merry children
> Grateful t'ward Providence, and heeding a slander against me
> Less than a rheum, think of me to-day, dear Lionel, and take
> This letter as some account of Will Stone's versification.[38]

That is very limber and winning, but happens to be the best single passage from sixty-four numbing pages in this revived quantitative measure contained in the *Collected Poems* (1953). Bridges seems to have perceived that this way of writing might be valid—as valid as Hopkins's way—to make a revision of the normative versification. But by the 1920s he was promoting his syllabics and the *Testament of Beauty* line as a happier and more daring construction upon the line. In *Milton's Prosody,* he had already noticed that "our classical verse is a hybrid, and cannot be explained exclusively by English or by classical rule; nor is much light thrown on it by straining the analogy of Greek and Latin quantitative feet."[39] And in that book, designed as he said "to provide a sound foundation for a grammar of English prosody, on the basis of Milton's practice," and "to combat the common opinion that there is no such thing as English prosody," Bridges had already perceived how in *Samson Agonistes* "every line may have a different rhythm," so that "if the stressed rhythm is the beauty of the verse, it is a sufficient account of it." When the laws of English stressed verse are recognized, he says amazingly, they will "explain all those irregularities of well-written free verse, to which metrists are now at pains to match the names of Greek quantitative feet, though these have no natural relation to them. . . . I will only add that when English poets will write verse governed honestly by natural speech-stress, they will discover the laws for themselves and will find open to them an infinite field of rhythm as yet untouched. There is nothing which may not be done in it, and it is perhaps not the least of its advantages that it makes excellence difficult." That passage is dated 1910, and utterly explodes all claims for Bridges as the one true Classicist of poetry since Tennyson; it is the most intelligent statement about free verse before the coming of Ezra Pound, and it is utterly at odds with the contemporary norms.

The fascinating thing about Bridges is that he should at once confirm those norms (in most of his poetry, in his treatment of Hopkins), and serve to contradict those norms—within the same year, usually, and even within the same book. Bridges worked to this position from knowing the practice of Milton and Hopkins, and from looking directly *away from* the current paradigms at the same time that he was able to show how Milton's blank verse is truly regular despite the seeming irregularities. His book began as a list of prosodic examples for an edition of Milton, and grew into a study that relies on the examples, thus in its monographic power making an important contribution to the reigning theory. But even within Milton, Bridges found anomalies, and in attempting to subsume these he was led a step beyond the ordinary. Bridges was made laureate for his reassuring scholarship and presumed regularity; yet there was something disturbing, and valuable, at work that undermined his ability to carry on the laureate tradition. This something led him into sympathy with formal innovation of a rather drastic sort, led him to tamper with both rhyme and meter in ways that would have been unsettling if anyone were to compare his performances with Tennyson's. *The Testament of Beauty* gets on tiptoe to be a poem of laureate pronouncement, but the discursive content is opposed by the technical invention in the line, its stubborn resistance to convention and euphony, and even by its resistance to the conventions of spelling. Where Tennyson knew perfectly well how he felt about such things, this particular laureate was deeply uncertain, up to the end of his life, what good poetry was, and he died still testing schemas of construction.

Bridges, then, is a faint innovator, driven to experiments from which he had to withdraw through hesitation. His fear and jealousy of Hopkins, and his friendship, manifest the divisions in a human and literary way. He is not the scourge of Modernism, but a nervous pre-Modern intelligence, experimenting along paths that were many of them bound to be unique. The poetry is admirable, the schemes are possible, yet Bridges does not break through to a new way of writing. He tried everything; and he succeeded fully at little. This is the explanation in history and theory of W. B. Yeats's famous motto on Bridges: "Every metaphor, every thought a commonplace; emptiness everywhere, the whole magnificent."

"Extremes Meet": The Relationship of Sprung Rhythm to Free Verse

Hopkins and Whitman are contemporaries. They are the major prosodic innovators of the second half of the nineteenth century. Each in his way responds to the crisis of versification, remaking poetry closer to a personal rhythm and an idea of speech. And we have explicit testimony that one knew the other's work and registered a profound affinity. A substantial Whitman selection was published in England by William Michael Rossetti in 1868, and there were periodical publications and reviews. In his own words, Hopkins by 1882 had seen "half a dozen pieces at most" by the American poet; yet he had seen enough of Whitman's work, he said, "to . . . influence another [poet's] style." Bridges having called Hopkins's "Leaden Echo" an imitation of Whitman, Hopkins responded (18 October 1882) by denying conscious appropriation.

Though long and defensive, the letter is a major document in my story. Here are its major parts:

> The question then [of influence] is only about the fact. But first I may as well say what I should not otherwise have said, that I always knew in my heart Walt Whitman's mind to be more like my own than any other man's living. As he is a very great scoundrel this is not a pleasant confession. And this also makes me the more desirous to read him and the more determined that I will not.
>
> Nevertheless I believe that you are quite mistaken about this piece ["The Leaden Echo"] and that on second thoughts you will find the fancied resemblance diminish and the imitation disappear.
>
> And first of the rhythm. Of course I saw that there was to the eye something in my long lines like this, that the one would remind people of the other. And both are in irregular rhythms. There the resemblance ends. The pieces of his read were mostly in an irregular rhythmic prose: that is what they are thought to be meant for and what they seemed to me to be. . . . In a matter like this [sprung rhythm] a thing does not exist, it is not *done* unless it is wittily and willingly done; to recognise the form you are employing and to mean it is everything. To apply this: there is . . . no sign that Whitman means to use paeons or outriding feet where these breaks in rhythm occur; it seems to me a mere extravagance to think he means people to understand of themselves what they are slow to understand even when marked or pointed out. If he does not mean it then he does not do it; or in short what he means to write—and writes—is rhythmic prose and that only. . . .

Extremes meet, and (I must for truth's sake say what sounds pride) this savagery of his art, this rhythm in its last ruggedness and decomposition into common prose, comes near the last elaboration of mine. For ["The Leaden Echo"] is very highly wrought. The long lines are not rhythm run to seed: everything is weighed and timed in them. Wait till they have taken hold of your ear and you will find it so. No, but what it *is* like is the rhythm of Greek tragic choruses or of Pindar: which is pure sprung rhythm. And that has the same changes of cadence from point to point as this piece. If you want to try it, read one till you have settled the true places of the stress, mark these, then read it aloud, and you will see. Without this these choruses are prose bewitched; with it they are sprung rhythm like that piece of mine.

Besides, why did you not say *Binsey Poplars* was like Whitman? The present piece is in the same kind and vein, but developed, an advance.[40]

Returning to his interest in the dramatically justified voice, Hopkins also denies influence by stating that "The Leaden Echo" is "not even spoken in my own person but in that of St. Winefred's maidens," but he does not deny all resemblance. The similarities include an avoidance of formal meter and rhyme traditionally defined, a "preference for the alexandrine" or at any rate for the long line, and actual speech stress or something simulating that. Most pertinent here is his statement that "extremes meet, and . . . this savagery of [Whitman's] art, this rhythm in its last ruggedness and decomposition . . . comes near the last elaboration of mine." Denying influence, he cannot deny affiliation. What he has seen but not fully stated—because of the limits of his terminology—is that with a more vigorous push his disruption of the normative accentual-syllabic line will fall over into free verse, where syntactic measures are the prosody. He agrees with Whitman that such a poetry is rather wild, he is forced to diminish Whitman's poems by assimilating them to rhythmic prose (like later misguided opponents of free verse), but he does not deny that Whitman makes a kind of art.

Avoiding one sort of rhetorical and rhythmic artifice meant, for both writers, creating another sort, or two related sorts, as the following comparison will show.

In the dooryard fronting an old farm-house, near the white-washed palings.
Stands the lilac bush, tall-growing, with heart-shaped leaves of rich green.
With many a pointed blossom, rising delicate, with the perfume strong I love,
With every leaf a miracle: and from this bush in the door-yard.
With delicate-colored blossoms, and heart-shaped leaves of rich green,
A sprig, with its flower, I break.[41]
                    ("When Lilacs Last in the Dooryard Bloom'd," 1865)

                         *   *   *

Come then, your ways and airs and looks, locks, maiden gear, gallantry and gaiety and grace,
Winning ways, airs innocent, maiden manners, sweet-looks, loose locks, long locks, lovelocks, gaygear, going gallant, girlgrace—

Resign them, sign them, seal them, send them, motion them with breath,
And with sighs soaring, soaring sighs, deliver
Them; beauty-in-the-ghost, deliver it, early now, long before death
Give beauty back, beauty, beauty, beauty, back to God, beauty's self and
    beauty's giver.[42]
             ("The Leaden Echo and the Golden Echo," 1882)

Let me point to the elements here that make Hopkins's "last elaboration" similar to Whitman's "last . . . decomposition into . . . prose." In both passages the verbs are deferred, held back by a form of left-branching sentence. Both have the habit of line-opening anaphora; listing of attributes to make many lines into catalogs; word splicing for effects of compression ("heart-shaped"; "gaygear"); paratactic stringing; inversion of syntax ("perfume strong"; "airs innocent"); and repetition of words and part lines, sometimes at line-end position ("rich green"; "grace"). Both these texts are highly worked with sound echo and refrains of syntax, and the returns of sound reinforce the main ideas of each poem.

Hopkins's lines are more steeped with the permutation of rhymelike equivalences, while those of Whitman have greater syntactical clarity and simplicity; the Whitman lines in fact break down into three syntactical lobes, each line with three parts roughly equal in length. Hopkins's syntax has far more abruptly the effect of juncture, the result, I think, of his turn-counterturn, load-every-rift conception of the poem—the saturation of the poetic line—which he mentions in his letter to Bridges as the quality that separates his work from Whitman's. "The Leaden Echo," he wrote, "is very highly wrought. The long lines are not rhythm run to seed: everything is weighted and timed in them. Wait till they have taken hold of your ear and you will find it so." And it is so. The lines are unpredictable. For instance, after a few similar lines of the first (Whitman) passage, one can begin to suspect the three-part division, but in the middle of Hopkins's final line the three-times-repeated "beauty" is striking. That sort of overing and aftering of the "instress" is never (or rarely) done elsewhere in English poetry, and its very excess is remarkable, perceptible—the more so because the line contains the same word three more times! The principle of emphasis is taken to another power in Hopkins, creating a texture of dense equivalence, a piling on of sound and a sense that works both forward and backward at once.

"The Leaden Echo," Hopkins writes in his letter, "is in the same kind and vein" as his poem "Binsey Poplars," "but developed, an advance." Let the reader compare three Victorian poems on trees: Whitman on lilacs (above), Hopkins on "Binsey Poplars," and Tennyson on yew trees in the second poem of *In Memoriam* (quoted in full in the previous chapter). The result of this comparison may well be a conviction that Hopkins and Whitman each pursue the defamiliarizing power of speech stress, but in different directions—each of them on a different side of the Tennysonian norm, one seeking diffusion of sense, the other saturation of sense. Curiously this speech-stress position on the table of prosodic possibilities can itself be divided in this way, so that *either side* of the range may be used to unsettle the rhythmical habits of the middle-range poetry.[43]

Urging poetry toward speech stressing, both poets encourage (in their different ways) a greater randomness of stress, an unpredictability of measure in the poem's rhythms. Yet both carve out a certain shape, Whitman's much weakened by comparison with traditional patterning. Both emphasize, Hopkins perhaps more so, an irregularity of segment size in the poem, irregularity of basic syntactic units, of equivalences that seem more scattered than regular. In both poets, grammar plays an obtrusive role, and tends to usurp versification, especially in the larger-than-the-line divisions of the poem. In both poets, the secondary features, especially those related to grammar and syntax, are raised in the hierarchy of importance. This creates the effect of a higher degree of attention in the reader, as the effects of crescendo, resolution, and the like are more tightly packed than in ordinary poetry (Hopkins), or much more loosely strung (Whitman). The spaces between expected elements are either more or less densely full, and *either* effect produces perceptibility in the text's form and meaning, by comparison with the Tennysonian norm. Yuri Tynjanov's phrase from Russian Formalism, "the crowdedness of the poetic line," applies positively to Hopkins, negatively to Whitman.

The more traditional poetry, with its greater number of unstressed syllables, left unfilled positions in the line, spaces between the expected prominences, between lines, rhymes, and caesuras. But the experimental poetry of form as proceeding seems to hate gaps in the reader's response. Rather than have spaces, this poetry arranges different densities of material, different rates of apperception. Repetition of sound features in Hopkins, of sense features of syntax in Whitman, structures this poetry; other poetry employs these devices, but not with such determination or intensity. In Hopkins, the number of verbal systems, the variety of the "oftening, over-and-overing, aftering of the inscape" is extremely in excess of the systems in the Tennysonian norm: syntactic systems, metrical systems, generic systems, sound-equivalence systems both extensive and short-term, part-whole relationships of extreme complexity, and so on. In Whitman, by contrast, the system of parallelism of syntax is basic, and infinitely changeable; this is clearly systematic enough for the creation of strong poetry, but less systematic than any poetry in the English tradition before its own arrival, with perhaps the exception of Macpherson's *Ossian* and other such sports and disasters.[44]

The structure of the work of verbal art, according to Jan M. Meijer, "is found to consist in the interference between a cognitive and an aesthetic structure"; and structural principles are "dynamic forces," their interference making the work cohere, propelling the work onward and taking the reader along. Cognitive structural principles can operate without the interference of aesthetic principles, but the reverse is impossible; this is why the seeming lack of interference of aesthetic principles with the dominating cognitive ones in Whitman has made his free verse subject to such grand traditional disdain. Certainly grammar, syntax, and syntactic measure had never before in the history of English poetry come so fully to acceptance within the art. The way was open, afterward, for a modification of Whitman's structures— for a new introduction of style and the aesthetic principle, but within, now, the free-verse medium that he had invented. Eventually, with Pound, Eliot, and Williams, this was to be the route that prosodic avantgardism explored after 1910, in the refinement of the free-verse line. It was a less central, less influential group of Modernists, including most notably Dylan Thomas and John Berryman, which elected to follow Hopkins in emphasizing above all else hyperbaton, heavy stress, and the repetition of sound features in the verse period.

5
The Prosodies of Free Verse

"How Beautiful Is Candor!"

Sprung rhythm and the prose poem are minority techniques in the English-speaking world, the former an astonishing and original minority of one. But free verse, in the century since *Leaves of Grass,* has become the major alternative mode of writing. Though in the understanding and the practice of poets, free verse has had full parity with metered verse since the seedtimes of T. S. Eliot and Wallace Stevens, scholars have been reluctant to talk about it, reluctant even to put chapters on the subject into introductory handbooks on poetic form.[1] If there was a reaction against free verse with Auden and others in the 1930s and 1940s, there was between the 1950s and the mid-1970s an almost overwhelming reaction to the reaction, which may be viewed either as a resurgence of the avant-garde prosodic impulse or as yet another vigorous renewal of the ancient, though undervalued, tradition of English accentualism. Poetry since the early 1970s has been undergoing yet another permutation. On one side of free verse, there has been a return to the track of rhyme and meter; on the other side, experimentation with the prose poem and new types of prose. This opening into a wider pluralism of styles has occurred largely for the reason given by Robert Hass in 1978: "Free verse has lost its edge, become neutral, the given instrument. . . . Once [it] has become neutral, there must be an enormous impulse to use it . . . to establish tone rather than to make form."[2] Poets have had a tendency to specialize in one subtype of free verse, thus to neglect the instrument's range of possibilities; thus also to bring to the foreground endemic weaknesses of free verse, notably the way it can favor bombast in long lines or trivial flatness in short lines. Energetic free verse is still being written in English, and doubtless a various and therefore strong free verse will once again make form, though never perhaps on the scale of the early Moderns. Meanwhile, the cross-lights of the present moment make it apt for a discussion of the instrument's capabilities, its candor.

The association of candor with free-verse prosody I have already traced back to the gigantic lineage of Coleridge and his idea of form as proceeding. In place of rhyme and the inherited construction with strophes, the first-generation Romantics established an inner rhythm, a language within language, an idea of a poetry that could subsist without the mediation of devices. What those manifestos propose is, I have insisted, an impossibility; but no matter, because practice has been deflected in the direction of the impossible. Wordsworth's contemporaries, but not Wordsworth himself, felt blank verse inappropriate for the treatment of working people; what bothered the Whig leader Charles James Fox about "Michael," as Robert Hass has said, is that the poem "democratized the imagination of spiritual order inside meter. That's why it's a short leap from Wordsworth to Whitman—one of the reasons why. It is why free verse appears as part of a consciously democratic poetic program."[3] And not only democratic; open-form poetry, as it emerges in the theory of Coleridge and his American heir Emerson, and in the practice of Whitman, expressed a fairly coherent, larger set of epistemological, cosmological, and metaphysical assumptions.[4] In America, those assumptions came out of an era of growing discomfort, so that, as Edwin Fussell has explained at some length, "nearly every ambitious American poem before 1855 reveals . . . unease in relation to the traditional techniques, and especially the traditional metric, of English poetry."[5] The line back to Coleridge and ahead to Whitman is evident in Emerson's epoch-making phrase from "The Poet" (1844): "It is not metres, but a metre-making argument that makes a poem." With that phrase, which defined the technical issues as the logical, ethical, and national issues, the scene of exploratory form making shifted from England to the North American continent.

For their own purposes, some American poets of the twentieth century deemphasized the metaphysics and politics of open form, but any approach to free verse must return, if only briefly, to the historical and cultural origins of American poetic technique. Walt Whitman was himself moved to flaunt the theoretical side of his achievement, in documents like his long letter to Emerson of August 1856—and especially the 1855 preface to *Leaves of Grass,* from which sentences that bring into a single aesthetics of candor the metrical and cultural issues of American poetry:

> The great poets are also to be known by the absence in them of tricks and by the justification of perfect personal candor. Then folks echo a new cheap joy and a divine voice leaping from their brains: How beautiful is candor! All faults may be forgiven of him who has perfect candor.[6]

For Whitman, "cheap" is a term of approbation; love of the truth is a free commodity in the States, not the privilege of one class. How beautiful is this large-spirited, democratic candor, how magnificent:

> I understand the large hearts of heroes,
> The courage of present times and all times,
> How the skipper saw the crowded and rudderless wreck of the steam-ship,
>   and Death chasing it up and down the storm,

How he knuckled tight and gave not back an inch, and was faithful of days
   and faithful of nights,
And chalk'd in large letters, on a board, *Be of good cheer, We will not
   desert you;*
How he follow'd with them, and tack'd with them—and would not give it
   up,
How he saved the drifting company at last,
How the lank loose-gown'd women looked when boated from the side of
   their prepared graves,
How the silent old-faced infants and the lifted sick, and the sharp-lipp'd
   unshaven men,
All this I swallow, it tastes good, I like it well, it becomes mine,
I am the man, I suffer'd, I was there.[7]

Whitman's subject is the common man and woman, his time the immediate present. He promises the reader that a journey is in prospect, but in the course of the journey no familiar signs are given, the reader has no "tricks," no cherished resources. So in this poem that will be a journey or transaction, the reader will be taken in, taken out of self, must loaf at ease. The poet depends on some powerful sources of affective power to sustain that; not only the sentiments of democracy, but wavelike surges of rhythm to carry poet and reader from the enumerative to the erotic to the meditative modes of the mind.

The assumption, of course, is that all traditional verse by accepting a formal, prescribed rhythm, accepts at least partial anonymity. The poet who chooses to write formally, who wants the "ring of authority," is abandoning some identity to an abstract conception of the poem. Writers of free verse are committed to a project of self-exploration or, less often, perfect candor of self-exposure, which makes its own demands on their language but which implies a more open, visionary, generous life.

Though I do not share this assumption, it has been my role as historian to show how it evolved as a means of self-justification for writers who wish to remove some prosodic obstacles from between themselves and the fulfillment of the laws of a design. Paul Fussell is everlastingly right when he says that " 'freedom' is not a virtue in meter—expressiveness is," and yet the idea of freedom is no embarrassment to the student of innovative prosodies. For the writer who is, in Hass's words, "making form," there is no need to oppose freedom to expressiveness. It is the task of the reader to make decisions about when a writer's forms and words are expressive, and it is true that readers of free verse have been unable to arrive at precise standards of judgment. This is because we have lacked a detailed understanding of how free verse (or any verse!) works with and against the structure of the English language, how free verse arouses and resolves the energies of attention. The present chapter, in conjunction with other recent studies, has tried to address the issue of method and its implications for judgment.[8] But beauty of candor is the prior issue, and requires that the critic remember, through scholarship, how the writer understands the contradiction of free verse.

This is how: There are indeed times when freedom as a moral category must be conceived as willing bondage, but there are other times when freedom will hardly seem itself if it must be defined solely as the negation of order and limit. Such times of choice, maximum uncertainty, and likely autonomy (prosodic as well as ethical) will be the explicit moments of the avant-garde, and eventually these moments will tend to anticipate tradition.

Free verse insists on at least an aura of candor, at least a myth of dangerous autonomy, poetic anarchy. Its ability to make form has been both enhanced and misunderstood by virtue of paradoxical associations of the term itself, and of related terms like *organic form, open form,* and *form as proceeding.* (Would there have been any achievement, any quarrels, if the denomination *nonmetrical poetry* had been the one that took hold at the origins of the mode?) Free verse is not virtue. It is a literary mode of the nineteenth and twentieth centuries, neither good nor evil, but decidedly possible, probable given the Romantic premises, and after the fact, necessary.

Renato Poggioli has pointed out that Modern art is often attacked for "denying those cultural ideals it never intended to serve," and its condemnation "*en bloc* by way of the concept of *degeneration*" is mere "pathological prejudice."[9] Graham Hough and J. V. Cunningham have argued that free verse is a detour from the traditional English versification; Yvor Winters has attempted to show its technical, and moral, degeneration. If we merely reverse these positions we are saying the same foolish things. It is, I imagine, dismaying to come to terms with a massive deflection in English versification if it calls into question one's ingrained beliefs about the kingly presence of poetry at the apex of the hierarchy of types, lording it over churlish prose. "Prose chopped up into lines" is the easiest and most frequent reproach, and is based on a misunderstanding of the relationship of prose to poetry, which I discuss at the beginning of the next chapter. The most difficult thing is to confront the literary fact with only the chance rightnesses of one's own unaided sensibility. Some aids do exist, however, and the present chapter intends to bring them forward.

To describe a range of free-verse styles from the most continuous to the most abrupt and dismembered, one must revise one's conception of patterning and deal with units of unfamiliar size and weight. That is the argument as regards technique; the historical story that accompanies the argument shows how Whitman's long and stable lines, waves that lose their energy on the shore, are dismembered from within, shortened, played with and against syntax in different ways to deflect attention. As the line narrows between Whitman and William Carlos Williams, the mouth tightens and the candor of voice is not oratorical but wry, more exact and exacting of discriminations, and yet more intimate with the reader.

Syllable, Word, Line, Sentence, Stanza, Poem

"The music of verse merits more attention than it has been honoured with. It is a subject intimately connected with human nature." Thus Lord Kames in his *Elements of Criticism* (1762). That the music of verse still merits attention, that more than ever we need to relate prosody to human nature is urged in the first lines of Charles Tomlinson's poem "The Chances of Rhyme" (1969):

> The chances of rhyme are like the chances of meeting—
> In the finding fortuitous, but once found, binding:
>
> . . . .
> To take chances, as to make rhymes
> Is human, but between chance and impenitence
> (A half-rhyme) come dance, vigilance
> And circumstance (meaning all that is there
> besides you, when you are there).

With his own poem as elaborate demonstration, Tomlinson proposes extending the category of rhyme to inside-the-line and impaired like sounds. Taking rhyme in its broadest sense, he relates prosody to the history of ideas by reaffirming the Modern tendency to isolate the fortuitous in artistic creation:

>   Yet why should we speak
> Of art, of life, as if the one were all form
>   And the other all Sturm-und-Drang? And I think
> Too, we should confine to Crewe or to Mow
>   Cop, all those who confuse the fortuitousness
> Of art with something to be met with only
>   At extremity's brink, reducing thus
> Rhyme to a kind of rope's end.[10]

Such lines are one measure of how far traditional poetry has modified itself to encompass the methods and prosodies of free verse. But because I have written elsewhere on rhyme I need only gratefully accept Tomlinson's reformulation of Mallarmé's "Toute pensée émet un coup de dés." With Tomlinson, I shall attempt to confine to Crewe or to Mow Cop those who speak as if poetic art were all form, most particularly certain prosodists who (like J. V. Cunningham in the title of his book of poems) disdain the chances for *The Exclusions of a Rhyme* (1960). In this enterprise I am not unaware of supportive definitions from the field of information theory, where unpredictability, or chance, signifies information, meaningfulness in the message.

Most poets before the Romantics, and many since, have required a body of exclusions or limitations that operate before the poem begins. Coleridge called the sum of these exclusions "shape as superinduced" and opposed it with a conception that prefigured the nature of avant-garde writing—form as proceeding. As Jean Rousset has remarked, "The great victory of modern art, or rather of the mode of concern this art has for the creative process," is that "conception and execution are contemporaneous, the image of the work is not anterior to the work."[11] For some works this is quite correct, but most often in Modern literature conception and execution are not literally contemporaneous—though we act as if they are. That is how we speak the discourse of the avant-garde, the discourse of form as proceeding; the works themselves teach us to speak it.

Searching for a private voice within a public language, for what D. H. Lawrence called "direct utterance from the instant, whole man . . . instantaneous like plasm,"[12] Modern poetry becomes an art of invention, not of expression. For the Classical writer, according to Roland Barthes, the poetic "never evokes any particular domain, any particular depth of feeling, any special coherence, or special universe"; but (Barthes exaggerates) Modern poetry "is a quality *sui generis* and without antecedents . . . opposed to classical poetry by a difference which involves the whole structure of language."[13] Insofar as Modern poetry is a French invention and Rimbaud's demand in the "Lettre du voyant"—"Il faut être absolument moderne"—is prototypical, the discoverer of vers libre in France is also (with Whitman) the founder of the literary avant-garde. The lucid violence of this credo, the logic of his abandonment of poetry, testify to a more radical questioning of the fact of literature than that of the first-generation English Romantic writers. Believing with Rimbaud that "les inventions d'inconnu réclament des formes nouvelles," the finest free-verse poets liquidate inherited form so as to emphasize randomness in their prosodies. As they abandon meter and rhyme and often metaphor, meanwhile inventing a variety of self-deflating rhetorical devices, a hatred of poetry—of the category of the aesthetic— comes into the poem itself, and thus the term *free verse* comes to speak of a poetry that defines itself by contradiction, an antipoetry. Thus, too, the contemporaneous and even bolder invention of the poem in prose.

Rimbaud's phrase, "formes nouvelles," obliges us to work through another, more immediately rewarding contradiction. If discoveries of the unknown call for new forms, these will still be aesthetic structures and recognizable as such. If the poem is to be more than asyntactical gibberish, more than the rudimentary configuration of type that is concrete poetry, the freedom must be partial, conditional. This brings us to T. S. Eliot's famous claim that "no verse is *libre* for the man who wants to do a good job" and to his related remark in a little-known article of 1917: "The ghost of some simple metre should lurk behind the arras in even the 'freest' verse; to advance menacingly as we doze, and withdraw as we rouse. Or, freedom is only truly freedom when it appears against a background of an artificial limitation."[14] Of course. Roland Barthes has written similarly that "writing as Freedom is . . . a mere moment" because, though today I can select a certain mode of writing, and in so doing assert my freedom, "it is impossible to develop it within duration without gradually becoming a prisoner of someone else's words and even of my own."[15] Since it is impossible to take a step toward the future without taking a step away from the past, the term *avant-garde,* like *free verse,* may seem a misnomer. How do one without the other? The process of rejecting and contributing is best described by the stylistic concept of deformation. The artist's distortions, we assume, are significant. If they are within the reigning paradigm, they constitute a variation; if they make a break with it, they constitute an innovation. John Thompson, in *The Founding of English Meter* (1961), describes a time in the late sixteenth century when meter and rhyme were variational distortions (so his title claims too much). If I am right, however, for Whitman and Rimbaud the dynamics of stylistic genesis required something like the obliteration of Classical meter—a process continuing down to the present by which norms of meter and rhyme, having become increasingly binding during the three preceding centuries, are gradually being themselves turned into deviants.

We have already seen how the late nineteenth century is a time of terrible quandary for traditional versification. To take the case of one representative figure not treated in the previous chapters: Intensely dissatisfied with the received system, Thomas Hardy could not see his way to breaking the molds and had to content himself with writing virtually every poem in homemade metrical and stanzaic forms. By contrast, the explicit intention of free verse was to do as much violence as possible to meter and rhyme, the two most legislative conventions of traditional poetry. Dissonance, deformity become stylistic ideals: "Dissonance / (if you are interested) / leads to discovery" writes William Carlos Williams in *Paterson* (4.2), and Robert Duncan praises in "old poets" like Pindar and Whitman "their faltering / their unaltering wrongness that has style" ("A Poem Beginning with a Line by Pindar"). "Move . . . out away from any declared base," Charles Olson wrote in a letter to Cid Corman. "It is almost exclusively when you have hewn to the pentameter that I have found fault."[16] The first flourishing of free verse in America, just after 1910, was in the moment of cubism and indeterminate music; but the medium of language proved resistant to the more thoroughgoing forms of experimentalism in the other arts, so that by and large, despite the deformation I have suggested, rhythm, sense, and structure as such are not abandoned in the best free verse. For this modest conservatism I shall adduce evidence, but first it is necessary to rule out of court one of the leading arguments by the adversaries of free verse.[17] Most prosodists wish to restrict the theory of expressive deviation to variants within the traditional system; they have not conceived that there might be a broader innovation, expressive in its way, which attempted demolition of that system. The principle of expressive variation from a metrical norm, according to Paul Fussell in *Poetic Meter and Poetic Form,* "is certainly the primary source of metrical pleasure for the modern critical reader." And thus, the argument runs, lacking any "counterpoint" between the fixed element of metrical regularity and the variants got by the poet's bucking against this the actual rhythms of language, free verse must offer inferior pleasures. John Crowe Ransom's assertion that the poet "is capable of writing smooth meters and then roughening them on purpose . . . of writing a clean argument, and then of roughening that too,"[18] cannot be disproved; but if it seems absurdly uneconomical to think this of the traditional poet, it will seem even less rewarding to condemn the experimental poet for not working within the metrical norms he is attempting to destroy.

The issue cannot be settled, as so much of extant literature on it assumes, in wholesale and a priori fashion—especially as the reader will doubtless derive another, equally valid source of pleasure from the perception in free verse of a far wider variety of rhythmic patterns than that achieved by expressive variation from the notional foot. Such patterns—of expectation, delay, and resolution—exercise the grasp of grammar and the delicacy of anyone's ear. So, to move toward a workable uncertainty principle, we must survey the main types of unpredictability in the prosodies of free verse. Then we shall be in a position to discriminate the pleasures of this body of poetry, to suggest standards for judging its success or failure, and to specify the cultural ideals it proposes to substitute for the ones associated with Classical versification.

It is much to his credit that Paul Valéry, a traditional poet highly conscious of the Modern plurality of styles, admits that if he were to be "seized by a desire to throw away rhyme and everything else . . . and to abandon myself completely to the desires of my ear," he should find "no truth essential to poetry" standing in his path.[19] Another poet who versifies, Donald Davie, writes of the professional poet as translator that he will "realize . . . in translating rhymed verse the rhyme is the first thing to go, and metre the second; whereas the amateur, wretched sceptic that he is, cannot be sure of having poetry at all unless he has these external features of it."[20] Of course, nobody would wish the considerations of meter and rhyme abolished for the study of poems consciously written in the traditional patterns; and some forms of rhyme are important in free verse, too. But at least two arguments—that the willing limitations of formal bondage "evoke" creative activity in the poet, and that meter as an absent norm has nothing to do with the real nature of poetry—seem foolishly overstated. Perhaps even my own provisional demonstration that metrical form is not the sine qua non of poetic shapeliness may serve to enliven the study of prosody. Valéry never abandoned himself completely to the desires of his ear, but if as reader I do so—if I assume that form as proceeding and individuality require each other, and that every poem creates its own convention—I think I will find it impossible to carry my strict empiricism very far. Affinities, limits, regularities begin to show up, and instead of doing absolute case law I find myself doing what Harvey Gross calls "prosody as rhythmic cognition."[21] And in so doing I may well discover that the ideal unit of poetic study is not the notional foot but the whole poem.

Along with Harvey Gross's chapter and the chapter entitled "Counterpoint" in Charles O. Hartman's book *Free Verse* (1980), Benjamin Hrushovsky's constitutive study, "On Free Rhythms in Modern Poetry,"[22] affords the most rewarding way into our discussion of the cooperative behavior, the convergence of forms in free verse. Hrushovsky takes the view that "a mere naming of the meter is as meaningless for the interpretation of an individual poem as the naming of its general idea; both are abstractions"; whereas rhythm, as an "organic" phenomenon, "can be appreciated fully by a phenomenological approach to the poem, that is, by going within it and moving in a hermeneutic circle from the whole to the parts, and vice versa." Working along these lines, the next step is to substitute a various and multiple prosody for a prosody comprised of one or two a priori units. Thereby we understand the poem, as Modern linguists understand language, as a system of relations rather than an addition of particles.

In the last chapter I discussed a scale of poetic elements stretching from the syllable to the whole poem. Probably the most interesting position on the scale is at the vexed middle rank of the line, which is equally liable to be taken downward to syntax and accent or upward in the direction of the whole poem. One suspects that this very unstableness will make study of the line rewarding. It affords a larger unit for analysis than the foot in traditional scansion, yet one not so large as the whole poem. Again, as Hrushovsky points out, the differentia of poetry from prose and the mark of poetry's "ontologically different framework" is the verse line: "It is hard to overestimate its importance in creating the poetic rhythm and very being of the poem" (page 186). (This is one view; it is modified in my next chapter.) Conservative prosodists have naturally argued that free verse blurs the distinction between prose and poetry, and they have shown only grudging interest when free verse makes its intermittent approaches to a "normal verse rhythm." Thus Yvor Winters claims little hope that many readers will understand the "scansion" he proposes for his own free verse in "The Bitter Moon," where a "free verse meter" and an iambic meter are said to be "running concurrently" and in counterpoint, and where several lines are "broken in two for the sake of emphasis." "The free verse foot," he says, "is very long, or is likely to be."[23] No more can Graham Hough, in his analysis of D. H. Lawrence's "Snake," lay the ghost of meter: "Alter the typography and break the line after 'mused,' and again we have two perfectly straightforward blank-verse lines."[24] Many prosodists would share Hough's "vulgar suspicion that much free verse is really prose," because traditional scansion permits them to see the line only as a distribution of relative stress values. In this way free verse may be reduced to the reflex of traditional poetry, a mere vers libre. Since, however, there is no free verse foot, and since it is strictly impermissible to alter typography in a genuine confrontation of all the linguistic features of the line, we must accept Zygmunt Czerny's axiom that each line in free verse is independent in structuring measures from the previous one, and Barbara Herrnstein Smith's that the line is "not a constant unit but the acknowledgement of a limit of variability."[25] In fact, the line is the notation of how the poem is to be read.

It is something of a scandal that we have not, in English at any rate, anything like a detailed defense of the postulate that prosody is meaning. The notion has been alive but unexamined for centuries. Any complete inquiry would have to find a logically coherent explanation of the arbitrariness of prosodic systems as processors of language, and of the way the aesthetic systems interfere with, and scissor, the cognitive processes that inhere in English grammar. Any complete inquiry would have to marshal theory and evidences against the contention of linguists and New Critics that the metrical stratum of the poem has no bearing whatever on content, that metrics must not (as they say) be vaporized into cognition. The inquiry might find much of promise in the Formalist-Structuralist idea of the interference of aesthetic and cognitive impulses in a poetic text, and in Hjelmslev's explanation of the way content substance relates to content form, expression substance to expression form.[26] As I take up the examples from English and American poets that follow, I am sensible that my own account is necessarily tentative.

My subject in this very practical inquiry is the relation between the line and the larger units of grammar—specifically, the coincidence and noncoincidence of line and sentence. There is no need to apologize for edging toward the linguist's province of prose rhythms and grammar, no need to fear a blurring of the distinction between prose and verse. Society or humanity is the outside term, within which is language (sometimes called *prose*), within which is *poetry* (variously defined). All these terms, from the largest meanings to local placement of a certain syllable, come within the view of this study; all these terms and their affiliations with one another stand as productive difficulties in the path, not as settled fixities.

Line and Sentence

Ezra Pound ends Canto II:

> And So-shu churned in the sea, So-shu also,
>   using the long moon for a churn-stick . . .
> Lithe turning of water,
>   sinews of Poseidon,
> Black azure and hyaline,
>   glass wave over Tyro,
> Close cover, unstillness,
>   bright welter of wave-cords.
>
> Then quiet water,
>   quiet in the buff sands,

> Sea-fowl stretching wing-joints,
>   splashing in rock-hollows and sand-hollows
> In the wave-runs by the half-dune;
> Glass-glint of wave in the tide-rips against sunlight,
>   palor of Hesperus,
> Grey peak of the wave,
>   wave, colour of grape's pulp,
>
> Olive grey in the near,
>   far, smoke grey of the rock-slide,
> Salmon-pink wings of the fish-hawk
>   cast grey shadows in water,
> The tower like a one-eyed great goose
>   cranes up out of the olive-grove,
> And we have heard the fauns chiding Proteus
>   in the smell of hay under the olive-trees,
> And the frogs singing against the fauns
>   in the half-light
> And . . .[27]

The critic as amateur metrist can scan this, as linguist can describe how the long, loose-jointed sentence is generated. I propose to do neither. Will these inquiries, taken singly, suggest what sort of fictional duration is portioned out for the mind's ear? Let us instead, neither scanning nor parsing, honor Pound's own determination of 1912 "as regarding rhythm: to compose in the sequence of the musical phrase, not in sequence of a metronome."[28] The grammetrical hypothesis offers a more appropriate accuracy for those prosodies which measure human time by sounding in the ear. One of the most sensitive grammetrical readers, Josephine Miles, rightly says that phrasal poetry such as this emphasizes "line-by-line progression, and cumulative participial modification in description and invocation without stress on external rhyming or grouping."[29] The passage is phrasal in its metric as in its grammar: cumulative, processional, Whitmanesque, with its verbs turned to participles and with an abundance of adjectives and nouns in heavy modifications and compounding of subjects. Like much free verse it aims for vigor, not solidity; for local detail and continuous transition, not (within reason) firmness of outline. A conscious preference for weakened shape accounts for the co-presence, here, of an extended sentence of dubious cohesion, and the concluding sentence fragment, "And . . . ," which conflates line rank with word rank.

The disposition of longer and shorter lines confirms one's sense that free verse veers toward extremes, testing limits of variability. In lines 2 through 6 and 9 and 10 of the passage, the poet seems to think of two half-lines making one line, so that the half-line is both bound and free, the first half-line proposing, the second half-line filling out. Perhaps there is some distant recollection of the half-lines that make a line in Anglo-Saxon poetry. The disposition of weaker and stronger accents tests metrical limits, too—in "of the rock-slide," we have two very weak followed by two forcible stresses, technically a four-syllable ionic *a minore* foot—but who cares about foot identification in such a context, where no line repeats a pattern from the line previous? Pound's lines are variable in meter as in grammar. With their elaborate, carrying repetition of sound and theme, their word jamming, the lines are anything but slack.

I have used the term *Whitmanesque,* a short reference to a group of attitudes at once moral and technical. In Whitman, as Leo Spitzer points out, ancient grammatical devices of anaphora and asyndeton are employed in a new prosody, a "chaotic enumeration" whose very eclecticism and inclusion of incomparables is the mark of its Modernity. At best, expressing separation as well as unity, "the stylistically heterogenous series becomes the expression of metaphysical coherence"; and since to catalog this democracy of things requires a human, democratic style, "Whitman has adapted the biblical verset and syntax for his bible of the flesh."[30] If in Pound the additive procedures are more various and complex, this is unquestionably the legacy of Whitman's powerful use of the coincident line and sentence, line and clause. Whitman's explosion of syllable-stress metric, foot unit, pentameter line—of that tradition of antagonism to English regularity which made an American free verse "as inevitable as the Declaration of Independence"[31]—is the occasion for Pound's 1916 tribute: "It was you that broke the new wood. / Now is a time for carving" ("A Pact"). Thus, as he begins his cantos, Pound has consciously decided to mark out more craftsmanly cadences upon or within Whitman's line. More recently William Carlos Williams has spoken of a "tremendous change in measure, a relative measure, which [Whitman] was the first to feel and embody in his works" though he hadn't enough power over his verses to turn them "this way, then that, at will."[32] On the strength of such testimony I assume that Whitman's end-stopped lines, rising to heavy accent as they close, with boundaries so often equivalent to those of the larger units of ordinary prose grammar, constitute almost the precondition of free verse in English.

A culminating moment for grammar and metrics is Pound's *Cathay* (1915), where Ernest Fenollosa's literal translations, along with his theories about the rapidity of English sentence order, are taken up and surpassed by an inventive metrist. The grammatical theories, summarized in Donald Davie's phrase, "the impetus with which a sentence drives through its verb from subject to object,"[33] are enacted in the one-line sentences of *Cathay*'s "South Folk in Cold Country" and in the superb line about the paired butterflies in "The River Merchant's Wife": "They hurt me. I grow older." But other lines in "The River Merchant's Wife" show Pound attempting to delay or withstand the impetus of the sentence while keeping his habit, virtually a norm for this poem, of the line equivalent to the sentence:

> At fourteen I married My Lord you.
> I never laughed, being bashful.

> Lowering my head, I looked at the wall.
> Called to, a thousand times, I never looked back.[34]

None of these sentences is ordinary. Only the second begins with the subject, and even there the right-branching participial construction is rare—usually considered, in fact, an "improper" subordination. The other lines even more unusually (such recoil being the signature of special premeditation) branch to the left by placing modifying clauses before the subject. Betraying Fenollosa's rather limited grammatical principle, Pound captures the delicate reticence of the Chinese woman who is the nominal speaker of the poem.

The numbered lines of Louis Zukofsky's "Poem beginning 'The' "—all but the first ("The") plundered from books and tags of speech and carefully noted in the epigraph—achieve another effect with the same device of stratification, different stripes of meaning laid on like colors, one line below another but not connected to it—the effect of clutter, of a mind that can barely begin to take stock of its contents. And Ted Hughes's mock metaphysics in his series of Crow poems finds the appropriate tone with a progression of unattached, staccato line-sentences, as in "Crow Communes":

> "Well," said Crow, "What first?"
> God, exhausted with Creation, snored.
> "Which way?" said Crow, "Which way first?"
> God's shoulder was the mountain on which Crow sat.
> "Come," said Crow, "Let's discuss the situation."
> God lay, agape, a great carcass.
>
> Crow tore off a mouthful and swallowed.
>
> "Will this cypher divulge itself to digestion
> Under hearing beyond understanding?"
>
> (That was the first jest.)
>
> Yet, it's true, he suddenly felt much stronger.
>
> Crow, the hierophant, humped, impenetrable.
>
> Half-illumined. Speechless.
>
> (Appalled.)[35]

First, six lines-equal-to-sentences, which give the contrast between the talking Crow and the sleeping God; then, seven more dispersed sentences, all different in structure, all but one equal to a line; last, three sentences of one or two word fragments, all adjectives for Crow's amazement, the last separated from the rest of the poem by line break, grammar, and closed parentheses. Crow's carnivorous relationship to the godhead is a malign jest; much of the poetic hilarity comes from the pointing of sentences and lines toward the catch in the voice that marks the parentheses around "Appalled" and makes the last dark joke (which is that such a human word can be used for Crow, an amoral force and, after all, a bird).

By contrast with the laconic inevitability of Hughes's lines, the end of David Gascoyne's "Salvador Dali" is an example chosen from the multitude of inferior free-verse poems that employ the technique of catalog, with the items in syntactic, semantic, and prosodic parallel:

> Heraldic animals wade through the asphyxia of planets,
> Butterflies burst from their skins and grow long tongues like plants,
> The plants play games with a suit of mail like a cloud.
> While the children are killed in the smoke of the catacombs
> And loves float down from the cliffs like rain.[36]

The lines, like their grammar, are loose, flaccid; for in his haste to yoke together surrealist images Gascoyne has not seen fit to turn his verses this way, then that, at will.

In Hughes's line

> Crow, the hierophant, humped, impenetrable,

the bold segmentation of rhythm into two halves halved creates a pouncing from word to word, a metrical exaggeration that reinforces the irony leveled against the presumptuous, quasi-human crow. It is a metric, moreover, which derives from the naked symmetry of grammar, subject + apposition balanced against predicate + predicate adjective. As Donald Davie has shown, it was Pound who among the Moderns insisted upon this method of disrupting the line from within, "throwing weight upon smaller units within the line. . . . slowing down the surge from one line into the next in such a way that smaller components within the line (down to the very syllables) can recover weight and value."[37] Once the line had been thus segmented and its smaller units dignified, early-twentieth-century prosodies could be enriched by a more meditative, discursive voice. This is precisely what occurs in *The Waste Land,* in *A Draft of XXX Cantos,* and in other poems since, which isolate and dismember the verse line—very often, I believe, intending to give prosody a symbolic form to express the thematic contrast between the historical moment and an imagined or lost moment of innocence and wholeness. The political section of Robert Duncan's "Poem Beginning with a Line by Pindar" is one instance:

> A stroke. These little strokes. A chill.
>   The old man, feeble, does not recoil.
> Recall. A phase so minute,
>   only a part of the word in- jerrd.
>
> *The Thundermakers descend*
>
> damerging a nuv. A nerb.

> The present dented of the U
> nighted stayd. States. The heavy clod?
> Cloud. Invades the brain. What
> if lilacs last in *this* dooryard bloomd?
>
> Hoover, Roosevelt, Truman, Eisenhower—
> where among these did the power reside
> that moves the heart? What flower of the nation
> bride-sweet broke to the whole rapture?
> Hoover, Coolidge, Harding, Wilson
> hear the factories of human misery turning out commodities.[38]

The contrast between the time of President Eisenhower's stroke and the "whole rapture" of Whitman's time of promise a century earlier is conveyed, here, by dismembered lines and deformed words and quotations. In the opening of Edward Dorn's "Hemlocks," lines and syllables are retarded to an entirely different rhythmic purpose, yet still the theme is loss:

> Red house. Green tree in mist.
> How many fir long hours.
> How that split wood
> warmed us. How continuous.
> Red house. Green tree I miss.
> The first snow came in October.
> Always. For three years.
> And sat on our shoulders.
> That clean grey sky.
> That fine curtain of rain
> like nice lace held our faces
> up, in it, a kerchief for the nose
> of softest rain. Red house.[39]

Repeating with slight change a few simple elements, Dorn achieves an elegiac monotone in which minute rhythmic and grammatical and lexical deflections—like "mist" that is missed—need to be registered, and in which statements like "How continuous" and "Always" are sadly controverted by the fragmentary form of the utterance.

Another, more emphatic dismemberment puts space between the lobes of the line, sending it across and down the page in clots of phrase. In the Canto II passage, Pound's indentation creates a doubling of lines that is only apparent; for where visually there are two distinct lines in

> Grey peak of the wave,
>   wave, colour of grape's pulp,

metrically, as I have said, it is neither one nor two, being both. Or, more precisely, since they are conceived and apprehended at once, the visual dismemberment is the rhythmical one, producing a poetry that as Davie says "moves forward only hesitantly, gropingly, and slowly; which often seems to float across the page as much as it moves down it" (page 119). There are antecedents in Mallarmé's "Un coup de dés"; Vladimir Mayakovsky arrived at the form independently in the 1920s; Pound has on occasion used it masterfully. But the method is best justified in the achieved "relative measure" of the later poems of Willliam Carlos Williams, for instance "To Daphne and Virginia":

> There is, in the hard
>   give and take
>   of a man's life with
>   a woman
> a thing which is not the stress itself
>   but beyond
>   and above
>   that,
>   something that wants to rise
>   and shake itself
>   free[40]

Grammetrically one must respond to the stress and its transcendence, to the cluster of accents in "the hard / give and take," and to the (perhaps too blatant?) energy of the final enjambment onto "free." The line breaking draws special attention to certain syllables (as to "thing"/"beyond"/"above," evidently a sequence), thus achieving emphasis less by traditional stress than by frequency of segmentation. The passage, though brief, is evidence for the contention that free verse recovers intensity at the rank of word and syllable.

That this method incites considerable delicacy of rhythm and tone can be illustrated by the affectionate formality of Williams's lines to his wife, which begin "Asphodel, That Greeny Flower":

> Of asphodel, that greeny flower,
>   like a buttercup
>   upon its branching stem—
>   save that it's green and wooden—
>   I come, my sweet,
>   to sing to you.[41]

Delaying its subject, the sentence syncopates its left-branching syntax against a typography that floats not only to the right but down, a zigzag for the reader's eye and mind, combining the echelon effect of the lines with the linear step by step of the sentence members, with the counterbalance or opposition of the meanings of separate phrases within the sentence. The pastoral decorum of the inverted phrasing ("Of asphodel . . . I come, my sweet, to sing . . ." to begin a Modern poem—how old-fashioned, how unlike prose syntax!) is playfully, impatiently modified by details packed into midsentence by apposition, simile, and dash. It seems that where the end and, less significantly, the beginning of the conventional verse lines are points of greatest interest, in free verse of this sort each of the phrasal members of the line gains identity and weight, producing climaxes of rhythm smaller but more continuous. The difference from traditional rhythms is not one of quality but of quantity; in such cases, there are more ends, more beginnings; more scissorings of the line by grammar, more of grammar by line, more pauses—thereby, arguably, more energy.

In an article published after his death, Williams said that when "the bracket of the customary foot has been expanded so that more syllables, words, or phrases can be admitted into its confines," the poetic measure will vary "with the idiom by which it is employed and the tonality of the individual poem."[42] Davie has shown that in Pound's *Cathay* and *Homage to Propertius* "the ear allows itself to be persuaded by the mind into regarding the lines as metrically equal because they are equal syntactically" (page 89). In somewhat the same way, Williams would presumably argue, ear and eye persuade the mind to regard the portions of the line as metrically equal because they are equal syntactically, thematically, or visually. Of course, such a relative measure once achieved can quickly become a stylistic trick, and the dismemberment and retardation of the line puts into harsh focus the inadequacies of a poet whose rhythms are derivative. Predictably, a number of imitators have reduced Williams's form to a formula with no rhythmic impulse beyond indentation and crude repetition; but typographical manipulation will not redeem woodenness of ear or poverty of lexicon.

The distinguished poem in free verse usually contains lines that are coincident with sentences and lines that are not. Even in the most disjunctive Imagist poems, revaluation of the syllable, word, and line are matched by shifts at the top of the rank scale, in the form of staza or poem. Indeed, Pound and especially Williams, feeling the special position of the line in the middle of the scale, are disposed equally to dismember it or to submerge it in stanza or whole poem—often dismembering and submerging one and the same line. And, in Williams especially, the abandonment of sentence boundaries is the exact reflex of the abandonment of line boundaries in his metric. Charles Olson, too, in the note to his poems written expressly for *Selected Writings,* paradoxically overstates the volatile nature of the free-verse line by declaring that his poems give the effect of enjambment with no enjambment: "The lines which hook-over should be read as though they lay out right and flat to the horizon or to Eternity."[43] As regards the poem's effect on a reader's attention, this perception of the contradictory isolation and submergence, retardation and speed of the verse line, brings us to the very center of our subject.

Only a lunatic would attempt to surmount the contradictions; that is why Robert Creeley, in a poem dedicated to Olson, calls the poet "Le Fou,"

> Who plots, then, the lines
> talking, taking, always the beat from
> the breath
>   (moving slowly at first

```
                 the breath
                       which is slow—
        I mean, graces come slowly,
        it is that way.
        So slowly (they are waving
        we are moving
                       away from (the trees
                              the usual (go by
        which is slower than this is
                              (we are moving!
        goodbye⁴⁴
```

This accords perfectly with Donald Davie's description of a Poundian poetry "in which, if the perceptions are cast in the form of sentences, the sentence is bracketed and, as it were, folded in on itself so as to seem equal with the disjointed phrase" (page 119); but when Davie presses further to call the Poundian style "a poetry (we might almost say) of the noun rather than the verb," Creeley's poem no longer seems to fit, so stubbornly does it celebrate both the aesthetic of meditative retardation ("graces come slowly") and the aesthetic of continuity or speed ("we are moving!"). What at first appears a random juxposition of theme and language, in Creeley's bracketed and un-bracketed sentence fragments, soon begins to look purposeful: differing syntaxes are understood separately yet together as they converge on one another toward agreement in the gesture of "goodbye." One would rather describe Pound-style as a poetry where extremes of dismemberment coexist with extremes of continuity, a poetry of process where at best the noun is teased into motion. Its main stylistic signature, with Whitman lurking behind Pound, is the cataloging of things by apposition, and of actions by accumulating present participles. "Graces come slowly," and yet we are, Creeley hopes, "moving away from" the usual versification—"which is slower than this," one assumes, because here one grammetrical perception is made to follow instantly on another by the exercise of that "progressive transition" Coleridge defined as method in poetry and in human intelligence. Since *method* in this sense means the ability to grasp wholes in imagination, the next step is to look at cases where line and sentence are not coincident, in groups of lines up to the last grouping that is the poem.

It was not the end of the matter then, if, after 1910, the line was isolated and dismembered to break the pentameter. Enjambment, avoided by the Imagists, was to return in the absence of meter; indeed, so powerfully that the free-verse poet's primary skill may be to prevent continuities from becoming torrents of language. At least as much as traditional versification, the relative measures lend themselves to triviality, imprecision, blather. Unless the poet breaks sentences over lines with care, patterns of movement will be wearyingly similar and prosodically as uninteresting as the despised second-order metered poetry. Yvor Winters's poems in free verse (so often do the lines end on the unkinetic particles of grammar) are textbook examples of spurious continuity. "The Rows of Cold Trees" is a rather extreme example:

> To be my own Messiah to the
> burning end. Can one endure the
> acrid, steeping darkness of
> the brain, which glitters and is
> dissipated? Night. The night is
> winter and a dull man bending,
> muttering above a freezing pipe;
> and I, bent heavily on books; the
> mountain iron in my sleep and
> ringing; but the pipe has frozen, haired with
> unseen veins, and cold is on the eyelids; who can
> remedy this vision?[45]

This is truncated iambic pentameter. Rewritten as rough blank verse, or as plausible free verse with perhaps one or more words from each line shifted right and down to begin the next line, this might gain the minimum of prosodic excitement. But because Winters has not decided between a metrical and a nonmetrical prosody, the poem remains slack as it stands. The passage is so outrageous as to seem quite deliberate. It might serve as an example of free verse out of hand, the rebellion seeming almost childish. Why create this kind of continuity except to show how one disdains the whole idea?

Continuation in prosody is motion toward a goal, it would seem; but neither the motion nor its completion are sufficient to give the shape of the poem a symbolic form that reinforces, indeed is, the meaning. To be fully significant the grammetrical motion must also be resisted, must make some show of encompassing and resolving discontinuities. Only then is displayed the mutual influence of one part on another within the whole. Kurt Koffka defines gestaltist laws of "good continuation" as the mind's craving for stable shapes, its tendency to perpetuate a motion and follow the line of least resistance: "Psychological organization will be as 'good' as the prevailing conditions allow. In this definition the term 'good' is undefined. It embraces such properties as regularity, symmetry, simplicity."[46] If we adapt gestalt notions to the arts, *good* does not and cannot mean "aesthetic"; for the better the psychological organization, the less likely is it that expectation will be aroused by discontinuity or by deviation from a norm. When Winters ends so many free-verse lines on hanging syllables, as above, isolating the lines rhythmically while submerging their grammar, he shows a residual need for the "good" psychological organization of stable shapes and small units. Since his method is inappropriate to the prevailing conditions of high unpredictability in nonmetrical prosodies, he botches his experiment.

In successful free verse, where expectation is aroused by the inhibition of a tendency to respond, it should be possible to imagine a poem that tests the grammetrical limits of continuity and its resistance. Such a poem might

consist of a single, relentless sentence, whose main clauses are split again
and again by the accumulation of detail, a sentence whose divergent members are seen to cooperate only when it is complete and whose division into
lines the reader finds a welcome impediment. Tony Harrison's "Isla de la
Juventud" is just such a poem:

> The fireflies that women
> once fattened on sugar
> and wore in their hair
> or under the see-through
> parts of their blouses
> in Cuba's *Oriente,*
> here seem to carry
> through the beam where they cluster
> a brief phosphorescence
> from each stiff corpse
> on the battlefield that looks
> like the blown-up towel
> of a careless barber,
> its nap and its bloodflecks,
> and if you were to follow,
> at Santa Fe's open-air
> cinema's Russian
> version *War & Peace,*
> the line of the dead
> to the end, corpses,
> cannons and fetlocks,
> scuffing the red crust
> with your snowboots
> or butt-end of your rifle,
> you would enter an air
> as warm as the blankets
> just left by a lover,
> yours, if you have one,
> an air full of fireflies,
> bright after-images,
> and scuffed Krasnoe snow
> like unmeltable stars.[47]

Harrison reveals hidden analogies between geographical places, war and
love, art and experience. Enabling these thematic connections is a prosodic
continuity that takes the reader's span of attention beyond even the embedded constituent sentence to its framing syntax, finally to resolve apparently unrelated lines and phrases within a frame where sentence, stanza, and
poem (perhaps too sweetly?) come to rest. Enjambed lines and highly recursive sentences are common in free verse, whose unstable structures often,
as here, force the reader to the temporal limits of the response to larger
groupings.

Or the same elements, employed as in W. S. Merwin's "In the Time of the
Blossoms," may force the reader into a sudden restructuring of the whole
verbal situation:

> Ash tree
> sacred to her who sails in
> from the one sea
> all over you leaf skeletons
> fine as sparrow bones
> stream out motionless
> on white heaven
> staves of one
> unbreathed music
> Sing to me[48]

As from figure to ground, with no piecemeal fumbling, Merwin's last line shifts the reader from the grammatical pattern of description to the pattern of invocation, from catalog to plea. Here and in Harrison's poem, lines end in strong particles and are given even more integrity by unobtrusive end or internal rhyme, most especially by the first and last lines. The lines remain, however, systematically run on, and as such are figures on the ground of the larger unit, the stanza that is the poem. By contrast, the dismembered line is the ground to the figures of its smaller units. Thus, to express in the language of gestalt psychology what I have described above as the volatility of the line: When a poem contains lines both isolated and submerged, the middle units on the rank scale engage in a protean series of identity shifts as between figure and ground.

The free-verse poet who abjures punctuation emphasizes such shifts in identity, but at the risk of incoherence. The finest of those who have attempted the unpunctuated poem—Apollinaire, Williams, Merwin, and Paul Blackburn—have realized the degree to which it puts pressure on grammar, and accordingly restrict their sentences to a single, clear meaning, or to several meanings, clearly articulated in their overlap. A minor lyric from Stuart Montgomery's *Circe* derives its success from the cohesion of its grammar, as well as from its happily random enjambment, assonance, and rhyme.

> Clear amber
> they say in Italy
> are tears of Circe but
>
> men in the act she wept over
> turned to insects and slept
> arms aching in amber for more
>
> than three thousand years
> now dangle mounted in silver
> as charms over their breasts or
>
> worn by women on the
> fourth or heart finger
> for love and against age[49]

Cohesion on a grander scale subsumes the inequalities of theme and rhythm, the sensory allure and physical weight, of Paul Blackburn's "The Watchers."

This is an extended meditation on the alphabet as the material basis of
writing, which takes as primary theme the right relation of scholarship to
poetry. These ideas are interspersed with and related to a narrative about a
mechanical crane hauling bedrock from a building site in Manhattan. I take
for comment the first of six pages, where the crane begins to be known as an
analogue to the scholar's mining of the actual for data:

> It's going to rain
> Across the avenue a crane
> whose name is
> > CIVETTA LINK-BELT
> dips, rises and turns in a
> > graceless geometry
>
> > But grace is slowness / as
> ecstasy is some kind of speed or madness /
> The crane moves slowly, that
> much it is graceful / The men
> > watch and the leaves
> Cranes makes letters in the sky
> > as the wedge flies
> > > The scholar's function is
>
> > > > Mercury, thief and poet,
> > > > invented the first 7 letters
> > > > 5 of them vowels, watching
> > > > cranes . after got
> The men watch and the rain does not come
> > > HC — 108B CIVETTA LINK-BELT
> In the pit below a yellow cat,
> > CAT–933
> > > pushes the debris
> and earth to load CIVETTA HC — 108B
> > Cat's name is PASCO and
> > there is an ORegon phone number,
> moves its load toward 3 piles
> Let him leave the building to us[50]

It takes the whole poem to complete all these suspended sentences, develop
the dropped hints, exemplify the alphabet's roots in the real ("Cranes fly in
V-formation"), its lovely arbitrariness. Capital letters ("CAT-933 / PASCO /
ORegon") return as refrains. The scholar's function turns out to be "fact –
Let him / quarry cleanly." The poet's function is to make the buildings, the
watchers of the crane (first called men) are at the end "the gods"—for men
must be gods who inherit such power from Cretan and Greek vowels and
consonants, and before that from "Mercury, thief and poet." What is broken
by indentation, slash mark, line breach, suspended predication, and dropped
theme is picked up, stitched, made sense of later. But the breaking off itself,
so frequent and abrupt, gives the sense of hieratic dignity, magic intonation;

and thus rhythm reinforces in its separate sphere the poem's unstated, pervasive assumption that language is the human link between world and mind, past and present. For Blackburn the divisions are massive but massively healed.

In fact, the effect of "breaking off" is so frequent and so marked in free verse generally, I might hazard that at midline or endline its prosodies require—even glorify—the Classical device of aposiopesis, or the dash construction actual or implied. To notice the importance of this, and of other grammetrical methods (for example, the high incidence of the present participle and of embedded clauses in the hearts of sentences), I must assume the poet's own perspective at the beginning of the utterance. When the reader notices the evolving unity of the sentences as a range of choices—a progressive transition from indeterminate toward determinate meaning, "in the finding fortuitous, but once found, binding" (Tomlinson)—the reader becomes especially alert to the eventfulness of grammatical and prosodic facts. And thereby the reader learns to identify the special way each element both displays and inhibits continuity. The free-verse stanza, for instance, may resist continuity with tight unrhymed forms such as fully punctuated, end-stopped quatrains, or at the other extreme it may seek pure transition with notional stanzas that are grammetrically "open" at either end. About the precise impact of the poem as a structure of relations there is much to learn if, registering the parts as at once exhibiting and resisting continuity, we can also understand the whole as both process and product.

About Kinetic

Vortex.

—Pound

A poem is energy transferred from where
the poet got it . . . by way of the poem
itself to, all the way over to, the reader. . . .
There's only one thing you can do about kinetic,
re-enact it.

—Olson

Lord Kames spoke of an intimacy between humanity and the music of the poem. In free verse, which Kames could never have imagined, the reason for such intimacy is that lines follow the grain of the English language, or at least lines do nothing to violate the structure of the language. Lines also justify themselves as units of sense by conforming to and extending habits of attention. Line integrity is determined by syntax, sense, rhythm or sound recurrence, sound values, intensity of sound, visual considerations, punctuation, and probably other, more subtle variables. For any line taken singly, whether run on or not has no bearing on the matter; whether the line can stand, and how it is resolved into the mass, are the main issues.

Focusing primarily on the relation of sentence and line, this chapter has isolated one of several factors in a counterpoint analysis. A complete study, such as we do not yet have, would offer factors above and below the prosodic unit of the line and the grammatical unit of the sentence. However, the narrowing of focus has given certain advantages. Much of previous work on poetic syntax has been restricted to accounts of repeated grammatical forms within sentences or from sentence to sentence in the poem; but here it has been shown that the figure of grammar is one of progressive transition, linear and directional (as well as recursive). The relationship of the line to the sentence is one of mutual scissoring, where the type and quantity of the pauses thus created make for a rhythm of phrase and of stress quite different from the (more regular) recurrences of metered poems. It has also been possible, through examples, to suggest why and how the energy of the meter-making argument leaks from lines that are mainly typographical.[51]

Free verse could not have become a valid measure of it had tried to will essential changes in the structure of Modern English or essential changes in the mind's tendency to find stable shapes, once the mind has been inhibited from responding. All reading is a process of transposing perspectives of attention. Perspectives can be arranged in counterbalance, opposition, echelon, and serial. Since free verse is marginally more vigorous than traditional verse in its demand for such transpositions, the open-field poem has often been described through an informal cognitive psychology of attention, and through physiological analogues like breathing and artistic analogues like music and dance. With the free-verse measure itself, these explanations of it are expressions of an immanentist poetics, where rules are not imposed upon the poetic material but are allowed to emerge and interact. The discovery of forms through attention is the Modern and post-Modern version of Romanticism's form as proceeding.

But what, Mr. Williams, is being measured? What, Mr. Olson, is motion in the kinetic of free verse? To what are poet and reader paying attention "by way of the poem itself"? How does poetry turn thought and language into energy? The short answer to the last question, which yet implicates the others, is that energy is passed over from the world and the poet's experience of it through the mutual interference of cognitive and aesthetic impulses in the poem's language. The interference of grammatical and prosodic systems that occupy the same site—the poem—acts to inhibit and to release the normal human tendency to respond—to, as we say, make sense. So energy is the end product of the frustration and the resolving of expectation. "There's only one thing you can do about kinetic, re-enact it." Easier said, of course. "The Compleat Prosodist, ideally equipped," as Harvey Gross has said, "should deal with the psychology of the creative process, the structure of the poem, and the reader's experience."[52] Like the poet, the

Compleat Prosodist as interpreter must reenact the motions of the writing and reading mind; and must also and in addition (something that can only be mentioned here because beyond this chapter's scope) study the wider historical conditioning of attention. For literary kinetic, as consciousness-in-action and therefore as free-verse prosody, is always informed, always overdetermined. The writer's family romance, class background, and education are factors that have indirect bearing on choice of genre, mode of address, style, even rhythm.

The period of "classic" free verse, I should say, stretches from Whitman through Pound and Williams to persons writing today in the Pound-Williams tradition. Most writers of free verse still inhabit this period and its aesthetic, though a significant and no longer small group is now attempting to surpass the classics. The members of the classic group may be identified by their devotion to the poetic line as a musical and gestural unit, their exploration of the meanings of measure as opposed to meter, and their expressivist aesthetics of reenactment, of the transfer of energy from world to poet and poem to reader. Within the classic group one might in the broadest terms distinguish two types of writers. The expansivists use the oratorical long line, evoke the abundance of their own verbal behavior, and invoke the reader. Examples would be Whitman, Robinson Jeffers, William Everson, parts of García Lorca and Neruda, Allen Ginsberg, and James Schuyler in *The Morning of the Poem* (1980). The precisionists write short lines and tight stanzas, employ heavy line breaking, and tend to be brief, lyrical, and descriptive. Examples are Williams, Robert Creeley, Cid Corman, Denise Levertov, Paul Blackburn, Charles Tomlinson, and George Oppen. Of course many poets, such as Edward Dorn and Ted Hughes, move from type to type as the single poem may demand. When the poem in classic free verse fails, it is usually because the syntax has no eventful relationship to the line, the syntax needs calisthenics both within the line and from line to line. In reenacting eventfulness, the more minimal precisionists have less chance to go wrong, perhaps simply because they give themselves fewer words to deploy in a smaller space.

One of the roles of reenactment in twentieth-century free verse has been in translations from relatively inaccessible languages. Neglected, but very much contributions to the distinction of classic free verse, are such works as Edwin Morgan's Mayakovsky, Charles Tomlinson's Tyutchev, Wai-lim Yip's Wang Wei—and Christopher Logue's brilliant versions based on the *Iliad*, from which these lines from three different passages:

> Rat,
> pearl,
> onion,
> honey:
> these colours came before the sun
> lifted above the ocean
> bringing light

   alike to mortals and immortals
. . . .
Cobalt in heaven,
        and below it
polar blue;
the body of the air is lapis, and
             where it falls
behind the soft horizon,
   the light turns back to Heaven.

A soldier pisses by a chariot;
   another
        sweetens his ax blade on a soapy stone,
and up between the dunes
      with ribbons, tambourines, and little drums,
come twelve white horses led by seven women,
Briseis in their midst,
her breasts so lovely that they envy one another. . . .
. . . .
Achilles stands; stretches; turns on his heel,
punches the sunlight, bends, then——jumps! . . .
and lets the world turn fractionally beneath his feet.

   Noon.
In the foothills melons roll out of their green hidings.
   Heat.

   He walks towards the chariot.
Greece waits.

   Over the wells in Troy mosquitoes hover.
   Beside the chariot.
Soothing the perfect horses; watching his driver cinch,
shake out the reins, fold, lay them across the rail;
dapple and white the horses are, perfect they are,
sneezing to clear their cool black muzzles.

   He mounts.[53]

Logue does not reenact Homer's hexameters, nor does he give the whole of Book 19, nor does he always reproduce Homer's images (he refers by calculated anachronism to tungsten armor and to Cape Kennedy!), but better than literal translations he gives the ethos, the energy of Homer's world. The stops and starts of free verse provide hieratic strangeness, impalpable archaism.

   At the outset I said many poets have veered from free verse to more traditional forms. But within the innovative poetries there has occurred also a division wherein an insurgent style has separated itself from classic free verse. For these newer writers, the open-form text is still too closed. In fact, these poets wish to eliminate the dichotomy between closed and open, and by this means, in Michael Davidson's words, "to investigate the inner workings of poetic structure and imposed form." Line, the normative English sentence, and sound value become subordinate to poetic figure or ecstatic image (Robert Bly), or to the varieties of declaration and their sleights (Michael Palmer), or to the undoubted power of chance combination (Jackson MacLow's work with aleatory methods; David Antin's "talk" pieces). Davidson's brief survey of this movement, which he participates in as both poet and commentator, is the best we have:

> What Emerson called a "meter-making argument" is very much at work in contemporary writing for which measure has become less a normative threshold and more of a boundary to be interrogated. By speaking of an exploratory use of form, I don't imply a new formalism. . . . For poets of the Fifties, the term "measure" was tied to an expressivist aesthetic; the recent generation looks to the material condition of language and to the function of mediation for its primary impulse. . . . One could point to at least five general areas: experimentation with conventional forms (Ted Berrigan's *Sonnets,* John Ashbery's sestinae); performance (MacLow, Steve McCaffery, David Antin, Jerome Rothenberg); non-generic prose (Ron Silliman's *Tjanting,* Ashbery's *Three Poems*); notational and concretist exercise (McCaffery, Bob Cobbing, Emmett Williams); and, for lack of a better term, "translation" (use of one text to generate another in Jack Spicer, Pound's *Propertius,* Louis Zukofsky's *Catullus,* parodies of corporate jargon in Edward Dorn's recent poetry, "total" translation in Rothenberg's "Horse Songs for Frank Mitchell").[54]

The sound poets in this grouping (for example, McCaffery and Cobbing) often isolate the sound elements in a work, submerging meaning, while the majority of the others show a somewhat reduced interest in grounding the poem in sound, or in the gold-balance precision of the classical free-verse line. The division of labor into sound poets and sense (and, elegantly, nonsense) poets would seem to be a fascinating development, a deliberate unwillingness to play the whole instrument. In this, however, the revisionists of free verse do nothing unusual but take further a dynamic that began when measure split away from meter at the time of Whitman's beautiful candor.

6

Narrative of Grammar in the Prose Poem

Inherited Definitions of Prose and Poetry

Bertrand, Baudelaire, Rimbaud, Mallarmé, Char, Eluard, Perse, Follain—merely to list the names is to admit that, in France, the prose poem has long been a major literary form. For a hundred years French writers have used the form as often as they have used traditional versification. Wider limits, greater freedom; yet withal, a system of constraints. In England and America, though, the current interest in this mode is rather a new impulse than a revival. Doubtless it is truer for England and America than for France that scholars have recoiled from the prickliness of the prose poem, and now as before our poets work the form without benefit of theory. More even for interpreters than for poets it is a treacherous genre, and it forces the most painful revisions of our literary beliefs.[1]

If we have not in English produced an adequate aesthetics of the prose poem, the reason is the curious slippage and deficiency of our speculative instruments. One "derives observations from the nature of the terminology" (Kenneth Burke), and the inquiry will not get far if the crucial concepts *prose* and *poetry* are quagmires of illogic and prejudice. So I would like first to sort out the inherited meanings of the terms, and then to show how the categories of narrative and of grammar have their use in the study of any and all prose poems—insofar as they can be isolated as poems. Since my subject is the narrative of grammar, I will be inspecting sentences and whole plots in "comprehensive and brief pieces" where, as Mallarmé said, "immediate thought rhythms [organize] a prosody."[2] But since my subject is also, more broadly, the grammar of narrative in the prose poem, I will be attempting to describe the range of types, the total morphology of a genre.

Roy Fuller, urging from his chair as professor of poetry at Oxford that "standards" be kept "during the course of revolutionary practice," is the conscious spokesman of poetic tradition.[3] He uses the terms *prose* and *poetry* in a fashion always polemical, but (on the showing of his printed lectures) never conscious of the full range of assumptions lodged in these common tags. Thus he denounces "the chopped-up prose that almost universally serves today as poetic form," and he forbids poets the right to take "the prolix and irregular liberties of prose to tease out their meanings. . . . Poetry cannot ignore all patterns: to do so would condemn itself to prose." The presence of rhyme or meter is the marker of literariness, according to such standards; hence the prose poem is unmentionable, and its contemporary cousin must always be qualified as "so-called free verse." Thus antagonists of the avant-garde will tend to describe prose poems and free verse as prose, will indeed argue that these forms are aesthetic scandals and logical impossibilities. This is not to complain that Fuller prefers poetry to prose, just to remark that he uses the terms as manifestos, aggressively and defensively.

For those who defend this venerable contrast of essences, the poem displays connotative language, a clustering of prominent equivalencies that remove it from the flat denotation of prose. If prose, for these writers, is fact, poetry is antiprose and the true home of emotion; hence their defensive disbelief that someone should claim to see "the same thing" in poetry and prose. A. Kingsley Weatherhead takes an article to defend William Carlos Williams against his own statements on the subject, anxious to show that the poet's prose is prose and that in the poems "there is no prose." Richard Howard describes a class at Yale where he wrote out in a single line on the blackboard a short poem by W. S. Merwin and asked students where this was cut by the free-verse line: "And—invariably—no one gets it 'right.' . . . It means that Merwin's poem is not in verse. When you cannot arrive at a consensus as to where the lines end, then you are writing in prose."[4] In both cases the term *prose* is used to withhold or award approbation, and certainly the same animus is implied in Randall Jarrell's mot on a certain poem by Pound: "The versification is interesting—there is none."

There is nothing unusual in this. The logically opposed face of this usage of the terms may be found in poets of the avant-garde who hope to abolish the prose-poetry distinction, but who depend on the distinction as the gauge of the originality, or perceptibility, of the text.[5] Each party to this dispute claims correctness and can argue with evidences; so merely to lay out in a range the variety of functions of these terms is not to settle disputes concerning their true definition. Moreover, the nonrecognition of the essentially contested quality of the terms *prose* and *poetry* would appear to be necessary to their use as centers of value on one side or the other of the disagreement. Very likely usage will become more delicate, disputes will tend to disappear, if as commentators we can obtain a stronger explanation of our role in this structure of disagreement.[6]

The relation of poetry to prose has always been a naive system of definitions in literary history. Even before we approach the tangled logic of the prose poem, a little device may be helpful: We begin with consciousness, then we edit to speech, then we edit to writing (ordinary language), then we edit to literary writing—at which last stage matters of genre begin to seem important. It seems pretty obvious that ordinary language *is* prose but that prose (literary) is *not* ordinary language; that is, the proposition is not reversible. So we have first ordinary language, then literary language, then literary language can be either in prose or in verse—two different relations to ordinary language, and to each other.

If the task of understanding the place of the prose poem has often been avoided or deferred, that is because for more than a century the presence of the form has disrupted a reciprocal correlation of meanings, the naive definitions that permit the polemic. It has been easier to overlook the form of the prose poem than to revise the definitions. It is possible that the prose poem as a form depends on this state of confusion.

The very existence of the prose poem demonstrates the likely impossibility of fixing such terms. Might it actually rely for its being on the instability of discourse types and genre terms?

Prose and *poetry* compound the difficulties inherent in single contested concepts because the two are in an unbreakable relation, which apparently depends on the resistance to definition of the key terms. Writers themselves have attempted to revise the oversimple contrast by claiming that prose and poetry are indeed different domains, distinguishable in many contexts but not, for literary purposes in an avant-garde era, unrelated. One of the first to do so was Wordsworth, who declined to say that the opposite of poetry was prose. There have also been times in history when it has seemed less necessary for writers to make a choice between prose and poetry—the period between Aloysius Bertrand and Stéphane Mallarmé in France, and the period from 1960 to the present in England and the United States. Informing and surrounding such moments is a whole system of literary assumptions, wherein prose and poetry cut each other into two different tracts, again and again, along different lines.

Since the first-generation Romantics, and especially since the invention of the prose poem by Bertrand in the 1830s, poetry has been "continually split open" by prose (Octavio Paz). On occasion, through a reverse procedure, poetry has operated upon prose. In the 1820s Pushkin introduced into a rarified poetic tradition the novel-in-verse, along with essayistic argumentation and a more direct and limber syntax. By this powerful example, artistic prose in novel and essay was enlivened in Russia during the second half of the century, but then prose conquered poetry to the extent of ceasing to be perceived in any kind of relation with it—and a new opening toward poetry was required after 1900 by Blok and Biely and others. Rather similarly, blank verse and Ossianic prose split the notion of rhymed verses that reigned between Dryden and Samuel Johnson, the more prolix forms actually carrying, for many of Johnson's contemporaries, more poetic feeling than the heroic couplet. One of those contemporaries of Johnson, Jean Jacques Rousseau, actually asked himself in a notebook, "How to be a poet in prose?"[7] The growth of a poetic prose in Rousseau, Chateaubriand, Goethe, Hazlitt, Lamb, De Quincey, disturbed the authority and balance of Neo-Classical prose. There developed the nervous personal voice, related to the more intrusive accent and flexible intonation in ballads and meditative poems in blank verse. Though these writers produced no prose poems, their changeable sentences and wavering intonations very likely prepared the coming of a new prose.

The new prose came as a result, directly and later, of a "crackup" [*brisure*] of the great literary forms, as Mallarmé has called his generation's crisis of prosody. In the prose poem, this violent regrouping of old elements meant "a necessary disjunction between poetry and versification," and, "under the banner of rhythm, a protest against meter" (Suzanne Bernard). Mallarmé called this kind of text, which questions even its very name its manner of existing, a "critical poem." His judgment comes in a note on sentences and the spaces between them, where the critical aspect of the poem, he says, will be shown through breaks in the text—through "immediate thought rhythms" that govern the prosody, and therefore do not belong to the domain of ordinary communication. Mallarmé believes that poetry is an activity of research.

Les cassures du texte, on se tranquillisera, observent de concorder, avec sens et n'inscrivent d'espace nu que jusqu'à leurs points d'illumination: une forme, peut être, en sort, actuelle, permettant, à ce qui fut longtemps le poème en prose et notre recherche, d'aboutir, en tant, si l'on joint mieux les mots, que poëme critique. . . .Sans doute y a-t-il moyen, là, pour un poëte qui par habitude ne pratique pas le vers libre, de montrer, en l'aspect de morceaux compréhensifs et brefs, par la suite, avec expérience, tels rythmes immédiats de pensée ordonnant une prosodie.[8]

(The breaks in the text, to set one's mind at rest, will need to harmonize with the meaning and trace an empty space, only up to their illumination point: a form may then emerge, up-to-date, thus allowing what was for a long time the prose poem, and our research, finally to manifest itself, putting it more aptly, as a critical poem. . . . For the poet who, out of habit, is not a devotee of free verse, this is probably a means of showing, eventually, with some experience, through comprehensive and brief pieces, those immediate thought rhythms governing a prosody.)

Mallarmé's experimental procedures, involving breaks in the skeins of consciousness and grammar, intend to do violence to literature and to the last and most stubborn of conventions, language itself. The breaks in the critical poem, on this showing, entail the whitening of the page by new and more varieties of continuity and discontinuity. Sentence revolts against paragraph, word against sentence.

Mallarmé implies another kind of disruption. Breaks partition the individual text but also, in literary history, divide one text from its parents and neighbors. That is why Mallarmé can hint that the prose poem was latent in literature for some time before it manifested itself "finally . . . as a critical poem." That is why J. K. Huysmans in his novel *À rebours* makes a special point of having his decadent hero des Esseintes praise the prose poems of

Mallarmé for giving the force of the novel but suppressing that form's dragging analytical and descriptive elements: "En un mot, le poème en prose representait, pour des Esseintes, le suc concrete, l'osmazôme de la littérature, l'huile essentielle de l'art."⁹ "Osmazôme," a culinary term, refers to the soluble-in-water oily essence of meats, and probably pertains to the prose poem's extreme foreshortening of narrative curve, the concentration of plot in this form. While to some the form might seem a weakening of shape, according to Huysmans, Mallarmé makes shapes denser, therefore more artful. Mallarmé, flattered, wrote "Prose pour des Esseintes," a poem in tight quatrains that mocks the whole prose-versus-poetry contrast with a title that alludes to the medieval Church's habit of calling a certain kind of verse liturgy a "prose."

In truth, writers of the prose poem like all writers of merit use the medium of their particular time and style in order to break from the medium. The only differences between the others and the writers of prose poems would be the intensity of the wish and the historical determinants of the technical means employed.

Narrative of Consciousness

When he advanced his concept of literary form as proceeding, Coleridge meant to supplement, not replace, the premises of Aristotle's *Poetics.* Unquestionably he agreed with Aristotle that "plot is the basic principle, the heart and soul, as it were, of tragedy, and the characters come second . . . it is the imitation of an action and indicates the persons primarily for the sake of their action."¹⁰ Coleridge's definitions of *plot, character, imitate,* and *action* did not precisely coincide with Aristotle's definitions, but the well-formed sequence of the text was Coleridge's central interest as it was Aristotle's. One of the ways Coleridge's poetics notably supplements Aristotle's is in taking the demand for strong plotting from tragic and epic actions to the lyric, to the act of the mind in a poem meditative, personal. The action of the text in the Coleridge tradition is a cognitive and linguistic sequence, where the events are thoughts, words. The prose poem is the extreme instance of this Romantic-Modern tendency to cede form sense from event to thought, from versification to grammar.

Every sentence in the poem is a narrative, insofar as it puts into an order the reader's acts of attention and habits of response to language; and the sequence of sentences makes up another, larger narrative. The narrative of the consciousness of author and reader is the same thing as the plot of the poem's sentences, taken singly and together.¹¹ In the way it engages the human impulse to find form and make sense amongst materials often disparate and intentionally obscured, the prose poem may stand for all other innovative poetries in the twentieth century. More than those other dispositions of the text, though, the prose poem plays on and against the reader's willingness to find plots when none are intended, to make sentence sense when none exists. Where in free verse the well-formed English sentence acted as a norm, a last resort of form, study of the prose poem must confront the possible obliteration of this last and most flexible of units. I think we will find, though, that the dethroning of the English sentence is an altogether more difficult revolution for writers to accomplish than the dethroning of the iambic foot.

The tale of the narrative of consciousness must properly start with sentences in French. Aloysius Bertrand thought he was renovating the medium of prose, making it denser, more telegraphic, with the images and rhythms of his *Gaspard de la nuit* (1842). The elements of this work are 1) diabolism, for the imagined author is shabby Gaspard, "un pauvre diable. . . . Ses cheveux longs comme un saule, et peignés comme des broussailles, ses mains décharnées, pareilles à des ossuaires, sa physionomie narquoise" (page 36); 2) delectation of the Gothic and odd in the old city of Dijon, locale of most of the seventy-four pieces; and 3) analogy with painted genre scene, evident in the book's subtitle, "Fantasies à la manière de Rembrandt et de Callot." I imagine that choice of a spatial, pictorial analogy for his writing enabled Bertrand to reconstitute the linear and unitary plot typical in his admired Walter Scott. Bertrand makes many smaller plots from diverse events and perspectives, yet keeps the work single by virtue of the city setting and the consistently bizarre quality of Gaspard's interests. The novel's recessive tendency to present the reader with tableaux is brought to the foreground, and fictional plot, a dominant tendency in the novel, is severely compressed. In the text called "The Mason," one of the set titled "Flemish School," plot is reformulated as a narrative not of events but of perceptions, thoughts:

Le maçon

Le maître maçon. "Regardez ces bastions, ces contreforts; on les dirait construits pour l'éternité."

—Schiller, *Guillaume Tell*

Le maçon Abraham Knupfer chante, la truelle à
la main, dans les airs échafaudé,—si haut que,
lisant les vers gothiques du bourdon, il nivelle
de ses pieds, et l'église aux trente arcs-boutants,
et la ville aux trente églises.

Il voit les tarasques de pierre vomir l'eau des
ardoises dans l'abîme confus des galeries, des
fenêtres, des pendentifs, des clochetons, des
tourelles, des toits et des charpentes, que tache,
d'un point gris l'aile énchancrée et immobile
du tiercelet.

Il voit les fortifications qui se découpent
en étoile, la citadelle qui se rengorge comme une
géline dans un tourteau, les cours des palais où le
soleil tarit les fontaines, et les cloîtres des
monastères où l'ombre tourne autour des piliers.

Les troupes impériales se sont logées dans le
faubourg. Voilà qu'un cavalier tambourine là-bas.
Abraham Knupfer distingue son chapeau à trois
cornes, ses aiguillettes de laine rouge, sa cocarde
traversée d'un ganse, et sa queue nouée d'un rouban.

Ce qu'il voit encore, ce sont des soudards qui,
dans le parc empanaché de gigantesques ramées, sur
de larges pelouses d'émeraude, criblent de coups
d'arquebuse un oiseau de bois fiché à la pointe
d'un mai.

Et le soir, quand la nef harmoniuse de la catédrale
s'endormit, couchée les bras en croix, il aperçut, de
l'échele, à l'horizon, un village incendié par des
gens de guerre, qui flamboyait comme une comète dans
l'azur.[12]

The Mason

The Master Mason: "Come look at these bastions, these buttresses; they
seem to have been built for all eternity."

—Schiller, *William Tell*

Abraham Knupfer, a mason, trowel in hand, sings from a scaffolded air,
so high that, reading the gothic inscription in a belfry, he sees between his
feet the church with thirty flying buttresses, and the town with thirty
churches.

He sees gargoyles pouring water from the slates into a canyon of bal-
conies, windows, vaults, turrets, towers, rooftops and beams, splashing a
small patch on the carved granite wing of one of the falcons gray.

He sees fortifications standing out against the sky, the citadel puffed up
like a hen on her nest, the palace grounds where the sun dries up fountains, and the monastery cloisters where shadows circle pillars.

Imperial troops are stationed in the neighborhood. There's a cavalry
drummer down there. Abraham Knupfer can make out his tricornered hat,
his red woolen epaulets, the braid decorating his cockade, and his long
ponytail gathered with a ribbon.

Later, he sees a band of veterans on the emerald greens of a park
bedecked with boughs, shooting their matchlocks at a mangled bird stuck
on top of the May pole.

And that night, while the musical nave of the cathedral was sleeping, at
rest with arms crossed, he saw, from his ladder, a village fired by soldiers
burning on the horizon like a comet in the blue.)[13]

Bertrand through Gaspard adopts the bird's-eye view of the mason, or the
view, perhaps, of the bell tower upon the city below. The revolutionary

troops are intruders on the Gothic city, impertinent, but they are cometlike, passing intrusions. So ephemeral are the troops that their violence is aesthetic, red flame against blue sky, when seen at the right distance and in the perspective of the eternal buildings. Every paragraph but one is a single long sentence, packed with perceptual detail, moving through several types of coordination and subordination in order to delay best details to last in paragraph and poem.

Charles Baudelaire, having read *Gaspard* (as he said) "for the twentieth time at least," imagined a reality "more abstract" and Modern than the painted-panel descriptions of Bertrand. If Bertrand was picturesque, *Le spleen de Paris* (1869; also a city book, but not about a medieval city) develops instead the "obsessive ideal" of a musical prose, taking its analogies from a less representational art—music. Baudelaire's prose poems consist of a texture ("croisement") of rhythm emerging from the innumerable connections ("innombrables rapports") self makes with world when we live in the gigantic cities ("villes énormes") of the nineteenth century. Neither poetry nor prose would seem to be sufficiently complex to display the multitude of significances in a swarming city. Thus, to fill a specific literary need, he invented a tertium quid, a form at the same time prose and poetry: "Which of us hasn't, during his days of ambition, dreamed the miracle of a flexible prose, musical without rhythm or rhyme, flexible and broken enough to adapt itself to the lyric movements of the spirit, to the undulations of reverie, and to the leaping of consciousness?"[14] When he writes meter, Baudelaire is unable to permit himself the untidiness of a line unconnected with another by rhyme; for his prose poem, he wants the flexibility of a different music, and a book as a whole with the form of a "serpent," which, he wrote, "has neither tail nor head, since on the contrary, everything there is at once head and tail, alternately and reciprocally." In a calligrammelike sketch of a tribute to Bertrand, Mallarmé in 1866 used the similar image of a ring for the prose poem's unusual plot:

Baudelaire thought novels dangerous, baggy indulgences, and yet with this collection of fifty prose poems he does hope to win for poetry something like narrative, as well as something of the forensic movement of essays. One need only glance at opening sentences to appreciate this intention: "Vauvenargues dit que...." ("Les veuves"); "Il est un pays superbe, un pays Cocagne, dit-on...." ("L'invitation au voyage"). He uses narrative and argumentative structures, here and in later prose poems, but for different reason and effect. Narrative defeats narrative, argument argument, in a text where concatenated feeling makes the whole plot. In the prose poem, "feeling gives importance to action" (Wordsworth), and the events are those of consciousness.

Despite the wide variation of surface structures and styles, Baudelaire's prose poems, and most others, too, share with all post-Romantic art the prompting to show the author's mind through acts of language—but to avoid the overpersonal they partition the voice and thereby multiply it. As with all post-Romantic poetry of value, the attempt is to understand, ultimately to cast out, the crippling effects of undue self-consciousness. In the process, the reader is brought close to the voices themselves, often, as in Baudelaire's "Enivrez-vous," by ambiguous reference of pronouns.

> Il faut être toujours ivre. Tout est là: c'est l'unique question. Pour ne pas sentir l'horrible fardeau du Temps qui brise vos épaules et vous penche vers la terre, il faut vous enivrer sans trêve.
> Mais de quoi? De vin, de poésie ou de vertu, à votre guise, mais enivrez-vous.
> Et si quelquefois, sur les marches d'un palais, sur l'herbe verte d'un fossé, dans la solitude morne de votre chambre, vous vous réveillez, l'ivresse déjà diminuée ou disparue, demandez au vent, à la vague, à l'étoile, à l'oiseau, à l'horloge, à tout ce qui fuit, à tout ce que gémit, à tout ce qui roule, à tout ce qui chant, à tout ce qui parle, demandez quelle heure il est; et le vent, la vague, l'étoile, l'oiseau, l'horloge, vous répondrent: "Il est l'heure de s'enivrer! Pour n'être pas les esclaves martyrisés du Temps, enivrez-vous sans cesse! De vin, de poésie, ou de vertu, à votre guise."[15]

Get Drunk!

> Get drunk and stay drunk. That's it; that's the sole solution to our greatest problem. So as not to feel the terrible burden of time breaking your back and bowing you ever closer to the earth, you must remain incessantly, relentlessly, constantly intoxicated.
> But intoxicated with what? With wine, with poetry, or with virtue: whatever you prefer. But get drunk!
> And if now and then you happen to come to, on the steps outside a palace, amid the green grass of some ditch or in the dreary solitude of your room; and you discover that your drunkenness is leaving you, or has already vanished, ask wind and wave, ask star, bird and clock; ask every fleeting thing, every flowing thing, everything that can sing or speak or croak or cry out:—ask them: "What time is it now?" And wind and wave, star, bird and clock will all answer: "It's time to get drunk! Yes, if you are not merely to live out your lives as the martyred slaves of Time, make sure you stay drunk too! With wine, poetry, or virtue, whatever you prefer.")[16]

This is not Baudelaire's best poem, but the darting in and out of unfixed pronouns, the interpenetration of voices, the recurrence of key phrases in different contexts, all have a measure of sophistication. Baudelaire else-where said that everything in life depends on the concentration, or the vaporization, of the consciousness ("moi"); either will do, and here the direction is all toward the latter impulse. The tone is expansive, driving. Why be drunken? To escape the oppressive self. Yet the urge to escape is at all points undercut by the acknowledgment of mutability and of memory. Thus the lyric impulse becomes urban, malign, and precarious.

Both the injunction and the question are the author's. Baudelaire is in dialogue with himself. His voice is diversified into two partial positions, catechizer and neophyte; but then at the end, five voices of nonhuman nature are imagined speaking in unison, and in their collective utterance they repeat phrases that have appeared in the earlier voices. The insistent commands are from the poem's speaker to the self that writes, but the "vous" also includes the reader as implied auditor of all the voices.

Several elements combine in the prose poem at this moment of historical origin: a narrative of consciousness in which feeling is more important than action; a fellowship of sorts between the poem's nominal speaker and the actual author, and between those two and the reader as actual auditor; a flexible yet broken phrasing that contains functional recurrences and discontinuities, as well as the significant absence of meter and rhyme (expectation frustrated, expectation unconventionally met). So described, except for the prosodic element, this genre corresponds in several particulars with the dramatic monologue, another nineteenth-century innovative genre and one whose rise is coextensive with the prose poem's. Both genres are products of the Romantic exploration into the role of the subject in the text; in both, as in the landscape poetry of the greater Romantic lyric, the tale is of the mind projecting itself onto the outer scene, and greeting itself there with an access of new knowledge about the relation of self to world. Robert Langbaum shows how the author of the dramatic monologue is able to dwell on personal materials indirectly through a fictional situation and in a voice nominally not his own, thus avoiding the imputation of egotism while extending the range of voices and the possibility for incident. Meanwhile the reader regards the nominal speaker with combined sympathy and suspicion, impressed by the fluent speech but aware that the utterance is only a refraction of the author's thought. Langbaum's title, *The Poetry of Experience,* might also apply to the prose poem as another version of the language of the Romantic self.

There is one major difference. In the prose poem, the auditor is not normally the overhearer, as might be the image for dramatic monologue. Such an analogue is not applicable to the prose poem, which puts the reader into the position of a second author, and the author into that of the first reader.[17]

Narrative is driven inward. In Baudelaire's "Les fenêtres," the poet imagines a whole history for an old woman seen "across waves of rooftops" and through a closed window; he sleeps "proud to have survived and suffered in others than myself," and if someone asks whether his tale is true the answer comes: "What does it matter whether the reality is situated outside of myself, if the story has helped me to live, to feel that I am and what I am?" The window in Charles Tomlinson's "The Daisies" is in the same way a transparent boundary between mind and world.

> All evening, daisies outside the window, have gone on flying, stalk-anchored, towards the dark. Still, vibrant, swaying, they have stood up through dryness into beating rain: stellar cut-outs, arrested explosions; too papery thin to be "flower-heads"—flower-faces perhaps; upturned hands with innumerable fingers. Unlike the field daisies, they do not shut with dark: they stretch as eagerly towards it as they did to the sun, images of flight. And your own image, held by the pane, diffuses your features among those of the daisies, so that you flow with them until your hand, lifted to close the window, becomes conscious of its own heaviness. It is their stalks thrust them into flight as much as their launching-out of winged fingers, all paper accents *grave* thrusting on acute, acute on *grave*. Cut the stalks and they fall, they do not fly; let them lose their bond and they, too, would grow, not lighter, but suddenly heavy with the double pull of their flower flesh and of the rain clinging to them.[18]

The poet finds many conceits for the daisies, and these are a witty form of definition. But the most complete evocation of the state of the flowers comes with the middle sentence of the poem, where the speaker's image "diffuses . . . among those of the daisies" in a double focus of similarity and difference between mind and world, enabled by the windowpane's combined transparency and mirroring qualities at evening. In the last sentence the performative verbs "cut" and "let them lose" mark a final stage of the similarity of flower to person, an imagination of violence that transfers the term "heavy" from human to flower. It is a little parable, really. Flowers are emblems of liberty and imagination, but also like humans must submit to the "pull of their . . . flesh." More narrowly, the method produces the double value of the pun, as when "grave" as the description of the angle of the flowers is a French accent, but in English an image of mutability. Such an effect reproduces in little the attempt of the whole: metaphoric transference of qualities from self to world and back, an action complete with the phrase "flower flesh" in the last clause. As a process of intellection, the poem represents a full revolution of the mind as it dwells on this subject and unfolds a web of connections both in meaning and sound (for example, "winged fingers"); because it is a complete turning of one parablelike thought, the poem is, though brief, comprehensive.

Sometimes, as with Rimbaud's "Les ponts," narrative is driven inward more violently.

Des ciels gris de cristal. Un bizarre dessin de ponts, ceux-ci droits,

ceux-là bombés, d'autres descendant en obliquant en angles sur les pre-
miers, et ces figures se renouvelant dans les autres circuits éclairés du
canal, mais tous tellement longs et légers que les rives, chargées de
dômes, s'abaissent et s'amoindrissent. Quelques-uns de ces ponts sont
encore chargés de masures. D'autres soutiennent des mâts, des signaux,
des frêles parapets. Des accords mineurs se croisent, et filent; des cordes
montent des berges. On distingue une veste rouge, peut-être d'autres
costume et des instruments de musique. Sont-ce ces airs populaires, des
bouts de concerts seigneuriaux, des restants d'hymnes publics?
Un rayon blanc, tombant du haut du ciel, anéantit cette comédie.[19]

Bridges

Crystal-grey skies. Bridges in weird designs, some straight, some convex,
others curving downwards, slanted across the first ones, and these figures
recur in the other illuminated windings of the canal which are so long and
light that the banks, laden with domes, slope downwards and diminish.
Some of the bridges are still lined with huts. Others are supporting masts,
signal lights, frail parapets. Minor chords criss-cross, and weave in and
out, ropes run upwards from the banks. A red coat can be distinguished
and perhaps other costumes and musical instuuments. Are they folk-
songs, scraps of manorial concerts, bits of public hymns? The water is
grey and blue, wide like an arm of the sea.—A shaft of white light, piercing
from high above, annihilates the performance.)

Up to the dash and last sentence, it is a vorticist cityscape, which might have
come from Wyndham Lewis, all leaping and overlapping arcs of circles,
bridge and reflection alike layered, with the gray color unrelieved except for
a flash of red or indeterminate snatch of music. Descriptive elements are
packed densely in a row, suggesting likely paths of narrative that are never
followed. We "make out" a red coat, we wonder what sorts of music ema-
nate from the scene, but these remain enigmas. Then everything is scrubbed
off the scene by the last sentence; the little description, with its narrative
leads, was building toward nothing, was in fact a comedy and instantly
expendable. The narrative elements were all tiny guises to keep alive a
certain interest in following the sentences, yet insofar as we responded to
this as plot we were being drawn into a trap. Abruptly the prose poem closes
on us, the descriptive and narrative elements proving to be pretexts for a
display of the writer's authority. What seemed genuine reference to the outer
world was in fact a joking allusion to our propensity to respond to a text as
scene and process; after all, the text proves to be only, but splendidly,
language. (And yet, the crucial thing about even this experimental sort of
language is the way it cannot finally eliminate meaning; the residue of reference is indestructible.) Here as elsewhere in *Illuminations,* Rimbaud uses
but disclaims complicity with the reader's habits of responding: if the events
produced in sequence are merely verbal, then all the leads and allusions are
dead ends, and the writer's position is a mockery of self and reader, yet at
the same time magisterial.

At the end of the ferocious, incongruous catalog titled "Side Show"
("Parade"), in a claim that defines the use of the form by other and later

writers, Rimbaud says, "I alone have the key to this savage side show." A
"savage procession" of images of anarchy, flashed on the mind of the reader,
a pseudonarrative of joke, pastiche, cock and bull—the form as a whole is
maxjacobien and biased in the direction of one of its major theorists and
minor practitioners. In the 1916 preface to *Le cornet à dés,* Max Jacob,
extracting laws from his own practice, said the prose poem must be short
("difficult to be beautiful for long"), must be situated by "a distancing from
the subject" or speaker, and must possess that style which is not the writer's
own speech but "the working of materials, the buildup of the whole."[20] By
means of the prose poem the reader will be not merely surprised but "trans-
planted," plunged into a different universe. Jacob's 1943 preface went
further to claim that the *Cornet* poems were wrested from the unconscious,
"words at liberty, chance associations of ideas, dreams and daydreams,
hallucinations."[21] At its simplest the form is a vehicle for the chaining of
wordplay and homophony, both of which are characteristics of the formal
babble some people call automatic writing:

> Cet Alemand était fou d'art, de foulards de la poulardes. Dans son pays, la
> Reine-Claude est peint sur les foulards; á table, on en sait aussi qui rôdent
> autour des poulardes.

Or again:

> Le toit, c'est quatre, quatre, quatre: il y en a quatre. Le perron est une
> pelouse qui nous opérons et qui les jalouse. Les toits sont amarante: reflet
> d'orage! rage! rage! et l'ensemble est un sucre, en stuc, en ruche, moche,
> riche.

The tendency for twentieth-century poets to engage in echolalia and verbal
jugglery often hides an anxious appeal to the unknown, a desire to see
established new connections between words approached in this way through
their sonorities. Through a suspension of the laws of space, time, and causality, the relations of the narrative are blurred.

Tranced, the poem plots its own logic, in Jacob more gentle and closed on
itself than in Rimbaud:

> Quand le sire de Framboisy revint de guerre, sa femme lui fit des grands
> reproches à l'église, alors il dit: "Madame, voici la clef de tous mes biens,
> je pars pour jamais." La dame laissa tomber la clef sur le pavé du temple
> par delicatesse. Une nonne, dans un coin, priait, parce qu'elle avait égaré
> la sienne, la clef du couvent et qu'on n'y pouvait pas entrer. "Voyez donc
> si votre serrure s'accommode celle-ci." Mais la clef n'était plus là. Elle
> était déjà au musée de Cluny: c'était une énorme clef en forme de tronc
> d'arbre.

> (When the lord of Raspberry came back from the wars, his wife re-
> proached him mightily at church, so he said: "Madame, here is the key to
> all my possessions; I depart for ever." Out of delicacy, she let the key slip

to the stone floor of the temple. A nun, in the corner, prayed, because she had mislaid her own, the key to the convent that no one could get into. "See, then, if your lock fits this one." But the key was no longer there. It was already at the Musée de Cluny—a gigantic key in the form of a treetrunk.)

The witty turn is the specialty of Jacob, who is always more successful with the surreal joke than an American writer similar in theme and approach, Russell Edson.[22] We are led into this poem by the plausibility of the fablelike opening; yet the first phrase, we remember, is lifted from an old French song, whose situation Jacob is reconstructing for his broad tale about a chastity belt. The sexual content is only thinly covered by the metaphors of keys and locks. The wife drops the key because she pledges good faith; she will be like the nun, who is searching for the key to her convent. At the end there is a wrenching out from this mock-narrative time to a Modern perspective. The germ of the prose poem was the poet's seeing the key of a chastity belt in a museum and imagining an explanation of its presence, its links with humanity in the past, the absurdity of a masculine-appearing object having a feminine gender ("la clef"). The temporal-logical breaks, the shifts of grammar, enable Jacob's false plot to inhibit, or complicate, the reader's response to the tale-telling of folksong and conversational narrative.

The expectations of normal narrative are necessary to the proper effect of the narrative of consciousness. Pseudonarrative or false plot over a long stretch is often, as in Bertrand or Rimbaud or William Carlos Williams, managed by the presentation of discontinuous panels of language, illuminations, slidelike patches of paragraphs recognizably connected by theme and style. Often within the single paragraph of Williams's *Kora in Hell: Improvisations* (1920) every sentence is laid on like a stroke, a new color of intention:

> Beautiful white corpse of night actually! So the north-west winds of death are mountain sweet after all! All the troubled stars are put to bed now: three bullets from wife's hand none kindlier: in the crown, in the nape and one lower: three starlike holes among a million pocky pores and the moon of your mouth: Venus, Jupiter, Mars, and all stars melted forthwith into this one good white light over the inquest table,—the traditional moth beating its wings against it—except there are two here. But sweetest are the caresses of the county physician, a little clumsy perhaps—*mais*—! and the Prosecuting Attorney, Peter Valuzzi and the others, waving green arms of maples to the tinkling of the earliest ragpicker's bells. Otherwise—: kindly stupid hands, kindly coarse voices, infinitely soothing, infinitely detached, infinitely beside the question, restfully babbling of how, where, why and night is done and the green edge of yesterday has said all it could.[23]

This story of officials at a police autopsy becomes a speech to the corpse. Moving from grim detail to lyricism, the sentences make sudden changes to partition, or to set in opposition, the details presented. "So-but-*mais-otherwise*": these are sentences perpendicular to one another, obliging the reader to invest strenuous mental activity to follow a brief passage. The narrative of an inquest becomes a pretext for calling forth the reader's minutest knowledge of grammar. Roy Fisher, though his earlier prose in *The Ship's Orchestra* (1966) made many connections with normal narrative, has more recently in *The Cut Pages* (1971) suppressed semantic links and proceded by one-line bursts of sentence fragment. Partitioning downward further than Williams in texts that resemble film scripts without dialogue, he has sacrificed certain tracts of obvious meaning in order to gain immediacy in the presentation of image and discourse. Aspects of a thing, event, or relationship are offered—never, even in the section "Stopped Frames and Set Pieces," anything approaching delineation of the implied whole.

Here as everywhere in the prose poem, those "breaks in the text" demanded by Mallarmé are discontinuities narrative as well as formal. This is dramatically true in one of the finest of recent prose-poem sequences, Geoffrey Hill's *Mercian Hymns* (1971). Hill maintains throughout a studied anachronism, a voice that comprehends a span of knowledge from what King Offa understood of the eighth century A.D. to Ruskin's *Fors Clavigera*, beer crates, and the construction of the M5 roadway up the spine of modern England. Hill presents his condensed paragraphs in the form of the long verset or line stanza, a technique that is employed more digressively and personally in Allen Ginsberg's *Howl* (1956) and Karl Shapiro's *Bourgeois Poet* (1964). In Shapiro and Ginsberg anecdote, phantasmagoria, catalog, and rant are all part of controlled self-revelation; yet they speak in their own voices, where Hill employs dramatic monologue. Shapiro's poem also resembles Williams's *Kora* and David Antin's "november exercises" in the way paragraphs seem to be diary entries, rearranged or invented perhaps, but related to real time; individual entries may violate conventions of time and causality, but not the outer framework. Antin's book *Talking* (1972), in addition to the diarylike form, employs improvisational dialogue transcribed from tapes, and, as here, the lyrical lecture:

```
           in my mind        but imagine a doug heubler
piece in which doug heubler        operates a system
        he operates a system in which      he      proposes
that you apprehend a criminal and he offers the
closed system       if the work is bought      if the
criminal is apprehended the buyer pays for the
apprehension
        now what kind of work is that? is it a piece
of sculpture?        its an art work to the degree
that it occupies your mind?        perhaps[24]
```

Among the least internally divided of long prose poems are the rhapsodies that blacken the page in John Ashbery. The justified margins of *Three Poems* contain immense sentences, seemingly endless ratiocination, mainly concerning the psychological, social, and linguistic conditions under which any sentences can be strung on a page. There is no claim of offering anything more than a narrative of sentences, themselves jerry-built from clichés and dead rhythms, a story that is no story, and therefore in a bland way boring. But Ashbery intends to bore, arguing in the text itself that the irritation is, if you persist, salutary:

> And as the discourse continues and you think you are not getting anything out of it, as you yawn and rub your eyes and pick your nose or scratch your head, or nudge your neighbor on the hard wooden bench, this knowledge is getting through to you, and taking just the forms it needs to impress itself upon you, the forms of your inattention and incapacity or unwillingness to understand. For it is certain that you will rise from the bench a new person, and even before you have emerged into the full daylight of the street you will feel that a change has begun to operate in you, within your very fibers and sinews, and when the light of the street floods over you it will have become real at last, all traces of doubt will have been pulverized by the influx of light slowly mounting to bury those crass seamarks of egocentricity and warped self-esteem you were able to navigate by but which you no longer need now that the rudder has been swept out of your hands, and this whole surface of daylight has become one with that other remembered picture of light, when you were setting out, and which you feared would disappear because of its uniqueness, only now realizing that this singleness was the other side of the coin of its many-faceted diversity and interest, and that it may be simultaneously cherished for the former and lived in thanks to the versatility for the latter.[25]

Utterly serious, consciously monstrous, in its technique—Ashbery's book is opposed to the careful methods of Williams and Fisher, yet in our day the extremes of continuity and discontinuity are equally experimental, equally contemptuous of normal narrative.

My description of the narrative of consciousness, as the prose poem's attempt to create less conventional conventions, has made passing and analogical reference to a range of types of prose. The assumption is that prose, whether literary or not, is inherently iconic and figurative, composed as it is of palpable grammar, with a determinate display in paragraphs and justified margins.[26] How prose moves from non-art to art is one of the most pressing unsolved difficulties of current poetics. Since there are not two separate grammars for art and non-art, and since not all rhythmical prose makes a prose poem, the author's intention to mark off a prose poem from other forms of writing will influence the way that poem is read and interpreted. Usually the prose poem will be marked off from other written discourse by a declaration of antagonism that would seem to disallow our use of prose forms as stylistic models for this type. But here again our notion of a linkage between prose formats and poetic formats must be used to interpret the statements poets make in their manifestos. Mallarmé, when he collected his prose poems in *Divigations* (1896), in an exemplary usage called them "Anecdotes ou poèmes," meaning not to assimilate poetry to prose but rather to specify the tendency of the work, and to acknowledge a continual oscillation or struggle between two formal types, both conventional. Let the anecdote stand for the whole range of written types on the side of simple prose: proverb, aphorism, joke, catalog, parable, fable, diary, travel narrative, memoir, meditation, rant, phantasmagoria, rhapsody, sketch, short story, and lyrical novel. The progress of the genre after Baudelaire would tend to confirm, as one of the major generic characteristics, a new aversion to the anecdote. The anecdote is not sufficiently a compound of incident and determinate style (though it certainly has its typical patterns, as speech-act sociologists have shown). It offers brevity but not comprehensiveness, and thus, as a lump of personal data, belongs in the sphere of non-art. By sheer antagonism to whatever is anecdotal, the prose poem wants increasingly to give to narrative that intensity which comes of the elimination of discursiveness.

Narrative of Grammar

In the prefatory materials to his great *Dictionary*, Samuel Johnson makes *Prosody*, as a set of rules for English stress, the last subsection under the vast heading, *Grammar*. With this Neo-Classical priority as with so many others, Romanticism attempts a revision. We are coming at last to appreciate what poets since Coleridge have known in theory and practice—the need to see in grammar a phrase of prosody.

No other form, mode, or genre before the prose poem has so called into question the literariness of the poetic device, thereby risking while enhancing and extending our notion of poetry. No one rhetorical element is certified as a marker of poetry, and yet there must be one or more patterns of language that cut shapes in time. To read or write the prose poem is to become rhetorician of a mode that detests rhetoric. Of course, for the interpreter any description of a structural plan is linked always to a loss of semantic richness from the text. That is why any writer of prose poems (or sprung rhythm or free verse) wants the apprehension of form to occasion the least possible loss of semantic value. By avoiding such overfamiliar (to them) devices as meter, rhyme, and the line, avantgardist prosodies hope to give more, and more unhackneyed, information in the sense of unpredictability. Density of information is possible in prose as well as in traditional verse if the chosen form signals ambiguities across all divisions from word through sentence to paragraph and whole poem. A great deal of practical prose discourse tends toward single meaning of the single word, and toward redundancy higher up the scale of abstraction at the message. But artistic prose, equally with Modern verse and certain kinds of criticism and philosophy, prefers figural words with many meanings, which (taken together in syntax) produce over-lapping types of information. The poetic plot of the sentences is thus logically subsequent to the narrative of consciousness treated above, because the narrative of grammar affords the local technique for the construction of a track of feeling.

As my two previous chapters have tried to show by practice, the task of the grammarian is first to classify words by broad function into the same or different form class; second, to describe the more or less systematic ways in which words are "modified" by the addition of prefixes or suffixes (or in more subtle ways); and last, to present the syntax—to state the rules for admissible (that is, grammatical) combinations of words. The development of formal criteria for the analyses of phrases, clauses, and full sentences is by far the most intricate project. Like Aristotle in sections 20 through 22 of the *Poetics,* on the elements of language, the Modern literary critic can also be a grammarian, though with formal criteria less rigorous than any linguist's.

In the prose poem, the relation between overall intent and actual units, between genre and particular poem, can be described with some show of adequacy. This morphological study is necessarily historical, because its first priority is to define the prose poem as a Modern mode; to inspect strictly Modern art sentences and to show how these extreme texts, poems that question poetry, generate a grammar whereby part, whole, and all intervening structures are possible metonymies for each other. William Carlos Williams goes so far as to think that "structurally, the form itself is a 'word'—that dominates every other word in the poem."[27] To deal with the mind that could conceive such a claim, we must trace unprecedented sleights of connection, conflation, expansion, and reweighting of verbal materials. For now the laws of the prose poem must remain partial and defective.

George Saintsbury seems to have suspected something about grammar in his futile attempt to analyze prose rhythm by identifying the long and short stresses of traditional poetic feet. *A History of English Prose Rhythm* (1912), like his three-volume *History of English Prosody* (1910), succeeds in defining and dating period styles, but only by opposing the author's perceptive ear to his eye's idée fixe for scansion.[28] The attempt at quasi-scientific accuracy with the foot hypothesis comes to grief everywhere as Saintsbury tries to apply rules of scansion to a rhythm he has defined as "diverse" by contrast with the "uniform" rhythm of verse. He must admit such monsters as "prose catalexis," and four- and five-syllable "bigger feet" that are "the absolute *sine qua non* of the best numerous prose," and an ornate style in Sir Thomas Browne, in whose scansion "no two identical feet ever follow each other." To push his argument a stage further is to perceive that "a variety of foot arrangement" is not the differentia of prose so much as the contradiction of his method of scansion. David Antin has abandoned all such scansion schemas in his reading of Gertrude Stein's "Miss Furr and Miss Skene" as "concrete poetry with justified margins . . . a traditional phrase poetry, in spite of the punctuation . . . in a profoundly traditional sense . . . a very elegant prosody; but . . . a prosody immanent in English intonation, not the arbitrary convention of meter."[29] Antin's view sorts with that of Mallarmé as quoted above: a prosody might be organized in the prose poem by "immediate thought rhythms." To assimilate prosody to grammar may be heretical, but to move even a few steps in this direction is perfectly in accord with the technical facts of the prose poem as a genre.

With his impressive auditory imagination Saintsbury has identified the following notebook entry from Coleridge as "prose rhythm of the highest quality":

> Leaves of trees upturned by the stirring wind in twilight—an image of paleness, wan affright.

Saintsbury comments, "The omission of the copula and the use of a kind of apposition at 'paleness, wan affright,' is something you will find practically never in Augustan prose, constantly in the nineteenth century; and it gives a rhythmical heightening of the most definite and peculiar kind."[30] Then in a footnote he betrays this accurate description by finding metrical feet in "in twi / light an im / age of pale / ness," and then by noting that the precedent and subsequent clauses entirely preclude such an arrangement for the whole sentence. For him this is proof that this is "*not* verse" in his definition of verse. But for us the issue as resolved may seem a diversionary one, preventing a more immediate inspection of syntax to gauge the energy of the utterance.

Failing the identification of feet, what basic unit of analysis will give richness to the categories of movement and voice? Any grammarian of the prose poem must answer, The sentence, as microcosm of a writer's language habits. (Phrase and clause, incomplete by themselves, cannot be considered relatively freestanding units.) For dissection and articulation, the two typical operations of structural analysis, the sentence offers special advantages. Since it is not a theoretical entity, its modes of possible realization are (in theory) infinite. Each of its instances shares the common feature of grammaticality, but possesses also in its syntax and diction an infinite number of identifiably different features. Again, larger than word or phrase but usually smaller than the whole text, the full stop, whole sentence enables the smooth performance of the skill of reading. Items kept in the reader's developing apprehension are neither too small nor too large; thus while certain elements are made automatic others remain optional, and the degree of anticipation is high but not, except in very extreme cases, sufficient to baffle the reader entirely. (The degree to which the sentence's limits are rendered automatic determines the degree of anticipation involved in the reader's response.) One prominent effect of the prose poem is to give sentences the greatest possible cognitive frustration and excitement. This is achieved by obscuring the internal and external relations of the sentence, a grammatical effect precisely correlated with the obscuring of events as we have already noticed it in the prose poem's narrative of consciousness.

Insofar as its conventions of grammaticality preexist any given utterance, the sentence is universal and anterior. Nonetheless the sentence, as meeting ground of rule-governed activity and creativity, is every time different. (Sentences composed of identical syntactic elements can, of course, be leaden, static; this is one characteristic of bad writing that tries to be experimental.) In the absence of rhyme and meter the sentence is the smallest unit that contains the complete convergence of the psychological, historical, and aesthetic as well as grammatical modes in the literary work. Between the work itself and any of its longer sentences the difference is one of degree only—a difference that disappears when the single sentence constitutes the whole poem.

The degree to which language is automatic in the sentence clearly determines the degree of anticipation involved in the reader's response. As a form the prose poem seems deeply engaged in warring against formulaic language, often by the very methods of "omission of the copula and the use of a kind of apposition" noted by Saintsbury in Coleridge and by my chapter on Hopkins, often by a miserliness with pronouns and conjunctions and a preference for parataxis. A closer look at the sentence from Coleridge might suggest a method for understanding the relation between syntax and lexis. Certain features stand out in relief, especially if we set it out with these (admittedly arbitrary) divisions:

1. Leaves of trees
2. upturned
3. by the stirring wind
4. in twilight
5. —an image of paleness,
6. wan affright

The journal entry first (1–4) presents perceptions, then (5) offers commentary, then (6) develops the commentary by apposition. In numbers 1 through 4 the language is cumulative and embedded; then at the dash the break turns this utterance, with some excitement, toward an ending in a taglike apposition. Coleridge works his prepositions hard, and gets a minimal coherence from them, but a disdain for logical connection and absence of personal pronouns contrive to turn this sentence into a small engine of functional frustration. The very "upturned" is embedded in syntax but operates both forward and back, toward noun and subject "leaves," and toward "wind" as agent of the sentence. The slight connection between "twilight / affright" catches a link of sound back from a previous part of the sentence, overleap-

ing grammar and adding an extra form of equivalence. "Paleness" and "wan"
are not redundant, but different, disjunct nuances with special force, joined
in meaning but separated by a break at the comma. Notation thus turns into
commentary and judgment in the course of Coleridge's little drama of description. The elements of the sentence may seem to be movable counters:
in numbers 1 through 4 and 5 and 6 the elements could have been many ways
transposed with no loss of syntactical coherence, or numbers 5 and 6 could
have come before 1 through 4. That these relations are not clarified makes
for the surprise and complexity of the sentence and the zest of the reader's
developing responses, which are organized by overlapping orbits of continuity and grammatical-rhythmical break. And after all, there are other
poetic constraints here, most obviously the argumentational movement from
concrete to general, and the prosodic brevity of the second half as accented
by the comma's pause.

Coleridge has not written a prose poem, but his sentence may be taken as
an indication. When grammar encroaches on versification in the Modern
poem, it obliges a redefinition of the idea of plot to include any text that
takes the reader's developing apprehension through a determinate process.
A sentence, like a full tragedy, can be woven into and upon itself. Aristotle's
term for the larger plot, *peplegmenos* ("inwoven; intricate"), also applies to
sentences that dispose their elements to elude a loosely episodic structure.
As in W. S. Merwin's poem, "A Thing of Beauty," plot in this widened sense
is still Aristotle's soul of the action, and at the same time the plot is the
grammar of a single sentence:

> Sometimes where you get it they wrap it up in a clock and you take it
> home with you and since you want to see it it takes you the rest of your life
> to unwrap it trying harder and harder to be quick which only makes the
> bells ring more often.[31]

One wants this sentence to end, to break partway and allow us to pause, or
at least to stop stringing new details. One wants definition in the reference of
pronouns, in the six-times-repeated "it" and in the "they-you" series. One
wants ironic references to be self-explanatory, as the mention of the bells
cannot be. One wants the landing place of a comma or semicolon. Is this
thing of Merwin's a sentence? Yes and no—that is the fascination. It fulfills
some of the criteria of a sentence but deliberately flouts others.

The speaker, for example, repeats himself with the "it it" construction at
midsentence, but this usage enables the physical expansion of the sentence,
the prolonging of meaning for "the rest of your life." The first "it" is a
pronoun, referring back to the first three uses of the same term (which have
no referents at all); but the second "it" in midsentence is the kind that in
English never has a referent, as in "it is raining." The same term has different shades of meaning, and what seems a barbarity becomes an ambiguity, as
such irresolvable. The hunt for referents will apparently be fruitless. In this
detail as throughout, local position is deemphasized and hurried past by the

urgent trajectory of grammar. In its meaning, but also in its breathless parataxis, the sentence conveys the frustration of a quest for beauty in a universe where time is racing.

Arguably, this informal text grammar works on longer texts, too. Charles Tomlinson's "Poem" appears to be a single sentence by virtue of its interknit construction, its return to the beginning in the final sentence:

> The muscles which move the eyeballs, we are told, derive from a musculature which once occupied the body end to end. . . . Sunblaze as day goes, and the light blots back the scene to iris the half-shut lashes. A look can no longer extricate the centre of the skyline copse. But the last greys, the departing glows caught by the creepers bearding its mass, prevail on the half-blinded retina. Branches deal with the air, vibrating the beams that thread into one's eye. So that "over there" and "in here" compound a truce neither signed—a truce that, insensibly and categorically, grows to a decree, and what one hoped for and what one is, must measure themselves against those demands which the eye receives, delivering its writ on us through a musculature which occupies the body end to end.[32]

Tomlinson has called "Processes" a small group of prose poems included in a book otherwise versified (1969). Whatever the outer form the theme of the genre as he practices it is usually, as here, the "truce" between perception and cognition. The special process here enacted is an extension of the first into the last sentence, a verbal elision or leaping of the anecdote of perception that is the middle part of the poem. Changing of verb tenses signals the development: "once occupied" has by the end become "occupies," a minimal grammatical change that is yet the key to the poem. By the agency of a veridical image of the world bodied against the self, what seems a notional, historical postulate becomes a present truth. The middle sentences, which linger on the necessary detail of sense experience, are dense with alliteration, repetition, internal prose rhyme ("sunblaze as day goes"), and indeterminate noun-verb shifting ("iris" and "glows"), whose full understanding requires the combined or alternate specifying of a word's type in diction and its place in the syntactic sequence. The interfusion of mind and world is progressively truce, decree, and writ, a local instance of how this kind of process, in verbal texture and meaning, has also the tone of witty argument and stately movement of procession.

Sentence-as-narrative has a very different movement in the first two of Geoffrey Hill's *Mercian Hymns* (1971):

I

> King of the perennial holly-groves, the riven sandstone: overlord of the M5: architect of the historic rampart and ditch, the citadel at Tamworth, the summer hermitage in Holy Cross: contractor to the desirable new estates: saltmaster, money-changer: commissioner for oaths: martyrologist: the friend of Charlemagne.
> "I liked that," said Offa, "sing it again."

II

A pet name, a common name. Best-selling brand, curt graffito. A laugh; a cough. A syndicate. A specious gift. Scoffed-at horned photograph.

The starting-cry of a race. A name to conjure with.[33]

Hill jams language with the equivalences of rhyme and off-rhyme, alliteration, outright redundant repetition, and word compounds (four in the tight space of Hymn II). A brokenness of syntax is conveyed in Hymn I by listing divided items separated by commas and colons; and in II by periods, semicolons, and the space between parts. Certain values of sound and sense, notably the theme-idea "name" three times repeated in Hymn II, persist despite continual new starts in sentence fragments that attempt to give the flavor of ancient English speech while remaining fiercely Modern. (The Joyce of *Ulysses* and *Finnegans Wake* seems the closest influence on the rhythms created by syntactic concisions.) These sentences are the narrative of Modern intelligence trying to repossess through style the excellence of a historically previous relationship among man, God, nature, and language. Offa, ruler of Mercia in the eighth century, is seen from 1970, but is also permitted by the poem's fiction to judge 1970. Hill's language of double vision, syntactically chopped and lexically distorted, correlates a style of sentencing with essential meaning: with the careful anachronisms and their warping and conflation of time.

In the early 1980s, the prose poem in English is more lively than at any previous time since William Carlos Williams's *Kora in Hell* (1920). It is revealing that in 1976 there was published, in English translation, the first anthology of the prose poem to be popular in format, comprehensive, and widely international. Among a younger generation of American writers, there is fruitful discussion of what might constitute a new prose. There have emerged from this ferment a handful of works that scorn the sentence-making methods of the immediate past in prose poems by Edson or Merwin or Bly, looking to what is productive in the discoveries of first-generation Modernists.

But enough examples of promise, and enough of arguments. I should like to quote a text so indisputably great that it must charm all mistaken proponents of metrical counting, vanquished difficulty, and the separate purity of verse language; one of the crowns and vindications of the genre, Mallarmé's "La pipe":

Hier, j'ai trouvé ma pipe en rêvant une longue soirée de travail, de beau travail d'hiver. Jetées les cigarettes avec toutes les joies enfantines de l'été dans la passé qui'illuminent les feuilles bleues de soleil, les mousselines et reprise ma grave pipe par un homme sérieux qui veut fumer longtemps sans se déranger, afin de mieux travailler: mais je ne m'attendais pas à la surprise que préparait cette délaissée, à peine eus-je tiré la première bouf-fée, j'oubliai mes grands livres à faire, émerveillé, attendri, je respirai l'hiver dernier qui revenait. Je n'avais pas touché à la fidèle amie depuis ma rentrée en France, et tout Londres, Londres tel que je le vécus en entier à moi seul, il y a un an, est apparu; d'abord les chers brouillards qui emmitouflent nos cervelles et ont, là-bas, une odeur a eux, quand ils pénètrent sous la croisée. Mon tabac sentait une chambre sombre aux meubles de cuir saupoudrés par la poussière du charbon sur lesquels se roulait le maigre chat noir; les grands feux! et la bonne aux bras rouges versant les charbons, et le bruit de ces charbons tombant du seau de tôle dans la corbeille de fer, le matin — alors que le facteur frappait le double coup solennel, qui me faisait vivre! J'ai revu par les fenêtres ces arbres malades du square desert — j'ai vu le large, si souvent traverse cet hiver-là, grelottant sur le pont du steamer mouillé de bruine et noirci de fumée — avec ma pauvre bien-aimée errante, en habits de voyageuse, une longue robe terne couleur de la poussière des routes, un manteau qui collait humide à ses épaules froides, un de ces chapeaux de paille sans plume et presque sans rubans, que les riches dames jettent en arrivant, tant ils sont déchiquetés par l'air de la mer et que les pauvres bien-aimées regarnissent pour bien des saisons encore. Autour de son cou s'enroulait le terrible mouchoir qu'on agite en se disant adieu pour toujours.[34]

(Yesterday I found my pipe as I was dreaming about a long evening's work, fine winter work. Throwing away cigarettes with all the childish joys of summer into the past lit by the sun-blue leaves, the muslin dresses and taking up again my earnest pipe as a serious man who wants a long undisturbed smoke, in order to work better: but I was not expecting the surprise this abandoned creature was preparing, hardly had I taken the first puff when I forgot my great books to be done, amazed, affected, I breathed last winter coming back. I had not touched the faithful friend since my return to France, and all London, London as I lived the whole of it by myself, a year ago, appeared; first the dear fogs which snuggly wrap our brains and have, there, a smell of their own, when they get in under the casement. My tobacco smelt of a dark room with leather furniture seasoned by coal dust on which the lean black cat luxuriated; the big fires! and the maid with red arms tipping out the coals, and the noise of those coals falling from the steel scuttle into the iron grate in the morning—the time of the postman's solemn double knock, which brought me to life! I saw again through the windows those sick trees in the deserted square—I saw the open sea, so often crossed that winter, shivering on the bridge of the steamer wet with drizzle and blackened by smoke—with my poor wandering loved one, in traveling clothes with a long dull dress the colour of road dust, a cloak sticking damp to her cold shoulders, one of those straw hats without a feather and almost without ribbons, which rich ladies throw away on arrival, so tattered they are by the sea air and which poor loved ones re-trim for a good few seasons more. Round her neck was wound the terrible handkerchief we wave when we say goodbye for ever.)[35]

The anecdotal opening, the accidental discovery of a household object, leads to a fully sustained revery in six sentences of amazing length and complexity. The pipe is, like the speaker's lady friend, a "fidèle amie," and both are connected in the memory of earlier events in London: the beloved fog, the room with its cat and English maid excitedly described, the sick trees and deserted square, and suddenly the shift to the open sea and the steamer at a seaport. The second and fifth sentences mime a speedup of sensations, in the attempt to pin down a line of feeling. The emotional center of the poem is the description of the lady's dress in the long sentence beginning, "J'ai revu par les fenêtres," for the outer marks of her poverty are touching but meaningless compared with the rich emotion the speaker has invested in her presence. Everything is leading toward and preparing the adjective in the last sentence: the "terrible" handkerchief or scarf, as emblem of irreparable erotic loss, fortunately around the woman's neck and not being waved in irreversible adieu. This image of loss is the final, summary tone, which condenses for the speaker all the winter emotion of London, fog, coal fires, meditative smoking, and erotic intensity. Images and whole sentences are here carefully managed in sequence to lead the reader from the opening anecdote to a remembered imagination of loss. The number of details and cross-lights picked out, the flagging or electrified string of syntax, but most of all the surprising distances traveled in feeling and in imaginary space and time, are indexes of how very greatly this poem exercises the reader's capacity to tolerate disequilibrium when it is rewarding enough. The poem is brief and intense, seemingly closed on itself; and yet its effect is to contain and convey, like "a . . . charged, irradiated block" (Suzanne Bernard), an infinity of suggestion, with meanings beyond its own universe of relations. It will stand comparison with the best versified lyrics in any language.

"La pipe" might be my definitive instance of the narrative of consciousness and of grammar—but it cannot have the last word, not only because the poem is a century old now and the prose poem is still developing, still, in fact, only emerging within the English-speaking contexts. It cannot have the last word because it is only one type of prose poem, a type with maximal closure that we can more aptly place at the center of this various form or genre that so readily blurs into its literary neighbors. Baudelaire's image for the prose poem was the snake, everything at once head and tail, and Mallarmé's image was the ring; accordingly their own work is heavily closed as a plot of consciousness and grammar, a method preferred also, among the texts here quoted, by Bertrand, Jacob, Tomlinson, Hill, Merwin, and even, rather surprisingly, David Antin. Other poets among those quoted in this chapter have with the set just listed a hidden argument about the nature of unity, coherence, and closure, and prefer instead what Marjorie Perloff has recently called a poetics of indeterminacy. The line runs from Rimbaud through Gertrude Stein to Williams and Ashbery, finally to certain writers not described here who have the most programmatic distrust of plot and self-enclosure.[36] In this latter set of writers, so much emphasis is placed on the actual structure of the linguistic utterance—sound, grammatical pattern, and imagery and its development—that continuous discourse is fractured. It is nearly impossible to read such work continuously. This is an attribute of the Modern and one made possible, while not anticipated or even imagined, by the Romantic premises I described earlier.

What, after all, is the prose poem? Not coyness but the inner nature of writing prevents an answer. Variety and division within the type, as just hinted, is one obvious difficulty. The definitive difficulty has to do with the procedures—exploration of the sentence, disruption of continuity, and tolerance for more than one voice and plot—these ways of writing share with fiction, which help to make the differences between literary types disappear (and which justify my chapter's title). David Antin's talk pieces are neither improvisation, nor narrative, nor poetry, nor writing. Franz Kafka's parables, Theodor Adorno's *Minima Moralia,* and fictions by Joyce, Faulkner, and Beckett put impossible pressures on existing terms and notions of genre. To go back and consult the premises of form as proceeding is to realize that this is a quandary prepared for us nearly two hundred years ago, at the origins of Romanticism.

On Poetry and Truth

The sentence in the prose poem is often a crossroads of sense, with words turning on double valences and a functional mystification of pronoun reference. Charles Tomlinson, himself "very much aware of the way a language stylizes our perception" (words from an interview), refers to this open-ended structure in "A Process," a prose poem that mentions

> that speech of islanders, in which, we are told, the sentence is never certainly brought to an end, its aim less to record with completeness the impression an event makes, than to mark its successive aspects as they catch the eye, the ear of the speaker.[37]

The effect of much Modern poetry is, on such a principle, to reemphasize the affiliation of language with perception, cognition, and the moral imagination.

Four final citations are the most thoroughgoing of all in this respect because, to make language ultimately more responsible to its referents, they depose the nominative sentence as a sacred form of thought. The sentence becomes itself a prime subject of basic research—not by the rejection of the world of reference, but rather by the insistence, almost terrorist in its relentlessness, on the relation between signifier and signified. With poems as examples, the writers-as-experimenters explore the proposition that the way language realizes is inseparable from the way it stylizes. Strange to say in view of the examples that follow, which some readers will detest, the writer-experimenter works with a heavy responsibility for language and its relation to what it signifies. It would seem as if the most experimental writers show the greatest care for language, the profoundest unwillingness to offer a debased coinage.

A Method of a Cloak

A single climb to a line, a straight exchange to a cane, a desperate adventure and courage and a clock, all this which is a system, which has feeling, which has resignation and success, all makes an attractive black silver.[38]

(Gertrude Stein)

A Dog

A little monkey goes like a donkey that means to say that means to say that more sighs last goes. Leave with it. A little monkey goes like a donkey.[39]

(Gertrude Stein)

Letting pin in letting let in let in in in in in in in in let in let in wet in wed in dead in dead wed led in led wed dead in dead in led in wed in said in said led wed dead wed dead said led led said wed dead wed dead led in led in wed in said in wed in led in said in dead in wed in said led led said wed dead in. That makes they have might kind find fined when this arbitrarily makes it be what is it might they can it fairly well to be added to in this at the time that they can candied leaving as with with it by the left of it with with in the funniest in union.

Across across across across coupled across crept a cross crept crept crept crept across. They crept across.[40]

(Gertrude Stein)

I changed my name not to be recognized. I change it to John, or Wanda. A wand chair is wicker. A wandering dune has moved. It passes the fixed stars in an ancient catalogue. It's gone too soon. Too little to choose. To you it all seems silly. But there once was a fiddler called Wandering Willie.[41]

(Michael Palmer)

The principle is to follow the buildup of the syntactic sequence, but only to evade the demands of sequence. Nearly every paradigm is transformed into a syntagm by the overlay of another, subversive sequence.

This overlay or surplusage prevents the good continuation of sentences that try to complete themselves normally. The reader's hopes for grammatical resolution are frustrated by the jingle of exact or rhymed repetition, by rephrasing with change, by punning, and by free association along the line of sense set up by an immediately previous word. This is not, however, automatic writing, if such a thing exists, but a conscious use of techniques of permutation. Stein and Palmer have arranged syntactic false leads and rhyming will-o'-the-wisps not in order to run every utterance into the ground of nonsense, but to discover surprising grammatical forms and, in turn, new logical connections and patterns of intonation. One must grant that the intense focus on the word seems to squeeze out of it nearly all meaning; indeed, because they are so peculiarly arbitrary such texts seem to be issuing from the mixing bowl of language itself. But language has no mixing bowl, and the residual meaning that collects at the bottom after language is thus broken down is alchemical and bestows validity on these extreme texts. The display of sentence plots is not devoid of sense and reference. One need not actually enjoy such writing to appreciate its renovative intent.

Art sentences like these, which aspire to textuality but must at last depend on commonsense reference and the historical senses inherent in words, can stand for the prose poem and prosodic avantgardism more generally. Even at its furthest reach Modernist language signifies outside the limits of language—and this reference, in turn, is a recognition that says something about the nature of poetry and about our abilities to follow its sentences. Poetry, as language, models something outside itself, in relation to which it makes claims of truth, albeit by means of signs conventional and arbitrary. Moreover, as language, poetry implicates the response of a reader or auditor who can be influenced by these claims of truth—even or especially, perhaps, if the claims are brought across by means of the indirect method of the counterfactual, the imaginative, which seems a kind of dream or lie. Post-Romantic poetry has taken its duty to the reader with immense seriousness, believing that the poet's awareness of order is reflected in the order of his or her syllables, and that by following the lines of form and the knowledge given in sequence by the voices in the text, a reader's physical and moral sensibilities may be enhanced. It is in this sense of refining perceptions through language that the great Romantic writers believed phenomenological reality might be discovered and even constructed by poets.[42] But there is more to it than that, for—to writers in this tradition—poetic speech earns its historicity by signifying outside itself to an ordinary universe, forever changing in the stream of historical time—and by communicating outside itself to auditors no less real because the forever changing community of their presence is imagined.

There has emerged in the midst of Anglo-American criticism a defense of poetry based on its privileged separation from denotation, scientific or objective language, and prose. Perhaps this position has weakened somewhat recently. The terms of this defense are accepted by critics otherwise various: I. A. Richards, F. R. Leavis, John Crowe Ransom, W. K. Wimsatt, and Murray Krieger, to begin the list with names of influential writers who could hardly object to see precisely their conviction adopted but reversed by someone who has such contempt for verses, Jean-Paul Sartre. In "What Is Writing?" (1947), Sartre condemns poetry to self-reflexiveness, a refusal to "*utilize* language," because it "considers words as things and not as signs."[43] "The man who talks is beyond words and near the object, whereas the poet is on this side of them. . . . The speaker is *in a situation* in language . . .

[whereas] the poet is outside language. . . . For the word, which tears the writer of prose away from himself and throws him out into the world, sends back the poet to his own image, like a mirror." Even if he grunts or babbles, however, no human speaker is conceivably outside language; and since prose is, as I have shown, only relatively more transparent to meaning than poetry, Sartre contradicts himself when he says that "the style makes the value of the prose. But it should pass unnoticed." But if what we have been looking at, and finding to say about it, is as it would appear, then those who defend and those who attack poetry with such an argument must be equally wrong, having notably misconstrued the relations between the historicity and the conventionality of poetic speech. Almost inevitably they go on to isolate poetry and literature (from *what*?), thus sadly placing the human studies out of contact with the world of action. If the basis of their argument is pernicious for poetry, it is also, in the strictest sense, false as well for prose.

Notes

Introduction

1. Donald Davie, *Collected Poems, 1950–1970* (London: Routledge, 1972), p. 59.
2. Roy Fisher, *Collected Poems* (London: Fulcrum Books, 1968), p. 62.
3. Geoffrey Hill, *Mercian Hymns* (London: Andre Deutsch, 1971), number XXVII.
4. Romantic writing down to the end of the nineteenth century wishes to abolish style, and thereby, through writing, to realize, to humanize. That is why this writing, especially in the emergent avant-garde prosodies, has recoiled in mock horror from the scandal of a preexisting formal structure. I have called this writing theoretically central because it uses and develops the dominant Romantic premises. However, resistance to the central mode has also been a feature of the whole period from 1795 to the present, as writers fight against the excesses of their own Romantic inheritance. The era of early Pound and Eliot and the imagists is an especially large eddy against and within the huge current of Romanticism. Hulme's defense of Classicism against Romantic humanism, Gaudier-Brzeska's and Wyndham Lewis's art of the surface, of emotion suppressed and expressed through lines and points and hard edges, all show the attempt to achieve a level of stylization, of dehumanization (and thus, eternity) that would place the work of art in the ontological status of self-sufficiency.
5. Roland Barthes speaks of rhyming as a "kind of structural scandal," because it "produces an associative sphere at the level of sound, that is to say, of the signifiers." According to Barthes, in the literary text there is "a defiance of the usual distribution syntagm/system, and it is probably around this transgression that a great number of creative phenomena are situated, as if perhaps there were here a junction between the field of aesthetics and the defections from the semantic system" (Roland Barthes, *Elements of Semiology,* trans. A. Lavers and C. Smith [London: Cape, 1967], pp. 86–87).
   In poetry, the operative principle is intentional selection, identity making, and selective spatializing. The selective, as Roman Jakobson has reminded us, subsumes the combinatory, projects the principle of equivalence on to the semantic, syntactic, and phonological elements in the text. Without in any way deemphasizing these facts, in recent studies of rhyme and meter I have tried to follow the lead of my chosen texts and authors by bringing forward the linear aspects of text making that literary criticism has neglected. Distribution, sequence, and movement of sentence become the major interest, because my purpose has been to show the beauties and limits of grammar as a replacement for poetic devices.
6. See Jonathan Culler's chapter on apostrophe in *The Pursuit of Signs: Semiotics, Literature, Deconstruction* (Ithaca, N.Y.: Cornell University Press, 1981).
7. Paul de Man's "Semiology and Rhetoric" appeared in *Diacritics* in 1973 and was reprinted as the first chapter of de Man's *Allegories of Reading* (New Haven, Conn.: Yale University Press, 1979). To pursue the debate with Paul de Man, and with the several critics who have in recent years written Deconstructionist studies of Romantic and post-Romantic literature, would have led me far from my subject. My task has been to foreground, theirs to minimize, the subject-centered and logocentric components of Romantic and post-Romantic poetry.
8. For a disagreement with de Man on the subject of voice, see my article, "Difficulties of the Bardic: Literature and the Human Voice," *Critical Inquiry* 8 (Fall 1981): 69–81.
9. Donald Davie's F. W. Bateson Memorial Lecture (February 1981) on personification has fighting words on this topic, as he insists that English poets remember they are rhetoricians. That way they separate themselves from the Americans, who are "much less critical of Roman-

ticism (theirs, as well as ours) than we can afford to be. This is reflected in their poetry, particularly in that poetry which some of them are now calling 'post-modernist.' . . . What vitiates [the post-Modern American poetry], I dare to suggest, is a renewed effort to surprise English into acting unrhetorically, the revival of a categorical distinction between the poet and the rhetorician. I have tried to suggest that if we attend to a feature of our language such as personification we are forced to think that all such attempts are doomed to failure because based on untenable notions about the relation between our human nature and our human arts" (see "Personification," *Essays in Criticism* 31 [April 1981]: 104). From a position outside Deconstruction, Davie agrees with Paul de Man's main point on the nature of literary language. I am less convinced than Davie that any writer anywhere can elude the major imperatives of Romantic poetics.

Chapter 1. The Transformation of Premises

1. W. K. Wimsatt, "Imitation as Freedom: 1717–1798," in his *Day of the Leopards: Essays in Defense of Poems* (New Haven, Conn.: Yale University Press, 1976), p. 139.

About history: My account of the avant-garde has drawn on Renato Poggioli's *Theory of the Avant-Garde* (1968) and on Marxian notions of culture derived from Marx himself, as well as those from Terry Eagleton, Fredric Jameson, and Herbert Marcuse. My version of the epistemological-prosodic break at 1795 affiliates with ideas of the history of the disciplines I have found in Michel Foucault and Thomas S. Kuhn, but more explicitly derives from studies of the Classic-Romantic transition by M. H. Abrams, Walter Jackson Bate, Harold Bloom, A. O. Lovejoy, Frederick Pottle, and A. N. Whitehead.

2. Geoffrey Tillotson, *The Continuity of Englilsh Poetry from Dryden to Wordsworth* (Nottingham: University of Nottingham Press, 1967), p. 19.

3. John Bayley, *The Romantic Survival* (London: Constable, 1957), p. 15. My quarrel is not with this passage as written, but with what is missing from it and from Bayley's book: exposition of the new ideas of form, and willingness to see that those ideas were the necessary condition to the coming of the innovative prosodies later in the nineteenth century. A more recent book that also minimizes the change and forgets the formal-technical issues altogether is Marilyn Butler, *Romantics, Rebels, and Reactionaries: English Literature and Its Background, 1760–1830* (New York: Oxford University Press, 1982).

4. Bayley, *The Romantic Survival,* pp. 15, 17.

5. Ian Watt, "Two Historical Aspects of the Augustan Tradition," in R. F. Brissenden, ed., *Studies in the Eighteenth Century* (Toronto: University of Toronto Press, 1968), p. 85.

The ethos of agreement and centralization was well expressed in the earl of Manchester's formal speech of welcome to Charles II: "You are the desire of three Kingdoms, the Strength and Stay of the Tribes of the People, for the moderating of Extremities, the reconciling of Differences, the satisfying of all Interests, and for the restoring of the Collapsed Honour of these Nations" (*The Earl of Manchester's Speech to His Majesty, in the Name of the Peers, at his Arrival at Whitehall, the 29th of May, 1660* [London, 1660]).

In the fascinating study, Howard Weinbrot has shown that eighteenth-century thinkers were skeptical of the analogy between their age and Augustan Rome (*Augustus Caesar in Augustan England: The Decline of a Classical Norm* [Princeton, N.J.: Princeton University Press, 1978]).

Partly as a response to an earlier published version of my pages on Augustan form, my colleague Don E. Wayne has argued a case for the contestatory nature of English classicism. See his powerful article, "Mediation and Contestation: English Classicism from Sidney to Jonson," *Criticism* 25 (Summer 1983): 211–37.

6. Quotations in this sentence from Ian Watt, "Two Historical Aspects," p. 85; and W. K. Wimsatt, "The Augustan Mode in English Poetry," in his *Hateful Contraries: Studies in Literature and Criticism* (Lexington: University of Kentucky Press, 1965), p. 164.

7. Here, as again below, I rely on my notes to quote from a lecture, "The Sot as Hero, Lunatic as King," given by Dr. J. S. Cunningham, at the University Teachers of English Conference, University of Kent, England, 1969.

8. The phrase is Harold Bloom's from *A Map of Misreading* (New York: Oxford University Press, 1975), p. 35.

9. Roland Barthes, *Writing Degree Zero,* trans. A. Lavers and C. Smith (London: Cape,

1967); Pierre Sollers, *Logiques* (Paris: Seuil, 1968), esp. p. 10, where Sollers states that the "rupture textuelle" occurs at the same time as Marx's discovery of dialectical materialism.

10. *The Burden of the Past and the English Poet* (Cambridge, Mass.: Harvard University Press, 1970), pp. 16–17.

11. Claudio Guillén, *Literature as System: Essays toward the Theory of Literary History* (Princeton, N.J.: Princeton University Press, 1971), p. 9.

12. William Bowman Piper, *The Heroic Couplet* (Cleveland, Ohio: Case Western Reserve University Press, 1969), p. 435.

13. Irène Simon, comp., introduction to *Neo-Classical Criticism, 1660–1800* (London: Edward Arnold, 1971), p. 33. To the objection that this may be said about any period prior to the eighteenth century, one may reply that no previous period was in possession of so many social and economic facts that so boldly challenged the premises of an elitist literature.

14. Piper, *The Heroic Couplet,* p. 153.

15. Quoted from Dennis's "Causes of the Decay and Defects of Dramatick Poetry," *Critical Works of John Dennis,* 2 vols. (Baltimore, Md.: Johns Hopkins University Press, 1939–43), 2:275–99.

16. Geoffrey Tillotson, *On the Poetry of Pope,* 2d ed. (Oxford: Oxford University Press, 1950); James Sutherland, *A Preface to Eighteenth Century Poetry* (Oxford: Oxford University Press, 1948); and Reuben Brower, *Alexander Pope: The Poetry of Allusion* (Oxford: Oxford University Press, 1959).

17. "Imitation as Freedom: 1717–1798," p. 118. Of course, Pope also wrote about snatching "a grace beyond the reach of art."

18. *The Classical Style* (New York: Viking Press, 1971), p. 174.

19. *The Classical Style,* p. 175.

20. Wimsatt, *Hateful Contraries,* pp. 158, 152.

21. This sentence, using some of Dr. Cunningham's key phrases, summarizes the lecture cited above in note 7. A related view of the period as a whole may be found in Donald Greene's welcome reminder about the century of Swift and Pope in the title of his *Age of Exuberance: Backgrounds to Eighteenth Century English Literature* (New York: Random House, 1970).

22. *The Classical Style,* p. 175.

23. *The Classical Style,* pp. 174–75.

24. I refer in particular to Rachel Trickett's excellent study, *The Honest Muse* (Oxford: Oxford University Press, 1967).

25. See René Wellek's *History of Modern Criticism, 1750–1950,* vol. 1, *The Later Eighteenth Century* (New Haven, Conn.: Yale University Press, 1955), introduction, p. 1. It is pertinent to quote Ian Watt's sentence from the essay cited in note 5: "Especially in the academy, Pope and Swift support the intellectual's image of himself as a passionate defender of the last citadels of human reason against the mounting tide of folly, vulgarity, and commercialism" (p. 87). On Augustan values, see Israel Kramnick's chapter, "The Nostalgia of the Augustan Poets," in his *Bolingbroke and His Circle: The Politics of Nostalgia in the Age of Walpole* (Cambridge, Mass.: Harvard University Press, 1968).

26. Written, 1953; reprinted, 1965 in *Hateful Contraries.*

27. Ralph Cohen, "The Augustan Mode in English Poetry," delivered as a paper in 1966, a year after the book publication of Wimsatt's essay, and published in Brissenden, ed., *Studies in the Eighteenth Century* (1968); this sentence quoted from p. 191.

28. This is Cohen's last sentence, p. 192.

29. Guillén, *Literature as System,* pp. 10–11.

30. M. H. Abrams, "The Greater Romantic Lyric," in H. Bloom and F. L. Hilles, eds., *From Sensibility to Romanticism* (New York: Oxford University Press, 1965).

31. See Roman Jakobson, "The Dominant," in Ladislav Matejka and Krystyna Pomorska, eds., *Readings in Russian Poetics: Formalist and Structuralist Views* (Cambridge, Mass.: MIT Press, 1971), pp. 82–87. Trickett, in *The Honest Muse,* argues pertinently that both nineteenth- and twentieth-century commentators on this period "have started from the style rather than the attitude behind it, and have thus missed the whole by paying too close attention to the parts" (p. 3).

32. See *Critics and Criticism: Ancient and Modern,* ed. R. S. Crane (Chicago: University of Chicago Press), p. 565 n.

33. *The Honest Muse,* p. 276. And yet, Pope plays magnificently with language; it is possible

that satire, because it is acknowledged to be a "lesser" genre, escapes some of these prescriptions.

Roland Barthes's anti-Classical tract, *Writing Degree Zero,* is in full agreement with Trickett's more modest formulation when it offers the following as elements of Classicism's "single language, which reflects the eternal categories of the mind":

—poetry as the decorative equation of a possible prose
—the "poetic" not as a separate universe, but only as the individual handling of a verbal technique
—the function of the poet not to find new words, but to follow the order of an ancient ritual
—classical conceits involve relations, not words
—no word has a density by itself, but is rather the means to convey a connection
—poet images are due to long custom, not to individual creation

These elements are culled from the section, "Is There Any Poetic Writing?" (*Writing Degree Zero,* pp. 47–58). I find Barthes's formulations provocative and useful, but because they are devised to fit the situation in France (do they?), they do not always describe the one in England. Also, his drastic and idiosyncratic redefinition of Classicism would encourage one to neglect, at peril, the contestatory qualities of Classicism in figures like Ben Jonson, Cowley, Swift, Pope, and Samuel Johnson.

34. *Writing Degree Zero,* p. 47. The following two quotations come from the same book, pp. 48, 9.

35. W. K. Wimsatt, "Rhetoric and Poems: Alexander Pope," in *The Verbal Icon: Studies in the Meaning of Poetry* (Lexington: University of Kentucky Press, 1954), p. 171. On the creative uses of literary imagination, see Trickett, *The Honest Muse,* p. 105; Bate, *The Burden of the Past,* p. 13.

36. The phrasing, taken because it so ably compresses a conventional point, is from Basil Willey, *The Eighteenth Century Background: Studies on the Idea of Nature in the Thought of the Period* (1941; repr. Harmondsworth, Middlesex: Penguin, 1962), p. 25. See also A. O. Lovejoy's constitutive study of this and related subjects in *The Great Chain of Being: A Study in the History of an Idea* (Cambridge, Mass.: Harvard University Press, 1936), esp. chap. 6.

37. Before the semicolon this sentence leans on W. K. Wimsatt (W. K. Wimsatt and Cleanth Brooks, *Literary Criticism: A Short History* [New York: Knopf, 1966], esp. p. 319); the final quotation is from Willey, *The Eighteenth Century Background,* p. 25.

38. Joseph Spence, *Anecdotes,* ed. S. W. Singer (London, 1820), p. 280.

39. "Innovation and Variation: Literary Change and Georgic Poetry," in *Literature and History* (Los Angeles: William Andrews Clark Memorial Library, 1974), pp. 3–4.

40. Geoffrey Tillotson, *On the Poetry of Pope,* 2d ed. (Oxford: Oxford University Press, 1950), p. 101.

41. The quotation is from Wimsatt, *The Verbal Icon,* p. 174; see also the pages on correctness in Trickett (140) and Bate (31).

42. Edward Bysshe, *The Art of English Poetry* (London, 1702), here cited from the 4th ed. (London, 1710). The definitive account of a manual poetics is A. Dwight Culler, "Edward Bysshe and the Poet's Handbook," *PMLA* 63 (1948): 858–85. See also, on Bysshe and his heirs, Paul Fussell, *Theory of Prosody in Eighteenth Century England* (Hamden: Connecticut College, 1954).

43. *Literature as System,* p. 61.

44. *A History of Modern Criticism* 1:19.

45. See Simon, *Neo-Classical Criticism,* pp. 18–19.

46. The univocal Classicism described by Roland Barthes may have existed in France, though I doubt it; certainly his strictures apply only part of the time to England. It would be wrong to emphasize the rigidities of English Neo-Classical criticism at the expense of more balanced versions, as in Pope's *Essay on Criticism.* See R. K. Root, "The Canons of Poetical Art," in *The Poetical Career of Alexander Pope* (1933; repr. Gloucester, Mass.: Peter Smith, 1962), pp. 1–31; and Irvin Ehrenpreis, "The Literary Value of Pope's Versification," in *Literary Meaning and Augustan Values* (Charlottesville: University Press of Virginia, 1974), pp. 63–75.

47. Wimsatt, *The Verbal Icon,* p. 171.

48. Brought out by Dr. Cunningham in the lecture cited in note 7.

49. Lines 309–12, from the edition of the poem given in Oliver F. Sigworth, *Criticism and Aesthetics, 1660–1800* (San Francisco: Rinehart, 1971).
50. *A History of Modern Criticism* 1:20.
51. See the final section of Cohen's "Innovation and Variation."
52. In Samuel Johnson himself, as well as in the bad fashionable critic he invents mainly to mock in two of the *Idler* essays (no. 60, 9 June 1759; and no. 61, 16 June 1759).
53. See my article, "An Ideal of Greatness: Ethical Implications in Johnson's Critical Vocabulary," *University of Toronto Quarterly* 34 (January 1965): 133–45.
54. Elements of the above paragraph restate and embroider points made by Simon in her introduction to *Neo-Classical Criticism*.
55. For these phrases and the one on Corneille, see Wellek, *A History of Modern Criticism* 1:19.
56. Simon, introduction to *Neo-Classical Criticism*, p. 27. My late colleague, Robert C. Elliott, was right to insist (in personal communication) that English satire, especially, had "a unique licence, a freedom from fixed rules."
57. Wimsatt and Brooks, *Literary Criticism*, p. 233. W. K. Wimsatt's passage has two rare terms for types of wordplay, both taken over from Puttenham's Renaissance treatise, *The Art of Poetry*. *Agnomination* is the change of a letter, syllable, or word to give a slightly different meaning the next time the item reappears. *Tranlacer* refers to the repetition of a word in the shape of its various derivatives or cognates. An elaboration of Wimsatt's point, which addresses a number of issues raised in the present section, is Maynard Mack's "Wit and Poetry and Pope: Some Observations on His Imagery," in J. L. Clifford, ed., *Eighteenth Century English Literature* (New York: Oxford University Press, 1959), pp. 21–41.
58. See text and editorial materials, *The Poems of Samuel Johnson*, ed. David Nichol Smith and Edward L. McAdam, 2d ed. (Oxford: Oxford University Press, 1974), pp. 204–5.
59. "The Augustan Mode," in Brissenden, ed., *Studies in the Eighteenth Century*, pp. 191–92.
60. Alan Roper, *Dryden's Poetic Kingdoms* (London: Routledge, 1965), p. 42.
61. *On the Poetry of Pope*, p. 159.
62. *Eras and Modes in English Poetry* (Berkeley: University of California Press, 1964), p. 11.
63. "Form and Defect of Form in Eighteenth-Century Poetry: A Memorandum," in *Eighteenth Century Studies in Honor of Donald F. Hyde*, ed. W. H. Bond (New York: Grolier, 1970), pp. 365–82.
64. "'Logical Structure' in Eighteenth-Century Poetry," *Philological Quarterly* 31 (July 1952): 329–32. George Sherburne says linear order in Pope's poems is not strong, because the poet continually moved couplets and verse-paragraphs around, rearranging units (see "Pope at Work," *Essays on the Eighteenth Century Presented to David Nichol Smith* [Oxford: Oxford University Press, 1945], pp. 49–64).
65. See the table in Miles's *Eras and Modes*, p. 8.
66. If, according to Roland Barthes, post-Romantic literature develops a body and hidden depths, a "second-order power independent of its economy and euphemistic charm," a "dramatic phenomenon of concretion," Neo-Classicism for its part rests on "the radical elimination of all virtualities in language" (*Writing Degree Zero*, pp. 9, 64). The wish to eliminate virtualities is everywhere on display in Neo-Classical poetry and poetics and language theory; also, however, the recognition that language will never permit such transparency. Barthes overstates.
67. Wellek, in *A History of Modern Criticism* (1:99), speaks of "Johnson's incomprehension of the centrally metaphorical character of poetry"; and yet, conceivably, that function only became central in texts and constructs about texts after 1795. Prominent among others on this subject, Mack in "Wit and Poetry and Pope" and Brower in *Alexander Pope and the Poetry of Allusion* have described the complicating function of allusion in Pope: the interlayer of metaphorical names like Sporus among names of real persons juxtaposes concrete and abstract, yielding a "more reticent mode of imaging" (Mack).
68. Patricia Meyer Spacks, introduction to her anthology, *Late Augustan Poetry* (Englewood Cliffs, N.J.: Prentice-Hall, 1973), p. 36.
69. The irony of these phrases from Johnson's *Life of Collins* may be turned against him, if we remark that Johnson's own play, *Irene*, is in blank verse with the syntaxes and pauses of antithetical couplets. Everything of couplets is there but the rhyme, a contrast with

Wordsworth's transitional poem of the 1790s, "Descriptive Sketches," where blank verse struggles under the cover of couplets.

70. Wimsatt, "The Augustan Mode," p. 152.

71. Roman Jakobson, "Concluding Statement: Linguistics and Poetics," in Thomas A. Sebeok, ed., *Style in Language* (Cambridge, Mass.: MIT Press and John Wiley, 1960), p. 358.

72. *Theory of Prosody in Eighteenth Century England.*

73. See T. R. Edwards, Jr., *This Dark Estate: A Reading of Pope* (Berkeley: University of California Press, 1963), p. 5.

74. Robert Langbaum, *The Poetry of Experience* (New York: Norton, 1963), p. 25.

75. The phrase is from Geoffrey H. Hartman, "Wordsworth, Inscriptions, and Nature Poetry," *Beyond Formalism* (New Haven, Conn.: Yale University Press, 1970).

76. This is the account of the Proustian *récit* given by Gérard Genette in *Figures* III (Paris: Sevil, 1972), p. 273 (my translation).

77. *Literature as System,* p. 488.

78. *The Subtler Language* (Baltimore, Md.: Johns Hopkins University Press, 1959), p. 11. The subject has been further explored in the long chapter, "Language within Language," in David Simpson's study of Romantic self and language, *Irony and Authority in Romantic Poetry* (London: Macmillan, 1979).

79. *Collected Letters of Samuel Taylor Coleridge,* ed. Earl Leslie Griggs, 6 vols. (Oxford: Clarendon Press, 1956–71), 2:812.

80. "Note to 'The Thorn'" in W. J. B. Owen, ed., *Wordsworth's Literary Criticism* (London: Routledge, 1974), p. 97.

81. *Biographia Literaria,* ed. J. Shawcross (Oxford: Oxford University Press, 1907), 2:262.

82. "On Poesy or Art," in *Biographia Literaria* 2:258.

83. *Biographia Literaria* 2:254–55.

84. *Shakespearean Criticism,* ed. Thomas M. Raysor, 2 vols. (London: Dent, 1960), 1:198.

85. "Observations on the Experimental," *Vision and Resonance* (Oxford: Oxford University Press, 1975), p. 244.

86. Bate, *The Burden of the Past,* p. 117.

87. *Vision and Resonance,* p. 186.

88. *The Poetry of Experience,* p. 227.

89. Jakobson, "The Dominant," p. 85.

90. *Prose Works,* ed. W. J. B. Owen and J. W. Smyser, 3 vols. (Oxford: Oxford University Press, 1974), 3:26.

91. See M. H. Abrams, *The Mirror and the Lamp* (New York: Norton, 1953), p. 84.

92. Miles, chaps. 5 and 6 of *Eras and Modes;* and see the more recent book-length studies of *Lyrical Ballads* by Stephen Maxfield Parrish (1973), John E. Jordan (1976), and Mary Jacobus (1976).

93. The only study I know of this crucial but neglected topic is Renato Poggioli's "Poetics and Metrics" in his book, *The Spirit of the Letter: Essays in European Literature* (Cambridge, Mass.: Harvard University Press, 1965), pp. 343–54.

94. *Vision and Resonance,* p. 164.

95. *The Mirror and the Lamp,* p. 118.

96. *The Poetry of Experience,* p. 33.

97. *History of English Prosody* (London, 1910), 3:508.

98. *Eras and Modes,* pp. 118, 122.

99. *Selected Writings of Charles Olson,* ed. Robert Creeley (New York: New Directions, 1966), p. 17.

100. See *Inquiring Spirit: A New Presentation of Coleridge,* ed. Kathleen Coburn (London: Routledge, 1970), pp. 110–11, for quotations in this and the next sentence.

101. See preface of 1815, *Prose Works,* ed. Owen and Smyser, 3:31; and "Prelude," 1805 version, book 1, line 341.

102. "The Poem as a Field of Action," *Selected Essays of William Carlos Williams,* ed. John Thirlwall (New York: Random House, 1954), p. 291.

103. *Shakespearean Criticism,* 1:197.

104. "The Delicacy of Walt Whitman," in R. W. B. Lewis, ed., *The Presence of Walt Whitman* (New York: Columbia University Press, 1962), pp. 177–78.

105. The veil image comes from C. S. Pierce; the onion image from Roland Barthes.

106. Quoted by Abrams, *The Mirror and the Lamp,* p. 117.
107. Stanley Fish, in his "Affective Stylistics," an appendix to his book *Self-Consuming Artifacts* (Berkeley: University of California Press, 1971), says "*anything* can be a stylistic device." True; but we then need categories, prominences, to help our interpretation reduce empiricism.
108. "Linguistics and Poetics," in Sebeok, ed., *Style in Language,* p. 356.
109. "On Seeing a Lock of Milton's Hair," a poem of 1818.
110. *The Poetical Works of John Keats,* ed. H. W. Garrod (Oxford: Oxford University Press, 2d ed., 1958), p. 472.
111. *Prose Works,* ed. Owen and Smyser, 1:134, 146, 146, 148, 150.
112. I refer in particular to Stephen Maxfield Parrish, *The Art of the Lyrical Ballads* (Cambridge, Mass.: Harvard University Press, 1973), esp. p. 24.
113. This is Coleridge on Wordsworth in chapter 18 of *Biographia Literaria,* and the next quotation below in this paragraph is from the same source.
114. Quoted by Samuel Hynes, "Whitman, Pound, and the Prose Tradition," in *The Presence of Walt Whitman,* p. 113. Note Pound's reservation, "I do not mean that [the prose tradition] is not equally common to the best work of the ancients."
115. For Coleridge, one of the marks of poetic genius (*Biographia Literaria,* 2:16).
116. Quoted from Samuel Taylor Coleridge, *Poetical Works,* ed. E. H. Coleridge (Oxford, 1912), 1:224–25. Next quotation following is from same edition, same page.
117. *Collected Letters,* 3:112.
118. *Wordsworth's Poetical Works,* ed. E. de Selincourt (Oxford: Oxford University Press, 1946; 2d ed., 1954), 3:284–85, lines 43–58.
119. Unsigned review in *Monthly Review,* January 1817; and Thomas Moore in *Edinburgh Review,* September 1816 (both in J. R. de J. Jackson, ed., *Coleridge: The Critical Heritage* [London: Routledge, 1970], pp. 245, 232).
120. *Eras and Modes,* p. 118.
121. In Geoffrey H. Hartman, ed., *New Perspectives on Coleridge and Wordsworth* (New York: Columbia University Press, 1972), p. 140.
122. *Vision and Resonance,* p. 286.
123. Harvey Gross, *Sound and Form in Modern Poetry* (Ann Arbor: University of Michigan Press, 1964), p. 18.
124. Walter Jackson Bate, *From Classic to Romantic* (New York: Harper Torchbook, 1961), p. 168.

Chapter 2.
Form as Proceeding—Romantic Form in History and in Cognition

1. *Eras and Modes in English Poetry* (Berkeley: University of California Press, 1964), esp. pp. 113, 122.
2. *Le livre à venir* (Paris: Gallimard, 1959), pp. 291, 241, 240, 244, 247 (my translation and emphasis).
3. Roland Barthes, *Mythologies,* trans. Annette Lavers (Frogmore, St. Albans, Herts.: Granada Publishing, Paladin Books, 1973), p. 133n.
4. *The New Naked Poetry: Recent American Poetry in Open Forms,* ed. Stephen Berg and Robert Mezey (Indianapolis, Ind.: Bobbs-Merrill, 1976), p. 426.
5. Gérard Genette, *Figures* I (Paris: Seuil, 1966), p. 144 (my translation).
6. Quotations in this sentence, in order, from Geoffrey H. Hartman, "Wordsworth, Inscriptions, and Nature Poetry," *Beyond Formalism* (New Haven, Conn.: Yale University Press, 1970); and Barthes, *Mythologies,* pp. 133–34.
7. *Le livre à venir,* p. 243 (my translation).
8. *The Oxford Anthology of American Literature,* ed. Benet and Pearson (New York: Oxford University Press, 1938), note 85, p. 156.
9. Claudio Guillén, *Literature as System* (Princeton, N.J.: Princeton University Press, 1971), pp. 63–66. Guillén goes on to write: "As long as one accepted the neoclassical equation of art with 'nature,' every formal convention could seem a hindrance. But if the value of art

consisted in a liberation from nature, or in an enrichment and a formal transfiguration of it, then every artistic convention could be turned into an ally. . . . Since the Romantic movement, modern art has rediscovered the paradox that without the struggle with strict forms and conventions, an important use of human freedom would disappear."

10. John Hollander, "Wordsworth and the Music of Sound," in Geoffrey H. Hartman, ed., *New Perspectives on Coleridge and Wordsworth* (New York: Columbia University Press, 1972), p. 62. On the wind harp, see pp. 61–67 and note 40 on p. 82. George Dekker has fine materials on wind harps in his chapter, "Nature's Music" in *Coleridge and the Literature of Sensibility* (London: Vision Press, 1978).

11. Samuel Taylor Coleridge, *Poetical Works,* vol. 1 ed. E. H. Coleridge (Oxford, 1912). The lines here quoted (lines 26–33) are not in the text of 1796; they first appeared in print in 1817; however, they are perfectly in keeping with the view of the wind harp developed in the earlier version, extending beyond the more fanciful earlier portion of the poem's second section, and deepening its reference.

12. For commentary on the relation of eye to ear in Romantic poetry, and on this period's special interest in the power of sound, see John Hollander's chapter, "The Poem in the Ear," *Vision and Resonance: Two Senses of Poetic Form* (New York: Oxford University Press, 1975), esp. p. 23.

13. *The New Naked Poetry,* p. 32.

14. "Wordsworth and the Music of Sound," *On Coleridge and Wordsworth,* p. 62.

15. *The Subtler Language* (Baltimore, Md.: Johns Hopkins University Press, 1959), p. 186. See also Wasserman's splendid survey, "The English Romantics: The Grounds of Knowledge," in Robert F. Gleckner and Gerald E. Enscoe, eds., *Romanticism: Points of View* (Englewood Cliffs, N.J.: Prentice-Hall, 2d ed., 1970).

16. René Wellek's definition of Romanticism occurs in his *Concepts of Criticism* (New Haven, Conn.: Yale University Press, 1963), p. 161, and is expounded in the following pages.

17. These two sentences attempt to give the leading idea of Coleridge's essay, "On Poesy or Art." Here and below I rely on the Coleridge commentary of Walter Jackson Bate: on lecture-notes from his Harvard lectures, on the section on Coleridge in his *Prefaces to Criticism* (1959), and on his essay on art and nature in Coleridge's aesthetics in Harry Levin, ed., *Perspectives of Criticism* (Cambridge, Mass.: Harvard University Press, 1950).

18. *The Mirror and the Lamp: Romantic Theory and the Critical Tradition* (New York: Norton, 1953), p. 119.

19. "Ludwig Binswanger and the Sublimation of the Self," in *Blindness and Insight* (New York: Oxford University Press, 1971), p. 39.

20. *The Mirror and the Lamp,* p. 25.

21. *The Prose Works of William Wordsworth,* ed. W. J. B. Owen and J. W. Smyser, 3 vols. (Oxford: Oxford University Press, 1974), 3:84.

22. *The Making of Wordsworth's Poetry, 1785–1798* (Cambridge, Mass.: Harvard University Press, 1973), p. 204.

23. *The Collected Poems, 1956–1974* (Bolinas, Calif.: Four Seasons Foundation, 1975). Context makes clear Dorn is not referring to a coterie audience. See, for further explanation, my "Bibliography for American on Ed Dorn," *Parnassus: Poetry in Review* (New York: Spring–Summer 1977); pp. 142–60.

24. *Shakespearean Criticism,* ed. Thomas M. Raysor, 2 vols. (London: Dent, 1960), 1:220–21.

25. *S/Z* (Paris: Seuil, 1970), pp. 10, 12, 11 (my translation).

26. *Poetic Closure* (Chicago: University of Chicago Press, 1968), p. 36.

27. *Man's Rage for Chaos* (Philadelphia, Pa.: Chilton, 1965), pp. 217, 310.

28. *Inquiring Spirit: A New Presentation of Coleridge,* ed. Kathleen Coburn (London: Routledge, 1951), pp. 110–11.

29. *Coleridge: The Critical Heritage,* ed. J. R. de J. Jackson (London: Routledge, 1970), p. 623.

30. *Counterstatement* (1931; 2d ed., Los Altos, Calif.: Hermes, 1953).

31. For Miles, see especially *Eras and Modes* (1964); *Style and Proportion* (Boston: Little, Brown, 1967); *Poetry and Change* (Berkeley: University of California Press, 1974).

32. *Man's Rage for Chaos,* p. 271.

33. A. Reeve Parker, "Wordsworth's Whelming Tide," in Reuben A. Brower, ed., *Forms of Lyric* (New York: Columbia University Press, 1971), p. 100.

34. Parker, "Wordsworth's Whelming Tide," p. 102. For an admirable, different reading, see Tilottama Rajan, *Dark Interpreter: The Discourse of Romanticism* (Ithaca, N.Y.: Cornell University Press, 1980), pp. 232–33.

Chapter 3. The Crisis of Versification, 1855–1910

1. Roy Harvey Pearce, "Whitman Justified: The Poet in 1860," in *The Presence of Walt Whitman*, ed. R. W. B. Lewis (New York: Columbia University Press, 1962), p. 80. In the course of emphasizing the originality of early Whitman, Pearce underestimates the quality of Whitman's work after 1860. See also Pearce's fine placement and analysis of Whitman in his classic study, *The Continuity of American Poetry* (Princeton, N.J.: Princeton University Press, 1961); and his "Whitman Justified: The Poet in 1855," in *Critical Inquiry* 8 (Fall 1981): 83–97.
2. The Whitman-Hopkins relationship is explored very well in F. O. Matthiessen's *American Renaissance* (London: Oxford University Press, 1941). Points first made by Matthiessen are in my chapters 3 and 4 drawn toward the realm of poetic technique. The relationship has also been the subject of Philip Dacey's peculiar poem of 1978, "Hopkins to Whitman: From the Lost Correspondence," in Jim Perlman, Ed Folsom, and Dan Campion, eds., *Walt Whitman: The Measure of His Song* (Minneapolis, Minn.: Holy Cow! Press, 1981).
3. Hans Robert Jauss, "Literary History as a Challenge to Literary Theory," in Jauss's book *Toward an Aesthetic of Reception,* trans. Timothy Bahti (Minneapolis: University of Minnesota Press, 1982), pp. 3–45.
4. "La musique et les lettres," *Oeuvres complètes* (Paris: Gallimard), pp. 360, 367.
5. "English Prosody and Modern Poetry," *English Literary History* 14 (June 1948): 77–78. Matters are not much advanced since Shapiro wrote, but the field should begin to be more unified now that we have a monumental historical and constructive reference guide in T. V. F. Brogan's *English Versification, 1570–1980* (Baltimore, Md.: Johns Hopkins University Press, 1981).
6. *The Structure of Scientific Revolutions* (Chicago: University of Chicago Press, 2d ed., 1970), esp. pp. 34, 42, 208, 52, 84 (in order of quotations used).
7. Roman Jakobson, "The Dominant" (1935), in *Readings in Russian Poetics: Formalist and Structuralist Views,* ed. Ladislav Matejka and Krystyna Pomorska (Cambridge, Mass.: MIT Press, 1971), pp. 82, 85.
8. Yuri Tynjanov, "On Literary Evolution," in *Readings in Russian Poetics,* pp. 71–72 (my emphasis).
9. *In Memoriam,* ed. Robert H. Ross (New York: Norton, 1973), p. 5.
10. *History of English Prosody* (London, 1910), 3 : 150.
11. *Theory of Prosody in Eighteenth Century England* (Hamden: Connecticut College, 1954), p. 63.
It must be mentioned that several of the practices of elision that Paul Fussell sees as hallmarks of the eighteenth-century meter existed earlier. They existed on a grand scale in Milton, to go no further back than the 1630s. These matters have been powerfully and exhaustively explored in Edward R. Weismiller's contributions to *A Variorium Commentary on the Poems of John Milton,* 4 vols. (New York: Columbia University Press, 1972–75). That the theory for these practices existed even before Milton has been shown by Eleanor Berry in her article, "The Reading and Uses of Elizabethan Prosodies," in *Language and Style* 14 (Spring 1981): 116–52.
12. See *Music, the Arts, and Ideas* (Chicago: University of Chicago Press, 1967), pp. 115, 116.
13. *Poetry and Change* (Berkeley: University of California Press, 1974), p. 60.
14. On this Edwin Fussell has commented (in private communication): "Isn't that because, in English, anyway, speech is itself close to being metered? Almost any bit of random prose is very close to how you choose to hear it, e.g., iambic pentameter. Approximately every 2–3 syllables there is a stress, and every 10 or so (or what you will) a break of sense, syntax, or a need to breathe."
15. "Literary History and Literary Modernity," in *Blindness and Insight* (New York: Oxford University Press, 1971), p. 162.
16. See Jiří Levý, "Contribution to the Typology of Accentual-Syllabic Versifications," *Poetics* 1 (Warsaw: Polish Scientific Publishers, 1961), esp. p. 187. One of Levý's diagrams locates national versifications between the two extreme types of accent and syllable-count:

Accentual	*Accentual-Syllabic*		*Syllabic*
Old English,	German		Polish,
Old Norse, and ◄ ------------ English	Czech ---------►		Spanish, and
Old High German	Russian		French

17. Quoted from William J. Stone, "Classical Metres in English Verse," included as a supplement in Robert Bridges, *Milton's Prosody* (Oxford, 1901), p. 115.

18. "The Present Relationship of Prose to Verse," *Seven Arts,* selected and edited by Fernando Puma (Garden City, N.Y.: Doubleday, 1953), p. 140.

19. Quoted by Louis Simpson from a 1946 statement, in Simpson's *Three on the Tower* (New York: William Morrow, 1975), p. 303.

20. *A History of English Rhythms* (1838; 1882, ed. Walter W. Skeat; repr. New York: Haskell House, 1968), quotations from the repr. ed. pp. 302, 561.

21. *Poems of Gerard Manley Hopkins,* 3d ed., rev. by W. H. Gardner (London: Oxford University Press, 1964). Hopkins is here quoted from the notes to this edition, p. 252 (letter of 25 September 1888). For quotations below in this paragraph, see in the same volume Hopkins's author's preface, pp. 6–7.

22. According to James Wright, Whitman's method is "not based on the repetition of the sentence structure": "he uses parallelism not as a device of repetition but as an occasion for development" ("The Delicacy of Walt Whitman," pp. 180–81 and, for the quotations below, p. 172).

Other and more recent accounts of Whitman's free-verse style are Harvey Gross, *Sound and Form in Modern Poetry* (1964); Edwin Fussell, *Lucifer in Harness: American Meter, Metaphor and Diction* (1973); and Jim Perlman, Ed Folsom, and Dan Campion, eds., *Walt Whitman: The Measure of His Song* (1981), especially the contributions by Allen Ginsberg, Galway Kinnell, and Robert Bly. The account of Whitman's technical skills in Walter Sutton's *American Free Verse* (1973) has no merit, and Charles O. Hartman's *Free Verse: An Essay on Prosody* (1980) is disappointingly thin on the inventor of his whole subject. Still provocative on Whitman's meters and measures is Gay Wilson Allen's old standby, *American Prosody* (New York: American Book Company, 1935). Impressive general accounts of Whitman may be found in Albert Gelpi's *The Tenth Muse* (1975), and in the *Leaves of Grass* section of Lawrence Lipking's *The Life of the Poet* (1981).

23. In 1880, Ruskin wrote "Elements of English Prosody" in fifty pages; his notation that of musical notes and time measures. Lanier's *Science of English Verse,* written 1879, was published in 1880 (see "Time and Stress in English Verse: With Special Reference to Lanier's Theory of Rhythm," by J. W. Hendren [Houston, Tex.: Rice Institute, 1959]).

24. *Poetics* 2 (Warsaw: Polish Scientific Publishers, 1966). I pursue Levý's ideas further in Chapter 4.

25. "Semiology and Rhetoric," *Allegories of Reading* (New Haven, Conn.: Yale University Press, 1979).

Chapter 4. *Sprung Rhythm and the Figure of Grammar*

1. I do not claim that works with this mode of thought only come on the scene after 1795— Plato's dialogues and the essays of Montaigne and Bacon may be defended as earlier examples. I do claim that this type of thought becomes conscious of itself as a mode, and begins to be pursued consistently, in the generation of Hegel and Coleridge.

2. The thing to try for, said T. S. Eliot in a lecture delivered in 1933, is "poetry so transparent that in reading it we are intent on what the poem *points at,* and not the poetry. . . . To get *beyond poetry,* as Beethoven, in his later works, strove to get *beyond music.* We shall never succeed perhaps" (from a lecture given at New Haven and reported by F. O. Matthiessen; see Matthiessen, *The Achievement of T. S. Eliot,* 3d ed. [New York, 1959], pp. 89–90, and the note, p. 96).

3. "Overthought" and "underthought" are terms from Hopkins himself, writing in an analogous context (*Further Letters of Gerard Manley Hopkins,* 2d ed., ed. Claude Colleer Abbott [London: Oxford University Press, 1956], pp. 252–53). Language as such is most certainly being

interrogated in Hopkins and Dickinson, as the means of representation in literature. Where earlier studies tended to examine the religious aspects of the two poets, three Deconstructionist readings place special emphasis on language as replacement for presence. Perhaps the emphasis makes the poets sound more like skeptical internationalists of the 1970s than like troubled Christian provincials of the previous century. I refer to J. Hillis Miller, "The Linguistic Moment in 'The Wreck of the Deutschland,'" in Thomas Daniel Young, ed., *The New Criticism and After* (Charlottesville: University Press of Virginia, 1976); Sharon Cameron, *Lyric Time: Dickinson and the Limits of Genre* (Baltimore, Md.: Johns Hopkins University Press, 1979); and Michael Sprinkler, *'A Counterpoint of Dissonance': The Aesthetics and Poetry of Gerard Manley Hopkins* (Baltimore, Md.: Johns Hopkins University Press, 1980).

4. The prosody of modified (but not abandoned) traditional metric has been described at length in Harvey Gross's *Sound and Form in Modern Poetry* (1964); I have nothing to add. Quantity and quality of work in syllabics, concrete, and other visual forms, and sound poetry would certainly earn for these types consideration in any exhaustive catalog. However, if a framework for historical and structural inquiry can be built up through the consideration of the major nonmetrical forms of sprung rhythm, free verse, and the prose poem, the role and effect of these other, less influential avant-garde prosodies can be situated in context. Also, with such a framework we should be better able to account for the mutual influence of metrical and nonmetrical prosodies.

5. The places in the table would seem to be filled—until the features that create the table are revised. Of course, this must be said with diffidence and not as a prediction of the imminent exhaustion of poetry's resources. A commentator making a similar claim in 1855 would have been proved a fool by the publication of *Leaves of Grass*.

6. Charles Rosen, *Schoenberg* (New York: Viking, 1975), p. 57.

7. *The Note-books and Papers of Gerard Manley Hopkins,* ed. Humphrey House (London: Oxford University Press, 1937), p. 96. Hereafter cited as *Note-books.*

8. *Poems of Gerard Manley Hopkins,* 3d ed., rev. by W. H. Gardner (London: Oxford University Press, 1964), p. 75. Hereafter cited as *Poems.*

It may be useful to note that *falling* means strong-weak syllable-stress pattern, that the *first paèon* is strong then three weaks, and that an *outride* is an extra syllable interposed, as in line 4, "drudgery" (which can be pronounced optionally with three syllables or two).

9. *The Letters of Gerard Manley Hopkins to Robert Bridges,* ed. Claude Colleer Abbott (Oxford: Oxford University Press, 1935), 2:46. Hereafter this edition and volume will be cited as *Letters* 2. The best brief account of sprung rhythm, aside from the poet's own author's preface, is Paul L. Mariani's "Note on Hopkins's Prosody," in Paul L. Mariani, *A Commentary on the Complete Poems of Gerard Manley Hopkins* (Ithaca, N.Y.: Cornell University Press, 1970), pp. 330–35.

10. *Poems,* p. 83.

11. Walter J. Ong, "Hopkins' Sprung Rhythm and the Life of English Poetry," in *Immortal Diamond: Studies in Gerard Manley Hopkins* (New York: Sheed and Ward, 1949), p. 143.

12. *Letters* 2:44.

13. "Poetry and Verse," *The Journals and Papers of Gerard Manley Hopkins,* ed. Humphrey House and Graham Storey (London: Oxford University Press, 1959), p. 289. Hereafter cited as *JP.*

14. "A Postscript to the Discussion of Grammar of Poetry," *Diacritics* 10 (March 1980): 24. Jakobson here calls Hopkins "that clear-sighted discoverer in world poetry and poetics." Hopkins's centrality as a proponent of the figure of grammar was emphasized by Jakobson as early as the constitutive essay of 1960, "Concluding Statement: Linguistics and Poetics," in *Style in Language,* ed. Thomas A. Sebeok (Cambridge, Mass.: MIT Press, 1960), pp. 350–77.

15. *JP,* p. 84. Of course, only physically is the sentence linear. Syntax embraces grammatical subordination, whose order is counterlinear, or vertical.

16. This is the analysis of Charles O. Hartman in *Free Verse: An Essay on Prosody* (Princeton, N.J.: Princeton University Press, 1980), pp. 32–33. See also Sister Marcella Marie Holloway's *Prosodic Theory of Gerard Manley Hopkins* (Washington, D.C.: Catholic University of America Press, 1947), and the excellent chapter, "Rhythm and Other Structural Parts of Rhetoric-Verse" (chap. 4), in Stephan Walliser, *That Nature Is a Heraclitean Fire . . . : A Case Study in G. M. Hopkins Poetry* (Berlin: Francke Verlag, 1977).

17. *Note-books,* p. 74.

18. In the letter to Coventry Patmore on meter, from Stonyhurst, 7 November 1883, Hopkins in passing speaks of Tennyson as the "great master of meter of his day."

19. *Gerard Manley Hopkins: A Selection of His Poems and Prose,* ed. W. H. Gardner (Baltimore, Md.: Penguin Books, 1963), p. 157.

20. One might ask, Why spring stresses and words from their expected places? To answer in our terms rather than those of 1880, the artist must obscure the form to prolong the perception of it; that way, the linguistic form is stored by the reader along with the paraphrasable meaning, and this to a greater degree than in ordinary discourse or in the usual kind of poetry. One reason that Hopkins's poems are mostly short (no longer than sonnet length) is that he manages to say so much in every line, every syllable—he prefers massing and saturation, explosive simultaneity.

21. The Star of Balliol was one of the great Victorian Classicists, whose undergraduate studies and later teaching career and proposed scholarly studies were all in the Classics, and especially Greek poetry—and whose syntax is the most like Greek of any English poet.

The reservations Hopkins has about Parnassian come down to something he never makes explicit, an unwillingness to accept the normative English sentence as one that drives from the subject through the verb onto the object. Todd Bender's chapter, "Non-Logical Syntax: Latin and Greek Hyperbaton," crucially points out Hopkins's intent in using this figure of transposition on a large scale: "He often admitted obscurity when it imitated the mental processes in action and he found the advantage of inversion to be that it allowed words to be arranged in a non-logical associative pattern which indicates the state of excitement of the speaker and induces a similar state in the reader." The common types of hyperbaton are the placement of important words early in the sentence in violation of the logical order of ideas; the postponement of interrogatives, relatives, and conjunctions; and the deliberate separation of logically cohering words in the line, as substantive from adjective, substantive from genitive. There is also the possibility of double splitting, so that one hyperbaton is included within another (see Todd K. Bender, *Gerard Manley Hopkins: The Classical Background and Critical Reception of His Work* [Baltimore, Md.: Johns Hopkins University Press, 1966], chap. 4). Also very useful in this regard is chap. 7, "Order and Purpose: Hopkins's Syntax," in James Milroy, *The Language of Gerard Manley Hopkins* (London: Andre Deutsch, 1977).

Michael Sprinkler's reading of Hopkins attempts, as he says (p. 64), "a transumptive revision of the logocentric, idealising, canonical tradition of Hopkins criticism." But if Bender, Milroy, and I are correct in seeing Hopkins as a poet who tries through syntax to put the reader's mind into the same ferment as his own (verisimilitude not as accurate reflection of the external world, but as imitation of the way the perceiving mind works), then the poet himself is inescapably logocentric and idealizing, giving more than a little footing for the canonical readings.

22. About grammar: Linguistics seems more riven with disputes about fundamental matters than even literary criticism. With the partial collapse of Noam Chomsky's paradigm of generative grammar and the absence of any fully developed alternative grammar, we lack adequate, explicit, and revealing definitions of concepts like noun, verb, modifier, subject, and subordination. Most supportive of my own view of the sentence is the conceptual framework developed by my colleague Ronald W. Langacker as space grammar, which is renegade in its claim that grammar has no existence in isolation from semantic structure (Professor Langacker's *Foundations of Cognitive Grammar,* chap. 1, "Orientation" [1982] is a prepublication monograph). Though Langacker's theories and evidences seem to me of great promise for future literary application, I do not base my study on his or any other single source.

Since literary analysis studies not only the sentence but relations of sentences in the whole text, the new fields of discourse analysis, text grammar, and composition theory may prove more relevant than formal linguistics.

For practical matters I have relied on two dependable basic reference works: Archibald A. Hill, *Introduction to Linguistic Structures: From Sound to Sentence in English* (New York: Harcourt, Brace, 1958); and Randolph Quirk et al., *A Grammar of Contemporary English* (London: Longmans, 1972).

23. "Verbal Art as Interference between a Cognitive and an Aesthetic Structure," in Jan Van Der Eng and Mojmír Grygar, eds., *Structure of Texts and Semiotics of Culture* (The Hague: Mouton, 1972), pp. 215, 313, 327.

24. Much in this and the next two chapters depends upon Jiří Levý, "The Meanings of Form

and the Forms of Meaning," *Poetics* 2 (Warsaw: Polish Scientific Publishers, 1966): 45–59. This virtually unknown article is, I believe, one of the foundations of any poetics that aspires to relate form to meaning.

25. M. A. K. Halliday, "Categories of the Theory of Grammar," *Word* 17 (December 1961): 241–92. The remainder of this paragraph relies on Halliday; see esp. pp. 253, 254, 256, 262, 286.

26. See "On the Grammetrics of the Classical Alexandrine," *Cahiers de lexicologie* 4 (1964): 61–72; and "Distich and Sentence in Corneille and Racine," in Roger Fowler, ed., *Essays on Style and Language* (London: Routledge and Kegan Paul, 1966), pp. 100–117.

27. Because grammar and meter inhabit the same attentional space in the poetic line, one or the other has always been invisible when it has come time for analysis of poetic effects. My terms *mutual scissoring* and *verse period* should not mislead the reader into thinking that the analytical process I am proposing can be as simultaneous as the processing of the poetic line in reading. In choosing lines or sequences of lines for analysis, I look for especially dramatic effects that show the convergence or divergence of the two systems in the same place, but in practice, in describing such a nexus, the inquirer is usually obliged to describe one system and then the other.

28. *Poems*, p. 106.

29. I owe much of this commentary on line 1 to notes on the line by Edwin Fussell. Doubtless there is also a pun on "knot," which connects with the second line's talk of strands and untwisting; the point is made by Paul L. Mariani in his commentary on the poem (see note 9, above).

30. On this issue of self-indulgence, Fred V. Randel has written (in private communication) of a context that is needed for understanding "Carrion Comfort"—Keats as the epitome of self-indulgence for Hopkins: "The major influence is, I think, Keats's 'Ode on Melancholy,' which provides a remarkably large amount of Hopkins's content and structure: including the repeated negatives at the beginning, the talk of twisting, the ingestive imagery, the paradoxical combination of final defeat and victory, the acquisition of 'joy,' the language of eyes and feeding, the religious or quasi-religious imagery at the close. Hopkins here identifies Keats's poem as that which needs to be negated: the first line is a rejection of the Melancholy-Ode's self-indulgence in Hopkins's view, a rejection which is the more powerful since it is phrased in the terminology of Keats's opening rejection of 'Lethe.' All this leads me to think that the norm from which Hopkins deviates may be Keats even more than Tennyson." Very plausible; this debate with Keats is also a debate with the side of himself and of Tennyson that finds Keats delectable.

31. *The Dream Songs* (New York: Farrar, Straus and Giroux, 1969). The poem "Anarchic Henry," quoted in full below, is Dream Song number 345, on page 367 of this book. There is also in this volume a whole poem on Hopkins's death in Dublin: "Father Hopkins, teaching elementary Greek / whilst his mind climbed the clouds, also died here / . . . where did they plant him, after / the last exam?" (p. 399).

32. *The Norton Anthology of English Literature*, 2 vols. (New York: Norton, 1968), 2:1739.

33. *The Shorter Poems of Robert Bridges*, enlarged ed. (Oxford: Oxford University Press, 1921), pp. 24–25, 32.

34. See *A Hopkins Reader*, ed. John Pick (Oxford: Oxford University Press, 1953), p. 92.

35. *The Shorter Poems*, p. 193.

36. *New Verse: Written in 1921* (Oxford: Oxford University Press), pp. 1, 16: the poems are, respectively, "Cheddar Pinks" and "Kate's Mother." In the first of these passages, "squander'd" resembles something Whitman does; Hopkins, never. The apostrophe is meaningless, not affecting the sound in the least, but looking elegant.

37. *Robert Bridges: Collected Essays, Papers, etc.*, vol. 2 (London: Oxford University Press, 1930), esp. pp. 36–37, 45, 47, 54–55. Earlier printed in the *North American Review*, November 1922; and in the *London Mercury*, November 1922. This fugitive essay, quoted here from the copy of the London Library, was apparently not known to Donald Stanford; see his "Robert Bridges and the Free Verse Rebellion," *Journal of Modern Literature* 2 (September 1971). Stanford discusses Neo-Miltonic syllabics as Bridges's considered answer to the free-verse rebels; that is not what Bridges says about it.

These late pamphlets also display Bridges's theories of spelling reform; in order to show these to be homologous with his prosodic theories in their willful but faint revision, I do not regularize.

38. *Now in Wintry Delights* (Oxford, 1903).

39. *Milton's Prosody* (Oxford: Oxford University Press, 1901), quotations in this order: pp. 72, iii, 76–77. Provocative materials on Bridges and on *Milton's Prosody* appear in chap. 6 and 7 of F. E. Brett Young's *Robert Bridges: A Critical Study* (London: Martin Secker, 1914). See also the anti-Modern polemic of Donald E. Stanford, *In the Classic Mode: The Achievement of Robert Bridges* (Newark: University of Delaware Press, 1978).

40. Hopkins to Bridges, 18 October 1882, *Letters* 2:154–58.

41. Walt Whitman, section 3 of "When lilacs last in the door-yard bloom'd" in *Leaves of Grass,* Reader's Edition, ed. Harold W. Blodgett and Sculley Bradley (New York: New York University Press, 1965), p. 329. An excellent reading, which emphasizes the larger meanings of grammar in Whitman, in Mutlu Konuk Blasing, "Whitman's 'Lilacs' and the Grammars of Time," *PMLA* 97 (January 1982).

42. *Poems,* p. 98.

43. The oppositions may be expressed in this way:

Whitman	*Hopkins*
Diffusion of sense	Saturation of sense
"Noise" or redundancy	"Information" (in the cybernetic senses)
Frustration effects	Explosive effects
One after the other; linear	One on top of another; spatial, repetitive
Linear	Counterlinear
Diffuse	Dense
Gigantism	Miniaturization
No rhyme	Profuse rhyme
Syntactic measure	Sprung rhythm
Suspended predication	Overlaid predication, hyperbaton
Preference for whole poem, or whole segment	Preference for stanza
Entropy	Redundancy

Even in this necessarily provisional form these oppositions do show a significant range of contrasts—what is omitted in the middle of this range being the paradigm norm of Tennysonian poetry, occupied by nearly all other poets of the period. As for the relaxed and tense ends of the range, F. O. Matthiessen's accounts of both poets begin to unravel the differences: "Whitman's demand for the direct presence of speaking tones in poetry would put him in accord with the revolt of modern poets against the artificial muffling of such tones by Tennyson and Swinburne . . . In [Hopkins's] intense precision of design, or 'inscape,' as he named it, he is in revolutionary opposition both to Whitman's happy diffuseness and to Bridges' conventional decorum" (*American Renaissance* [London: Oxford University Press, 1941], pp. 555, 587). Whitman's preference for the whole poem is explained in the wider context of a specifically American poetics by Edwin Fussell, in his pages on "the constituting metaphor"; see *Lucifer in Harness: American Meter, Metaphor, and Diction* (Princeton, N.J.: Princeton University Press, 1973), pp. 49–55, and esp. pp. 61–68.

44. I have already summarized Hopkins's view of Tennyson in the account of his letter on Parnassian poetry; see also note 30 above. Hopkins loved Tennyson's poetry, admitted he was a helpless admirer from an early age; but he was also locked in a productive struggle against the laureate—against Tennyson's all-purpose style, against his religious uncertainties, against the misplaced public-historical gestures of the *Idylls.* Whitman's early break from conventional form has no direct reference to Tennyson, whom he inordinately admired and wished to visit, Tennyson having given him an open-ended invitation. Hopkins as stylist was explicitly warring with Tennyson, but Whitman is against British poetry in toto, especially Shakespeare.

Chapter 5. The Prosodies of Free Verse

1. Recognizing only later that free verse is part of the disciplinary field, Paul Fussell and Harvey Gross added material on free verse in the second editions of their standard books. See Paul Fussell, *Poetic Meter and Poetic Form,* rev. ed. (New York: Random House, 1978); and Harvey Gross, ed., *The Structure of Verse: Modern Essays on Prosody,* rev. ed. (New York: Ecco Press, 1979).

For convenience, we write of free verse as one method; actually it is several—or many—methods; hence my chapter title, hence my purpose here to describe essential gestures the several methods share.

2. Robert Hass, "One Body: Some Notes on Form," *Antaeus* 30/31 (Spring 1978): 341–42. Hass is right to add that "metrical poetry is used in the same way."

3. "One Body: Some Notes on Form," p. 339.

4. This was Albert Gelpi's point in his (unpublished) lecture on poetic form at the Conference on the San Francisco Renaissance, University of California, San Diego, February 1982. Tilottama Rajan uses deconstructive theory to analyze these and other idealisms of Romantic discourse, in her *Dark Interpreter: The Discourse of Romanticism* (Ithaca, N. Y.: Cornell University Press, 1980).

5. *Lucifer in Harness: American Meter, Metaphor, and Diction* (Princeton, N.J.: Princeton University Press, 1973), p. 28. See chap. 1, "The Meter-Making Argument."

6. Quoted from Whitman's 1855 preface, reprinted in *Leaves of Grass,* Reader's Edition, ed. Harold W. Blodgett and Sculley Bradley (New York: New York University Press, 1965), p. 722.

7. *Leaves of Grass,* Reader's Edition, p. 66.

8. T. V. F. Brogan's reference guide, *English Versification, 1570–1980* (Baltimore, Md.: Johns Hopkins University Press, 1981), lists and evaluates a number of studies (pp. 402–16), giving a place from which to start. To his list I would add a few items, mainly recent, which I recommend: Enikö Bollobás, "New Prosodies in 20th Century American Free Verse," *Acta Litteraria Academiae Scientiarum Hungaricae* 20 (1978): 99–121; Clive Scott, *French Verse-Art: A Study* (Cambridge: Cambridge University Press, 1980); and Alan Golding, "Charles Olson's Metrical Thicket: Toward a Theory of Free-Verse Prosody," *Language and Style* 14 (Winter 1981): 64–78.

The above are all scholarly studies, but there are also many collections by poets on poetry in open forms, such as *Naked Poetry: Recent American Poetry in Open Forms* (1969) and *The New Naked Poetry* (1976), both ed. Stephen Berg and Robert Mezey; *The Poetics of the New American Poetry* (1973), ed. Donald M. Allen and Warren Tallman; *American Poets in 1976* (1976), ed. William Heyen; *Towards a New American Poetics: Essays and Interviews* (1978), by Ekbert Fass; *A Field Guide to Contemporary Poetry and Poetics* (1980), ed. Stuart Friebert and David Young.

Also, Paul Mariani has edited an important set of notes for various talks and readings given by William Carlos Williams from May 1940 to April 1941: "Studiously Unprepared," *Sulfur* 4 (Pasadena: California Institute of Technology, 1982).

9. *The Theory of the Avant-Garde* (Cambridge, Mass.: Harvard University Press, 1969), pp. 157–58.

10. *The Way of a World* (London: Oxford University Press, 1969), p. 59.

11. Quoted in Pierre Daix, *Nouvelle critique et art moderne* (Paris: Éditions du Seuil, 1968), p. 148 (my translation).

12. "Poetry of the Present," *Complete Poems,* ed. V. de Sola Pinto and F. V. Roberts (New York: Viking, 1963), 2: 184–85.

13. *Writing Degree Zero,* trans A. Lavers and C. Smith (London: Cape, 1967), pp. 48–49.

14. "Reflections on Vers-Libre," *New Statesman,* 3 March 1917, p. 519.

15. Barthes immediately adds; "But this moment is one of the most explicit in history, since history is always and above all a choice and the limits of this choice."

16. *Letters for Origin, 1950–1956,* ed. Albert Glover (London: Cape Goliard, 1969), p. 85.

17. The following chronology lists a fair sampling of the adversaries, nearly all of whom argue the principle of expressive variation from a metrical norm: Henry Lanz, *The Physical Basis of Rime* (Palo Alto, Calif.: Stanford University Press, 1931); Yvor Winters, *In Defense of Reason* (Denver, Colo.: Swallow, 1947); Graham Hough, "Free Verse," collected in his *Image and Idea* (London: Duckworth, 1960); W. K. Wimsatt and Monroe Beardsley, "The Concept of Meter: An Exercise in Abstraction," *PMLA* 74 (December 1959): 585–98; John Hollander, "Experimental and Pseudo-Experimental Metrics in Recent American Poetry," in *Poetics* 1 (Warsaw: Polish Scientific Publishers, 1961): 127–35; J. V. Cunningham, "The Problem of Form" in *The Journal of John Cardan* (Denver, Colo.: Swallow, 1964); and Martin Dodsworth, introduction to *The Survival of Poetry,* ed. Martin Dodsworth (London: Faber, 1970).

18. "Wanted: An Ontological Critic," in Seymour Chatman and S. R. Levin, eds., *Essays on the Language of Literature* (Boston: Houghton Mifflin, 1967), pp. 281–82.

19. *The Art of Poetry* (New York: Bollingen, 1961), p. 195.

20. *The Poems of Dr. Zhivago* (Manchester: Manchester University Press, 1965), p. 3.

21. See chap. 1 of Harvey Gross's *Sound and Form in Modern Poetry* (Ann Arbor : University of Michigan Press, 1964); and the same author's "Introduction: Toward a Phenomenology of Rhythm," in Harvey Gross, ed., *The Structure of Verse,* rev. ed. (New York: Ecco Press, 1979).

22. In Thomas A. Sebeok, ed., *Style in Language* (Cambridge, Mass.: MIT Press, 1960), p. 180.

23. See "The Influence of Meter on Poetic Convention," *In Defense of Reason,* pp. 103ff.

24. *Image and Idea,* esp. pp. 95ff.

25. Zygmunt Czerny, "Le vers libre français et son art structural," *Poetics* 1 (Warsaw: Polish Scientific Publishers, 1961), p. 249 (my translation); and Barbara Herrnstein Smith, *Poetic Closure: A Study of How Poems End* (Chicago: University of Chicago Press, 1968), p. 95.

26. These are matters I take up at some length in my forthcoming book, *The Scissors of Meter: Grammetrics and Interpretation.* The elements of a strong new approach to poetry, structural and historical, are to be found in the epilogue to Marianne Shapiro's *Hieroglyph of Time: The Petrarchan Sestina* (Minneapolis: University of Minnesota Press, 1980).

27. *The Cantos* (New York: New Directions, 1934), pp. 9–10.

28. *Literary Essays of Ezra Pound,* ed. T. S. Eliot (New York: New Directions, 1954), p. 3.

29. *Eras and Modes in English Poetry* (Berkeley: University of California Press, 1964), p. 11.

30. *La enumeración caótica en la poesía moderna* (Buenos Aires: Casa Editora Coni, 1945), pp. 9, 35 (my translation).

31. The phrase is Edwin Fussell's: "Given the nature of poetry, and the facts of American history, free verse was as inevitable as the Declaration of Independence" (see Fussell's "Meter-Making Argument" chapter in *Lucifer in Harness*).

32. See Williams's contribution to Milton Hindus, ed., *Leaves of Grass 100 Years After* (Stanford, Calif.: Stanford University Press, 1955), pp. 28, 22.

33. *Ezra Pound: Poet as Sculptor* (London: Oxford University Press, 1965), p. 250.

34. *Personae: The Collected Poems of Ezra Pound* (New York: New Directions, 1950), p. 130.

35. *Crow* (New York: Harper and Row, 1971), p. 18.

36. *Collected Poems,* ed. Robin Skelton (London: Oxford University Press, 1965), pp. 21–22.

37. *Ezra Pound: Poet as Sculptor,* pp. 45, 246.

38. *The Opening of the Field* (New York: Grove Press, 1960), pp. 63–64.

39. Edward Dorn, *The Collected Poems, 1956–1974* (Bolinas, Calif.: Four Seasons Foundation, 1975), p. 70.

40. *Pictures from Brueghel: Collected Poems, 1950–1962* (New York: New Directions, 1962). See also the preface to "Un coup de dés" (in *Poems,* trans. R. Fry [New York: New Directions, 1951], pp. 156–58), where Mallarmé says his "subdivisions prismatiques de l'Idée" are spaced so as to speed or retard his lines, a method that does not transgress the older French versification, "seulement la disperse." For an instance of the three-tier line in Mayakovsky, see his "Brooklyn-Bridge" (1925) in *The Bedbug and Selected Poetry,* facing-text trans. by M. Hayward and G. Reavey (Cleveland, Ohio: Meridan Books, 1960), p. 173.

41. *Pictures from Brueghel,* p. 153.

42. *Princeton Encyclopedia of Poetry and Poetics,* ed. Alex Preminger (Princeton, N. J.: Princeton University Press, 1974), p. 289.

43. *Selected Writings,* ed. Robert Creeley (New York: New Directions, 1966).

44. *The Collected Poems of Robert Creeley; 1945–1975* (Berkeley: University of California Press, 1982), p. 111.

45. *Collected Poems* (Denver, Colo.: Swallow, 1960), p. 33.

46. Kurt Koffka, *Principles of Gestalt Psychology* (London: Keegan Paul, Trench, Trubner and Co., 1935), p. 110.

47. *The Loiners* (London: London Magazine Editions, 1970). The Harrison poem comes close to syllabic verse, on a module of 5 to 7 syllables per line.

48. *The Carrier of Ladders* (New York: Atheneum, 1970). Some may regard capital *A* and *S* in the opening and closing lines of Merwin's unpunctuated poem as punctuation liberally construed. The poem has a rather subtle rhyme structure on basic sounds: 1-a; 2-b; 3-a; 4-c (sk) and b; 5-b; 6-b; 7-b; 9-c (ic); 10-a.

49. *Circe* (London: Fulcrum Press, 1969), p. 37.

50. Paul Blackburn, "The Watchers," *In . On . Or about the Premises* (New York: Grossman, 1968), no pagination.

51. The account of line integrity in these paragraphs relies on hints from Edwin Fussell, "The Power of Negative Thinking, Minimally Construed," *Parnassus: Poetry in Review* 7 (Spring–Summer 1979), esp. pp. 255–56.

52. Introduction to *The Structure of Verse*, p. 12.

53. Christopher Logue, translator, *Pax*, Book 19 of *The Iliad* in *War Music* (London: Jonathan Cape, 1981), pp. 68, 75–76, 80. See also *Wi the Haill Voice*, twenty-five poems by Vladimir Mayakovsky, translated into Scots by Edwin Morgan (Manchester: Carcanet Press, 1972); *Versions from Fyodor Tyutchev, 1803–1873* by Charles Tomlinson (London: Oxford University Press, 1960); and *Hiding the Universe: Poems of Wang Wei*, translated by Wai-lim Yip (New York: Grossman, 1972).

54. Michael Davidson's "Advancing Measures: Conceptual Quantities and Open Forms" is to be found in a book on alternative ideas of prosody: Norma Procopiow, ed., *The New American Prosody* (Washington, D. C.: Sun and Moon Press, 1983).

Chapter 6. Narrative of Grammar in the Prose Poem

1. In France the prose poem is the subject of a monumental literary-historical survey, Suzanne Bernard, *Le poème en prose de Baudelaire jusqu'á nos jours* (Paris: Nizet, 1959). See also Monique Parent's introductory chapter, "Un fait littéraire moderne," in *St.-Jean Perse et quelque dévanciers: Etudes sur le poème en prose* (Paris: Klincksieck, 1960); and Barbara Johnson, "Quelque conséquences de la différence anatomiques des textes: Pour une théorie du poème en prose," in *Poétique* 28 (Paris: Seuil, 1976).

A collection of French prose poems with a decent introduction is Maurice Chapelan, *Anthologie du poème en prose* (Paris: Grasset, 1959). Better for its selections than for its critical essay is Guillermo Diaz-Plaja's *El poema en prose en España: Estudio critico y antologia* (Barcelona: G. Gili, 1956).

Recent contributions to the theory of the prose poem in English have all come from the United States, not England. See Michael Benedikt's introduction to his anthology, *The Prose Poem* ("over 500 selections by 70 authors from Baudelaire and Mallarmé to Solzhenitsyn and Shapiro") (New York: Dell, 1976); Russell Edson, "The Prose Poem in America," *Parnassus: Poetry in Review* (Fall–Winter 1976); and Robert Bly, "What the Prose Poem Carries with It," *American Poetry Review* (May–June 1977).

However, by far the best descriptions of a poetry in sentences are Stephen Fredman, *Poet's Prose: The Crisis in American Verse* (on William Carlos Williams, Robert Creeley, and John Ashbery) (Cambridge: Cambridge University Press, 1983); Ron Silliman, "The New Sentence," in *Talks: Hills 6–7* (San Francisco: Bob Perelman, 1980), and "What is the Prose Poem?," a talk given at the New College of California, 1 November 1982 (manuscript); and Richard Terdiman's chapters on the prose poem in his book on discourse and counter-discourse, forthcoming from Cornell University Press in 1984.

Two splendidly opinionated American anthologies are *A Little Anthology of the Poem in Prose*, ed. Charles Henri Ford, *New Directions* 14 (New York: New Directions, 1953); *Fifty-Four Prose Poems*, ed. Greg Kuzma and Duane Ackerson (Crete, Neb.: Best Cellar Press, 1974).

2. *Oeuvres complètes*, ed. Henri Mondor et G. Jean-Aubry (Paris: Pléiade, 1945), p. 1576 (my translation).

3. *Professors and Gods: Last Oxford Lectures on Poetry* (London: Andre Deutsch, 1973), esp. pp. 27, 88, 89.

4. A. Kingsley Weatherhead, "William Carlos Williams: Prose, Form, and Measure," *English Literary History* 33 (March 1966): 118–31; Richard Howard in *Ohio Review* 16 (Fall 1974): 57. The short answer to Howard is that you are not writing in prose. You are writing badly.

5. When John Ashbery titles a book of 118 pages in justified margins *Three Poems* (1971), he strictly adheres to ordinary usage by precise reversal of the reader's habits of text identification. So, too, William Carlos Williams when he denies that the prose passages in *Paterson* are an "antipoetic device": "I want to say that prose and verse are to me the same thing" *(Selected Letters of William Carlos Williams,* ed. John C. Thirwall [New York: McDowell, Oblensky, 1957], p. 263).

6. For a description of the idea of "essentially contested concepts," see W. B. Gallie, *Philosophy and the Historical Understanding* (New York: Schocken Books, 2d ed., 1968), esp. pp. 190, 157, 158.

7. Cited in passing by Suzanne Bernard.

8. *Oeuvres complètes,* p. 1576 (my translation).

9. Quoted in Chapelan, ed., *Anthologie,* p. 366 (my translation).

10. Aristotle, *Poetics,* trans. with an introduction by Gerald F. Else (Ann Arbor: University of Michigan Press, 1970), p. 28.

11. A fuller account of poetic consciousness would have to analyze the reader's role as subject. Consciousness cannot be so free-roaming or so passive as many accounts of poetry assume, because consciousness is bound by language and history and family training—consciousness is ideological consciousness. See Wolfgang Iser, *The Act of Reading: A Theory of Aesthetic Response* (Baltimore, Md.: Johns Hopkins University Press, 1978); and Ron Silliman, "Identification, Reference, Mode," in *Perception,* edited for *O.ARS* by Don Wellman (Cambridge, Mass.: Don Wellman, 1982).

12. Aloysius Bertrand, *Gaspard de la nuit: Fantasies à la manière de Rembrandt et de Callot,* ed. Jean Richer, Nouvelle Bibliothèque Romantique (Paris: Flammarion, 1972), pp. 60–61. The Mallarmé calligramme tribute to Bertrand, shown below, is quoted in this edition, p. 21.

13. Translated by Merrill Gilfillan in *This 11,* ed. Barrett Watten (Oakland, Calif.: Spring 1981), no pagination.

14. *Oeuvres complètes de Baudelaire,* ed. Y.-G. Le Dantec (Paris: Pléiade, 1954), pp. 281–82 (my translation). See Barbara Johnson's comparison of Baudelaire's metrical and nonmetrical versions of the "Invitations au voyage" poem in her book, *The Critical Difference: Essays in the Contemporary Rhetoric of Reading* (Baltimore, Md.: Johns Hopkins University Press, 1980), chap. 3.

15. *Oeuvres complètes de Baudelaire,* p. 338.

16. Translated by Michael Benedikt in *The Prose Poem,* ed. Michael Benedikt, pp. 65–66.

17. I owe this point to a letter from Ron Silliman.

18. *The Way of a World* (London: Oxford University Press, 1969), p. 53.

19. Original and translation from the facing-text bilingual edition, Rimbaud, *Illuminations,* trans. Daniel Sloate (Montréal: Editions Maisonneuve, 1971), pp. 40–42.

20. Quoted by Suzanne Bernard, p. 635 (my translation).

21. *Le cornet à dés* (Paris: Gallimard, 1945), pp. 110, 69, 63, 110. A Max Jacob Centennial (1876–1976) edition of *Folio* (Brockport, N.Y.) has been edited by Judith Morganroth Schneider (October 1976). For an excellent selection from Jacob, see the translations by John Ashbery and others in Michael Brownstein, ed., *The Dice Cup* (New York: Sun Books, 1979)—see, too, the able review of this volume by Marjorie Perloff, *Sulfur* 6 (Pasadena: California Institute of Technology, 1983). See also S. J. Collier, "Max Jacob and the 'Poème en Prose,'" *Modern Language Review* 51 (1956): 522–35.

The translation of "La clef" ("Quand le sire . . ."), below, is my own. The poems beginning "Cet Alemand" and "Le toit" are left untranslated; the play of sound will be evident from the original, while the play of sense is untranslatable.

22. Russell Edson, *The Clam Theater* (Middletown, Conn.: Wesleyan University Press, 1973).

23. *Kora in Hell: Improvisations* (1920), reprinted in Williams Carlos Williams, *Imaginations,* ed. with an introduction by Webster Schott (New York: New Directions, 1970), p. 39.

24. *Talking* (New York: Kulchur Foundation, 1972), p. 174.

25. *Three Poems* (Harmondsworth, Middlesex: Penguin, 1977), p. 80. The definitive reading of *Three Poems* is by Stephen Fredman (see note 1, above).

26. See David Antin, "Some Questions about Modernism," *Occident* 8 (Spring 1974). On page 27 Antin writes, "Prose is the name for a kind of notational style."

27. "The Basis of Poetic Form," a manuscript at the University of Buffalo; quoted by

Joseph N. Riddel, *The Inverted Bell: Modernism and the Counterpoetics of William Carlos Williams* (Baton Rouge: Louisiana State University Press, 1974), p. 131.

28. George Saintsbury, *A History of English Prose Rhythm* (London, 1912), esp. pp. 103n., 463, 191.

29. Antin, "Some Questions about Modernism," pp. 14–15.

30. *A History of English Prose Rhythm,* pp. 300–301.

31. *The Miner's Pale Children* (New York: Atheneum, 1970), p. 115.

32. *The Way of a World,* p. 53.

33. Published in London by Andre Deutsch (no pagination).

34. *oeuvres complètes,* pp. 275–76.

35. Translated by Keith Bosley, in *Mallarmé: The Poems,* a bilingual edition (Harmondsworth, Middlesex: Penguin, 1977), p. 217.

36. A very capable study of the Rimbaud-to-Cage tradition of anticlosural Modernism, which touches on several of the writers and texts in my chapter, is Marjorie Perloff's *The Poetics of Indeterminacy* (Princeton, N.J.: Princeton University Press, 1981). She brings her study up to David Antin. A continuation would inspect at least these important works from newer writers: Lyn Hejinian, *My Life* (Providence, R.I.: Burning Deck, 1980); Michael Davidson, *The Prose of Fact* (San Francisco: The Figures, 1981); Michael Palmer, *Notes for Echo Lake* (San Francisco: North Point, 1981); and Ron Silliman, *Tjanting* (San Francisco: The Figures, 1981). With respect to these last four writers in particular, it seems pertinent to remark that free verse and the prose poem can act within the limits of prosodic avantgardism to criticize each other. When, for instance, the French prose poem declined in the late 1880s, free verse was both the cause and the remedy; and in the 1980s, when much free verse in England and America has come to seem thin, unable to carry enough detail and energy, the prose poem and related forms have become workable, taut, and insurgent.

37. "A Process" is quoted from *The Way of A World,* p. 55. The interview mentioned, conducted by Jed Rasula and Mike Erwin, appeared in *Contemporary Literature* 16 (Autumn 1975), quotation from p. 408.

38. Gertrude Stein, from *Tender Buttons: Objects, Food, Rooms* (1914) as reprinted in *Gertrude Stein: Writings and Lectures, 1909–1945,* ed. Patricia Meyerowitz (Baltimore, Md.: Penguin Books, 1971), p. 164.

39. *Tender Buttons,* from *Writings and Lectures, 1909–1945,* p. 174.

40. Gertrude Stein: part of a scene from *Four Saints in Three Acts* (New York: Random House, 1934).

41. This is the last half of Michael Palmer's "Prose 1," from *Blake's Newton* (Los Angeles: Black Sparrow, 1972); consciously based on the example of Stein.

42. This sentence borrows some of its phrasing from David Antin's way of making the same point in "Some Questions about Modernism."

43. *What Is Literature?,* trans. Bernard Frechtman (London: Methuen, 1967), pp. 5, 6, 7, 8, 15.

Selected Bibliography

Romantic Theory of Poetry

Abrams, M. H. *The Mirror and the Lamp: Romantic Theory and the Critical Tradition.* New York: W. W. Norton and Company, 1953.

————. *Natural Supernaturalism: Tradition and Revolution in Romantic Literature.* New York: W. W. Norton and Company, 1971.

Armstrong, Isobel. *Language as Living Form in Nineteenth Century Poetry.* Totowa, N.J.: Barnes and Noble Books, 1982.

Barrell, John. *The Idea of Landscape and the Sense of Place, 1730–1840: An Approach to the Poetry of John Clare.* Cambridge: Cambridge University Press, 1972.

Bate, Walter Jackson. *The Burden of the Past and the English Poet.* Cambridge, Mass.: Harvard University Press, 1970.

————. *From Classic to Romantic.* New York: Harper Torchbook, 1961.

Bloom, Harold. *The Anxiety of Influence: A Theory of Poetry.* New York: Oxford University Press, 1973.

————. *A Map of Misreading.* New York: Oxford University Press, 1975.

Bloom, Harold, and F. I. Hilles, eds, *From Sensibility to Romanticism.* New York: Oxford University Press, 1965.

Coleridge, Samuel Taylor. "Essay on Method." In *The Collected Works of Samuel Taylor Coleridge.* Vol. 1, *The Friend,* edited by Barbara E. Rooke. London: Routledge, 1969.

————. "On Poesy or Art." In *Biographia Literaria,* vol. 2, edited by J. Shawcross. Oxford: Oxford University Press, 1907.

Dekker, George. *Coleridge and the Literature of Sensibility.* London: Vision Press, 1978.

Hartman, Geoffrey H., ed. *New Perspectives on Coleridge and Wordsworth.* New York: Columbia University Press, 1972.

Langbaum, Robert. *The Poetry of Experience.* New York: W. W. Norton and Company, 1963.

Perkins, David. *Wordsworth and the Poetry of Sincerity.* Cambridge, Mass.: Harvard University Press, 1964.

Rajan, Tilottama. *Dark Interpreter: The Discourse of Romanticism.* Ithaca, N.Y.: Cornell University Press, 1981.

Sheats, Paul. *The Making of Wordsworth's Poetry, 1785–1798.* Cambridge, Mass.: Harvard University Press, 1973.

Simpson, David. *Irony and Authority in Romantic Poetry.* London: Macmillan, 1979.

Wasserman, Earl. *The Subtler Language.* Baltimore, Md.: The Johns Hopkins University Press, 1959.

Verse Form and General Poetics

Altieri, Charles. *Act and Quality: A Theory of Literary Meaning and Humanistic Understanding.* Amherst, Mass.: University of Massachusetts Press, 1981.

———. *Enlarging the Temple: New Directions in American Poetry During the 1960s.* Lewisburg, Pa.: Bucknell University Press, 1979.

Attridge, Derek. *The Rhythms of English Poetry.* London: Longman, 1982.

Barthes, Roland. *Writing Degree Zero.* Translated by A. Lavers and C. Smith. London: Cape, 1967.

Berry, Eleanor. "The Reading and Uses of Elizabethan Prosodies." *Language and Style* 14 (Spring 1981): 116–52.

Blackmur, R. P. *Form and Value in Modern Poetry.* Garden City, N.Y.: Doubleday Anchor Books, 1957.

Brogan, T. V. F. *English Versification, 1570–1980: A Reference Guide with a Global Appendix.* Baltimore, Md.: The Johns Hopkins University Press, 1981.

Bruns, Gerald. *Modern Poetry and the Idea of Language.* New Haven, Conn.: Yale University Press, 1974.

Cohen, Ralph. "Innovation and Variation: Literary Change and Georgic Poetry." In *Literature and History.* Los Angeles: William Andrews Clark Memorial Library, UCLA, 1974.

Culler, Jonathan. *The Pursuit of Signs: Semiotics, Literature, Deconstruction.* Ithaca, N.Y.: Cornell University Press, 1981.

———. *Structuralist Poetics: Structuralism, Linguistics, and the Study of Literature.* Ithaca, N.Y.: Cornell University Press, 1975.

Davie, Donald. "Personification." *Essays in Criticism* 31 (April 1981): 91–104.

de Man, Paul. *Allegories of Reading.* New Haven, Conn.: Yale University Press, 1979.

Dillon, George L. *Language Processing and the Reading of Literature: Toward Model of Comprehension.* Bloomington: Indiana University Press, 1978.

Fussell, Paul. *The Theory of Prosody in Eighteenth-Century England.* Hamden: Connecticut College, 1954.

Gross, Harvey, ed. *The Structure of Verse: Modern Essays on Prosody.* Rev. ed. New York: Ecco Press, 1979.

Guillén, Claudio. *Literature as System: Essays toward the Theory of Literary History.* Princeton, N.J.: Princeton University Press, 1971.

Halliday, M. A. K. "Categories of the Theory of Grammar." *Word* 17 (December 1961): 241–92.

Hartman, Geoffrey. *Beyond Formalism.* New Haven, Conn.: Yale University Press, 1970.

Hollander, John. *The Figure of Sound: A Mode of Allusion in Milton and After.* Berkeley: University of California Press, 1981.

———. *Rhyme's Reason: A Guide to English Verse.* New Haven, Conn.: Yale University Press, 1981.

———. *Vision and Resonance: Two Senses of Poetic Form.* New York: Oxford University Press, 1975.

Jakobson, Roman. "Concluding Statement: Linguistics and Poetics." In *Style in Language,* edited by Thomas A. Sebeok. Cambridge, Mass.: MIT Press, 1960.

———. "A Postscript to the Discussion of Grammar of Poetry." *Diacritics* 10 (March 1980): 22–35.

———. *Questions de poétique.* Paris: Seuil, 1973.

Jameson, Fredric. *The Political Unconscious: Narrative as a Socially Symbolic Act.* Ithaca, N.Y.: Cornell University Press, 1981.

Jauss, Hans Robert. *Toward an Aesthetic of Reception.* Translated by Timothy Bahti and with an introduction by Paul de Man. Minneapolis: University of Minnesota Press, 1982.

Kristeva, Julia. *Desire in Language: A Semiotic Approach to Literature and Art.* Edited by Leon S. Roudiez. Translated by Thomas Gora, Alice Jardine, and Leon S. Roudiez. New York: Columbia University Press, 1980.

———. *La Révolution du langage poétique.* Paris: Seuil, 1974.

Kuhn, Thomas S. *The Structure of Scientific Revolutions.* 2d. ed. Chicago: University of Chicago Press, 1970.

Lawler, Justus. *Celestial Pantomime.* New Haven, Conn.: Yale University Press, 1979.

Lévy, Jiři. "Contribution to the Typology of Accentual-Syllabic Versifications." In *Poetics* 1. Warsaw: Polish Scientific Publishers, 1961.

———. "The Meanings of Form and the Forms of Meaning." In *Poetics* 2. Warsaw: Polish Scientific Publishers, 1966.

Lotman, Yuri. *Analysis of the Poetic Text.* Edited and translated by D. Barton Johnson. Ann Arbor, Mich.: Ardis, 1976.

———. *The Structure of the Artistic Text.* Translated by Ronald Vroon. Michigan Slavic Contributions No. 7. Ann Arbor: University of Michigan Press, 1977.

Marcuse, Herbert. *The Aesthetic Dimension: Toward a Critique of Marxist Aesthetics.* Boston: Beacon Press, 1978.

Matejka, Ladislav, and Krystyna Pomorska, eds. *Readings in Russian Poetics: Formalist and Structuralist Views.* Cambridge, Mass.: MIT Press, 1971.

Meijer, Jan M. "Verbal Art as Interference between a Cognitive and an Aesthetic Structure." In *Structure of Texts and Semiotics of Culture,* edited by Jan Van der Eng, and Mojmír Grygar, The Hague: Mouton, 1972.

Meschonnic, Henri. *Critique du rhythme: anthropologie historique du langage.* Paris: Verdier, 1982.

Meyer, Leonard B. *Music, the Arts, and Ideas: Patterns and Predictions in Twentieth-Century Culture.* Chicago: University of Chicago Press, 1967.

Miles, Josephine. *Eras and Modes in English Poetry.* Berkeley: University of California Press, 1964.

———. *Poetry and Change: Donne, Milton, Wordsworth and the Equilibrium of the Present.* Berkeley: University of California Press, 1974.

————. *Style and Proportion: The Language of Prose and Poetry.* Boston: Little, Brown and Company, 1967.

Pearce, Roy Harvey. *The Continuity of American Poetry.* Princeton, N.J.: Princeton University Press, 1961.

Perkins, David. *A History of Modern Poetry: From the 1890s to the High Modernist Mode.* Cambridge, Mass.: Harvard University Press, 1976.

Perloff, Marjorie. *The Poetics of Indeterminacy.* Princeton, N.J.: Princeton University Press, 1981.

Poggioli, Renato. *The Theory of the Avant-Garde.* Translated by Gerald Fitzgerald. Cambridge, Mass.: Harvard University Press, 1968.

————. "Poetics and Metrics." Essay in *The Spirit of the Letter: Essays on European Literature.* Cambridge, Mass.: Harvard University Press, 1965.

Pratt, Mary Louise. *Toward a Speech Act Theory of Literary Discourse.* Bloomington: Indiana University Press, 1977.

Riffaterre, Michael. *Semiotics of Poetry.* Bloomington: Indiana University Press, 1978.

Roubaud, Jacques. *La vieillesse d'Alexandre: essai sur quelques états récents du vers français.* Paris: Maspéro, 1978.

Said, Edward W. *Beginnings: Intention and Method.* New York: Basic Books, 1975.

Saintsbury, George. *History of English Prosody.* London: 1910.

Tynianov, Yuri. *The Problem of Verse Language.* Translated and edited by Michael Sosa and Brent Harvey, with an afterword by Roman Jakobson. Ann Arbor, Mich.: Ardis, 1981.

Wayne, Don E. "Mediation and Contestation: English Classicism from Sidney to Jonson." *Criticism* 25 (Summer 1983): 211–37.

Wesling, Donald. *The Chances of Rhyme: Device and Modernity.* Berkeley: University of California Press, 1980.

————. "Difficulties of the Bardic: Literature and the Human Voice." *Critical Inquiry* (Fall 1981): 69–81.

————, with Enikö Bollobás. "Verse Form: Recent Studies." *Modern Philology* 81 (August 1983): 53–60.

Wexler, Peter. "On the Grammetrics of the Classical Alexandrine." *Cahiers de lexicologie* 4 (1964): 61–72.

————. "Distich and Sentence in Corneille and Racine." In *Essays on Style and Language,* edited by Roger Fowler, 100–117. London: Routledge, 1966.

Williams, William Carlos. "The Poem as a Field of Action." In *Selected Essays of William Carlos Williams,* edited by John Thirlwall. New York: Random House, 1954.

Wimsatt, W. K. *Day of the Leopards: Essays in Defense of Poems.* New Haven, Conn.: Yale University Press, 1976.

————. *Hateful Contraries: Studies in Literature and Criticism.* Lexington: University of Kentucky Press, 1965.

————. *The Verbal Icon: Studies in the Meaning of Poetry.* Lexington: University of Kentucky Press, 1954.

———, ed. *Versification: Major Language Types: Sixteen Essays.* New York: Modern Language Association and New York University Press, 1972.

Sprung Rhythm, Free Verse, and the Prose Poem

Allen, Donald M., and Warren Tallman, eds. *The Poetics of the New American Poetry.* New York: Grove Press, 1973.

Antin, David. "Some Questions About Modernism." *Occident* 8 (Spring 1974): 7–38.

Bender, Todd K. *Gerard Manley Hopkins: The Classical Background and Critical Reception of His Work.* Baltimore, Md.: The Johns Hopkins University Press, 1966.

Berg, Stephen, and Robert Mezey, eds. *The New Naked Poetry: Recent American Poetry in Open Forms.* Indianapolis, Ind.: Bobbs-Merrill, 1976.

Bernard, Suzanne. *Le poème en prose de Baudelaire jusqu'à nos jours.* Paris: Nizet, 1959.

Bly, Robert. "What the Prose Poem Carries with It." *American Poetry Review* (May–June 1977): 44–45.

Bollobás, Enikö. "New Prosodies in 20th-Century American Free Verse." *Acta Litteraria Academiae Scientiarum Hungaricae* 20 (1978): 99–121.

Caws, Mary Ann, and Hermine Riffaterre, eds. *The Prose Poem in France: Theory and Practice.* New York: Columbia University Press, 1983.

Eliot, T. S. "Reflections on Vers Libre," *New Statesman,* 3 March 1917.

Fredman, Stephen. *Poet's Prose: The Crisis in American Verse.* Cambridge: Cambridge University Press, 1983.

Fussell, Edwin. *Lucifer in Harness: American Meter, Metaphor and Diction.* Princeton, N.J.: Princeton University Press, 1973.

Fussell, Paul. "Free Verse." *Antaeus* 30/31 (Spring 1978): 296–308.

Gelpi, Albert. *The Tenth Muse: The Psyche of the American Poet.* Cambridge, Mass.: Harvard University Press, 1975.

Golding, Alan. "Charles Olson's Metrical Thicket: Toward a Theory of Free-Verse Prosody." *Language and Style* 14 (Winter 1981): 64–78.

Gross, Harvey. *Sound and Form in Modern Poetry.* Ann Arbor: University of Michigan Press, 1964.

Hall, Donald. *Goatfoot Milktongue Twinbird: Interviews, Essays and Notes on Poetry, 1970–76.* Ann Arbor: University of Michigan Press, 1978.

———. *To Keep Moving: Essays 1959–69.* Geneva, N.Y.: Hobart and William Smith Colleges Press, 1980.

Hartman, Charles O. *Free Verse: An Essay on Prosody.* Princeton, N.J.: Princeton University Press, 1980.

Hass, Robert. "One Body: Some Notes on Form." *Antaeus* 30/31 (Spring 1978): 329–42.

Holloway, Sister Marcella Marie. *The Prosodic Theory of Gerard Manley Hopkins.* Washington, D.C.: Catholic University of America Press, 1947.

Johnson, Barbara. *Défigurations du langage poétique: la seconde révolution baudelairienne.* Paris: Flammarion, 1979.

————. *The Critical Difference: Essays in the Contemporary Rhetoric of Reading.* Baltimore, Md.: The Johns Hopkins University Press, 1980.

Lewis, R. W. B., ed. *The Presence of Walt Whitman.* New York: Columbia University Press, 1962.

Mariani, Paul L. "Note on Hopkins's Prosody." In *A Commentary on the Complete Poems of Gerard Manley Hopkins,* edited by Paul L. Mariani. Ithaca, N.Y.: Cornell University Press, 1970.

Milroy, James. *The Language of Gerard Manley Hopkins.* London: Andre Deutsch, 1977.

Ong, Walter J. "Hopkins' Spring Rhythm and the Life of English Poetry." In *Immortal Diamond: Studies in Gerard Manley Hopkins.* Edited by Norman Weyand. New York: Sheed and Ward, 1949.

Pearce, Roy Harvey. "Whitman Justified: The Poet in 1855." *Critical Inquiry* 8 (Fall 1981): 83–97.

Perlman, Jim, Ed Folsom, and Dan Campion, eds. *Walt Whitman: The Measure of His Song.* Minneapolis, Minn.: Holy Cow! Press, 1981.

Perloff, Marjorie. "Between Verse and Prose: Beckett and the New Poetry." *Critical Inquiry* 9 (December 1982): 415–33.

Procopiow, Norma, ed. *The New American Prosody.* Washington, D.C.: Sun and Moon Press, 1983.

Rothenberg, Jerome, ed. *Revolution of the Word: A New Gathering of American Avant Garde Poetry, 1914–1945.* New York: Seabury Press, 1974.

Scott, Clive. *French Verse-Art: A Study.* Cambridge: Cambridge University Press, 1980.

Silliman, Ron. "The New Sentence." In *Talks: Hills 6/7.* Edited by Bob Perelman. San Francisco: Bob Perelman, 1980.

Sprinkler, Michael. *'A Counterpoint of Dissonance': The Aesthetics and Poetry of Gerard Manley Hopkins.* Baltimore, Md.: The Johns Hopkins University Press, 1980.

Terdiman, Richard. *Discourse/Counter-Discourse: Symbolic Resistance in Nineteenth Century France.* Ithaca, N.Y.: Cornell University Press, 1984.

Williams, William Carlos. "The Present Relationship of Prose to Verse." In *Seven Arts,* selected and edited by Fernando Puma. Garden City, N.Y.: Doubleday, 1953.

————. "Studiously Unprepared: Notes for Various Talks and Readings, May 1940 to April 1941," edited by Paul Mariani. *Sulfur* 4 (1982): 4–35.

Index

226